EVERYBODY'S
BUSINESS

EVERYBODY'S BUSINESS

Managing risks and opportunities in today's global society

DAVID GRAYSON

ADRIAN HODGES

London, New York, Munich
Melbourne and Delhi

Project Editors
Clare Hill, Hazel Richardson
Editors
Jeff Groman, Lucian Randall
Editorial Assistant
Richard Gilbert

Project Art Editors
Amir Reuveni,
Lee Riches, Brian Rust
Design Assistant Paul Drislane

DTP Designer Julian Dams
Production Controller
Elizabeth Cherry
Picture Researcher
Louise Thomas

Managing Editor Adèle Hayward
Managing Art Editor Karen Self
US Editors Gary Werner,
Margaret Parrish

First American Edition, 2002.
Published in the United States by
DK Publishing, Inc.
375 Hudson Street
New York, NY 10014

A CIP record for this book is available
from the Library of Congress.
ISBN 0-7894-8391-2

Color reproduction by GRB Editrice,
Verona, Italy
Printed and bound by
Butler & Tanner, Somerset

see our complete product line at
www.dk.com

CONTENTS

Introduction   6

Foreword: HRH The Prince of Wales   8

GLOBAL FORCES FOR CHANGE

The Revolution of Technology   12

The Revolution of Markets   26

The Revolution of Demographics and Development   40

The Revolution of Values   62

Signposts   91

THE EMERGING MANAGEMENT ISSUES

The Emerging Management Issues Defined   94

The Impact on Business Strategy   128

The Impact on Company Functions   162

The Impact on Industry Sectors   176

The Impact on Small and Medium Enterprises   192

Signposts   205

Seven Steps to Minimizing Risks and Maximizing Opportunities

Introduction   208

Step 1 Recognizing the Trigger   214

Step 2 Making a Business Case   218

Step 3 Scoping the Issues   229

Step 4 Committing to Action   242

Step 5 Integrating Strategy   248

Step 6 Engaging Stakeholders   260

Step 7 Measuring and Reporting   287

Signposts   302

References   304
Index   307
Acknowledgments   316
Authors and Sponsor   319
Partners   320

INTRODUCTION

The job of the manager just got more difficult. Issues that were once peripheral to decision-making and incidental to business success are now fast becoming critical, yet few managers have been briefed as to what these issues are, or how they can affect their jobs and the companies they work for.

Everybody's Business explains how knowledge of the emerging management issues of ecology and environment, health and well-being, diversity and human rights, and of communities can improve business performance and make the manager's job more satisfying. Conversely, it shows how ignorance of these issues makes good managers flounder, wastes time, adds to operating costs, hurts company reputation and sales, and drives talented employees away.

The publication of *Everybody's Business* coincides with a period of anticapitalist demonstrations and increasing concern about the unequal distribution of the benefits of trade liberalization and globalization. This is despite the fact that business is the principal motor for growth in the world and that open markets contribute to sustainable social and economic development.

However, in our view, this level of contribution is not what it could or should be. We show that when managers and executives openly recognize that business can have both positive and negative impacts, and learn how to manage those impacts effectively, it can be significantly enhanced.

We are under no illusions that our objectives in writing this book are ambitious. On the one hand, we hope to help individual managers, struggling in an age of uncertainty, to build successful and rewarding careers. On the other, we want to show that, through individual actions, they can make a difference to some of the world's seemingly intractable problems.

For us, the front line in the struggle to overcome inequality, poverty, disease, and pollution is not formed by the rows of masked protesters in Seattle, Genoa, or Washington, but by the legions of frontline managers, who every day contribute to the creation of wealth.

WHY EVERYBODY'S BUSINESS?

There is a business imperative for managers to know how to respond to the emerging risks in today's global society. These risks cannot be sidelined to a specialized department because they impact upon, and are impacted by, all business functions. Every manager concerned with the profitability of his or her unit or enterprise needs to be concerned with the prosperity of the communities that feed those profits. Each of us, whether as an investor, employee, customer, parent, or neighbor, has a stake in the success of business.

The first part of the book, Global Forces for Change, is about the big picture. The manager's job is affected by powerful, yet seemingly remote, global forces for change. These are summarized as revolutions in technology, markets, demographics and development, and values. Business must respond to rising expectations from stakeholders for there to be greater transparency and accountability. There is no lessening of these expectations in times of economic downturn. In fact, it sharpens the message that what happens to business matters to society, so what happens to society should matter to business.

The next section deals with the emerging management issues. What were once regarded as "soft" business issues are now "hard" – hard to predict, hard to ignore, and very hard to manage when they go wrong. The risks and opportunities they represent for business strategy, corporate functions, industry sectors, and for small- and medium-sized enterprises are spelled out here.

The last part is titled Seven Steps to Minimizing Risks and Maximizing Opportunities. It is structured around the win-win Seven Steps, a management process designed to minimize risks and maximize opportunities for both business and society, stretching existing management techniques whenever possible to achieve this.

A VALUABLE RESOURCE

We have had the privilege of working for and with business leaders of many successful companies, and have seen their desire to convey to colleagues the importance of the topics covered in this book. *Everybody's Business* is written for the manager and from the manager's perspective. It will be a valuable resource for corporate advisers, those in government, and those in the nonprofit sector. We are pro-business, but not business as usual. We quote attacks on business not because we necessarily agree or endorse them, but because managers need to understand what is being said and by whom. And we agree with the sense of urgency for action suggested by The Prince of Wales in his foreword to this book.

Some label the actions we recommend as "corporate social responsibility" or "good corporate citizenship." However, the biggest impetus for change in business practices is not a growing sense of social responsibility, but market forces – concerned customers, vocal employees, and pragmatic investors who are worried about the value of their holdings. What was once regarded as nice-to-do has now become have-to-do.

To update the Nobel Prize-winning economist Milton Friedman's famous dictum of the 1970s: "Today, the business of business is everybody's business."

David Grayson and Adrian Hodges, August 2001

ST. JAMES'S PALACE

For the business community of the twenty-first century, 'out of sight' is no longer 'out of mind'. Global communications and media operations can present every aspect of a company's operations directly to its customers in stark, unflattering and immediate terms. Those customers increasingly believe that the role of large companies in our society must encompass more than the traditional functions of obeying the law, paying taxes and making a profit. Survey after survey reveals that they also want to see major corporations helping 'to make the world a better place'. That may be in some respect a naïve ambition, but it is, nevertheless, a clear expectation, and one that companies ignore at their peril.

In a rapidly changing world, my own view is that the globalisation of opportunity for major companies is not yet being matched by an equal globalisation of responsibility. There are certainly <u>some</u> companies who genuinely seek to operate responsibly and demonstrate respect for the long-term interests and aspirations of all the communities and localities where they base their operations. They understand that sustainable businesses can only operate profitably, over the long-term, in sustainable communities, and they play an informed, engaged and responsible role in those societies.

Tragically, there are all too many examples of businesses operating on a totally unsustainable basis, either directly or through their investments. Traditional communities and indigenous cultures, established over thousands of years, are being destroyed by agricultural intensification, by plantation forestry and by grandiose infrastructure projects imposed from afar. Those displaced rural populations then add to the immense problems of already overcrowded and under-serviced towns and cities, while new opportunities for developing genuinely sustainable livelihoods are largely ignored.

At the same time, important natural habitats, providing valuable biological services, such as mangrove swamps and estuaries, are being cleared to make way for ill-judged aquaculture schemes and port developments. In many parts of the world, new roads and pipelines are giving easy access to previously pristine areas, leading to the uncontrollable illegal exploitation of timber and minerals, and immense damage to wildlife. And issues like climate change and the loss of biodiversity receive only lip service in too many quarters, despite all the evidence of the potentially disastrous consequences if we go on as we are.

With few exceptions, businesses cannot be expected to take sole responsibility for tackling these issues. Those who operate in countries where corrupt administrations do not enforce the law, or where land rights are a matter for negotiation rather than a matter of fact, or where their competitors have no reputation to lose, face particularly intractable problems. But the old adage still applies in that those who are not actively seeking to be part of the solution are most certainly part of the problem.

Over the last two decades, as President of Business in the Community and of my International Business Leaders Forum, I have seen and heard many inspiring examples of companies working in partnership with communities, governments and NGO's to develop sustainable methods of operation. But they are still, I believe, an exception to the general rule.

It is immensely encouraging to find that there are business leaders who recognise the challenge of running their companies in ways that make a positive and sustainable contribution to the societies in which they operate. It is a huge task, not least in finding ways of reaching out to the thousands of managers at the 'sharp end' of the business who, every day, take the decisions that have real impact on employees, on whole communities and on the environment.

I hope this handbook will help in this task and I am delighted that my International Business Leaders Forum and Business in the Community are collaborating in its production and dissemination. 'Everybody's Business' is full of practical advice, examples and ideas which I hope will equip busy managers with the understanding and the practical tools they need to play their role in building sustainable business operating in successful communities. All managers should have it on their desks.

Charles

GLOBAL FORCES
FOR CHANGE

Gilbert Awekofua, Kampala, Uganda.

"The spread of markets far outpaces the ability
of societies and their political systems to adjust
to them, let alone to guide the course they take."

Kofi Annan, UN secretary general, World Economic Form, Davos, January 1999.

THE REVOLUTION OF TECHNOLOGY

The convergence of telecommunications and information technologies has created unprecedented levels of connectivity – within companies, between businesses and supply chains, between businesses and customers, and among consumers.

This connectivity transforms the way business operates: in manufacturing by affecting what, where, how much, how quickly, and with how many employees a product can be made; in the service sector by transforming how data is collected, stored, and analyzed; and between customer and business by the ways in which communications are transacted.

In addition, further waves of technological innovation in the life sciences are already generating major consumer and ethical debates, for example in the fields of genetics and animal cloning.

The capacity of business to do things in the first decades of the twenty-first century will have less to do with technological constraints and more to do with how far business can win popular support for the use of the new technologies – from both consumers and society in general.

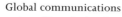

Global communications
Advances in satellite technology have made the military and space agencies' global positioning and tracking capabilities accessible to consumers, as well as enabling continual real-time communication around the world.

Information and Communications Technology

Our ability to access, transmit, and process information has increased dramatically because of the rise in telecommunications capacity, computing power, and the development of internet technology.

Technological advances and deregulation have reduced the price of phone calls dramatically, and innovation in cellular and mobile phones has produced extraordinary levels of communication.

- "A transatlantic telephone call in 1999 cost less than 1.5 percent of the 1939 price." Charles Dunstone, founder and CEO, Carphone Warehouse, March 1999.

- "When mobile phone text messaging first became available, some 20 million messages were sent worldwide in a month. Eighteen months later, the figure had risen to 3.5 billion messages a month." Susan Rice, CEO, Lloyds TSB Bank (Scotland), November 2000.

- 64 billion text messages were sent world-wide in 2000 – and by January 2001 the figure was a staggering 10 billion per month. Mobile Data Association.

Computing costs have also fallen, allowing powerful applications that were previously available only to governments and large businesses to be within the reach of small businesses and individuals.

- "Computer power is 8,000 times cheaper than it was 30 years ago." Charles Dunstone, founder and CEO, Carphone Warehouse, March 1999.

Faster communications

The phenomenal growth in the speed of electronic communications is graphically shown by calculating the time it would have taken in previous years to transmit the entire contents of the Library of Congress.

YEAR	TRANSMISSION TIME
1950	158,000 years
1980	661 years
1990	113 years
1992	53 days
1997	51 hours
And today?	*Woosh…there it goes!*

KPMG Peat Marwick, 1997.

The consequence of these developments for individuals and institutions is that the only certainty is greater unpredictability.

"One could reasonably expect the chairman of AT&T to know what his corporation will be in 10 years from now. He doesn't. One could, within reason, expect the chairman of AT&T to be able to predict how technology will transform his business a decade hence. He can't. At the least, he should know who his major competitors will be in 2002. Stumped again. But here is what he does know: something startling, intriguing, and profound is afoot." Robert Allen, then chairman of AT&T, quoted in Frances Cairncross, *The Death of Distance*, 1997.

Mobile power
The power of a computer that once required a room of its own in the 1960s can now be accessed on a park bench.

The accelerated pace of life

The speed of economic and domestic activities has accelerated with the advent of new technologies.

ONE YEAR OF	HAPPENS TODAY IN...
Growth in US economic output in 1830	a single day
World trade in 1949	a single day
Science done in 1960	a single day
Foreign exchange trading in 1979	a single day
Telephone calls in 1983	a single day
Emails in 1989	a single day

Dr. Oliver Sparrow, *Navigating Uncharted Waters*, Report from the Chatham House Forum, 1997.

"The newest innovations, which we label information technologies, have begun to alter the manner in which we do business and create value, often in ways not readily foreseeable even five years ago." Alan Greenspan, chairman, US Federal Reserve, May 1999.

THE IMPACT OF THE INTERNET

Bill Gates of Microsoft famously remarked in his book *Business at the Speed of Thought* (1999), "The internet changes everything."

● By summer 2000, there were 360 million internet users worldwide – up almost 100 percent from the 185 million users in July 1999. *Global Business Dialogue on e-Commerce*, September 2000.

● In China, internet growth is even faster: from four million users at the end of 1999 to 17 million in September 2000. *Ibid.*

Governments are making internet access and the development of electronic commerce a policy priority. Businesses of all shapes and sizes are getting to grips with its implications.

"I don't think there's been anything more important or more widespread in all my years at GE. Where does the internet rank in priority? It's number one, two, three, and four." Jack Welch, then CEO of GE, quoted in *Business Week*, June 28, 1999.

New communications technologies are coming onstream at an extremely rapid pace, moving from the research and development phase into operational use in a fraction of the time it took their predecessors.

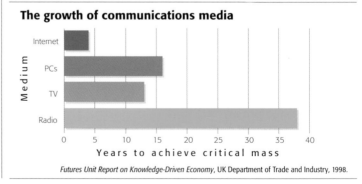

The growth of communications media

Medium / Years to achieve critical mass

Futures Unit Report on Knowledge-Driven Economy, UK Department of Trade and Industry, 1998.

Rapid uptake of the internet
The internet achieved 50 million regular consumers in the US in only four years, compared to, for example, radio, which took 38 years to reach critical mass.

CLICKS AND BRICKS

The convergence of new information and communications technologies has opened up a new way of conducting business, namely e-commerce. The internet allows the user to log on to the network and trade, sell, or buy. Some predict that this will end conventional "bricks and mortar" businesses. However, what is more likely to happen is that all businesses will need to develop e-commerce strategies on top of conventional strands of commerce.

"*Any business which is not an e-business within five years simply will not exist.*" Andy Grove, CEO Intel, quoted in *The Economist e-Business Supplement*, June 24, 1999.

In the mental geography of e-commerce, distance has been eliminated. There is only one economy and only one market. Peter Drucker, "Beyond the Information Revolution," *Atlantic Monthly*, October 1999.

For example, the building and construction industry is being revolutionized by e-companies that allow architects, suppliers, contractors, and customers to collaborate online from the initial design to the completion of projects.

● Sixty percent of US businesses now have a website. At the start of this millennium, there were one billion web pages. The fifth largest travel agent in the US exclusively conducts business on the internet. Microsoft Small Business Taskforce, 1999.

This combination of factors is having a dramatic effect on business processes and strategies. The growth of e-commerce will force businesses to develop new ways of differentiating their brands online, and developing online brands. The further enhancement of brand value will mean brands become more vulnerable to consumer and activist campaigns.

As more business becomes information- and data-oriented, rather than requiring raw materials and production facilities, jobs will be rapidly shifted to different locations and at little cost. One consequence is the growth of new business sectors in emerging economies.

● In Barbados, as many people now work in the IT industry as there are in the sugar-growing industry.

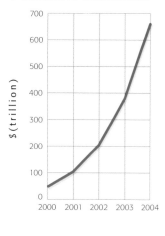

The value of global e-commerce transactions

Forrester Research Inc., 2000.

One hundred
and thirty-fold growth
Worldwide e-commerce was worth just over $50 billion in 1998. Research now suggests that this will be in the region of $6.79 trillion by 2004.

- Texas Instruments designs its most sophisticated computer chips in India.
- Motorola has equipment design centers in both India and China.

Another consequence of the growth of the information and data business in the employment sector is the loss of work that has occurred in the traditional sectors of the industrialized world. Even in developed countries, dramatic shifts are taking place toward the new economy, forcing policymakers to examine the elements which contribute to the high comparative costs of labor.

Intel microchip plant
The economic impact of Intel's investment in a new microchip plant in Costa Rica is estimated to be equivalent to a 15 percent increase in the country's level of domestic output during 2001.

When Asians write about the European welfare system for those of working age, they write with incredulity. They just cannot believe it. Five weeks vacation! One month Christmas bonus! Eighty percent of wages replaced when on unemployment insurance! Their disbelief is one of the reasons why the system cannot continue. Firms can move to the Far East and avoid all those European fringe benefit costs. **Lester Thurow, *The Future of Capitalism*, 1996.**

LIVING IN A 24X7X365 WORLD
The nonstop 24x7x365 world, which technology makes possible and which globalization requires, intensifies a long-hours culture that puts added pressure on business employees, and creates new management challenges to respond to employee stress and concerns for work/life balance. Competition for talented employees, especially in the IT sector, intensifies issues for employers of how to motivate and retain staff, and how the underlying culture and values of the business may help or hinder this.

WORKING PRACTICES
The convergence of the new information and communications technologies has created other changes in where we work, when we work, how we work, and for whom we work.

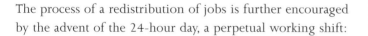

The process of a redistribution of jobs is further encouraged by the advent of the 24-hour day, a perpetual working shift:

> A group of computer programmers at Tsinghua University in Beijing is writing software using Java technology. They work for IBM. At the end of each day they send their work over the internet to an IBM facility in Seattle, where programmers build on it and use the internet to zap it 5,222 miles to the Institute of Computer Science in Belarus and Software House Group in Latvia. From there, the work is sent to India's Tata Group, which passes the software back to Tsinghua, by morning back to Beijing, then back to Seattle, and so on, in a great global relay that never ceases until the project is done. It's like we've created a 48-hour day through the internet. *USA Today*, April 24, 1997.

MEDIA EXPOSURE

Information and communications technology, and particularly the widespread use of the television, has helped to fuel the worldwide availability of media. Consumers have responded by expecting news and information on demand.

● During the Gulf War in 1991, CNN was available in eight million households outside the US; in 2000 the figure was 151 million households.

News exposure
Instant news from around the world at the touch of a button is a reality. Citizens are now better informed and more up to date, with access in real-time to sound and images of global events.

In a CNN world there is no hiding place. With this access to information, together with the power of visual images, transmitted instantly by cable and satellite TV around the world, businesses, as well as governments and other institutions, are subject to relentless scrutiny.

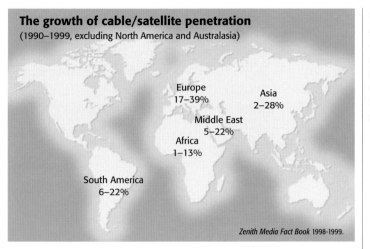

The growth of cable/satellite penetration
(1990–1999, excluding North America and Australasia)

Europe
17–39%

Asia
2–28%

Middle East
5–22%

Africa
1–13%

South America
6–22%

Zenith Media Fact Book 1998-1999.

Production and Manufacturing

Information, rather than manufacturing, is now a growing proportion of the world's economy; and although it has been the impact of technology for the "new" knowledge economy that has grabbed headlines, the effect on the old economy has been no less profound.

Increased automation and use of computers has led to the major restructuring of most industries.

- "New technologies, such as advanced electronics, ultralight materials, computer-aided design, and a host of others could change cars more radically in the next 10 or 20 years than in the last hundred." Sir Alex Trotman, then chairman, Ford Motor Company, quoted in *Shell Global Scenarios 1995/2020* presentation, 1996.

- Percy Barnevik, ex-chairman of ABB, claimed that only 10 percent of the economy would be in manufacturing by 2010.

Natural resources that were previously uneconomical to access because of their remote location, or the difficulty of the terrain, are now physically accessible, at an economic rate, due to advances in extraction technology. Similarly, the transportation and distribution systems required after extraction have improved.

- "BP believes that the application of new technology has cut the cost of producing oil and gas by at least 30 per cent during the 1990s." Chris Gibson, managing director, BP Regions & Technology, 1999.

Although there have been advances in fuel efficiency, there has also been a rise in the level of fuel extraction. This has led to economic development in some producing markets, but has also endangered previously untouched natural environments and has affected indigenous communities.

The ability to develop cleaner energy technology and alternative energy sources is creating new industries.

● Worldwide, environmental industries are worth $280 billion per annum and are set to reach $640 billion by 2010, an almost eight percent growth per annum. The EU Commission estimates that this will result in an extra 500,000 jobs across the EU by 2010. Jonathan Porritt et al., *Committee of Inquiry into a New Vision for Business,* 1999.

Alternative energy sources
Cleaner, cheaper energy sources, such as wind power, are being sought as dwindling fossil fuel resources, the escalating costs of their retrieval and refinement, and the pollution they cause becomes of ever-increasing concern.

Such developments have enabled governments to impose new regulations that stipulate that companies are responsible for the environmental impact of their products.

● The EU passed legislation early in 2000 that holds car manufacturers liable for the final disposal of vehicles and for the setting of parameters for the use of recyclable materials in car manufacture.

The revolution of technology is affecting the way that companies are structured. Thanks partly to increased sophistication in communications, companies are able to outsource noncore business operations. One of these consequences is the potential exposure to mistakes by subcontractors or the negative impacts they could cause. This risk is greater when there are several levels of subcontractors, making control much harder.

Global investment in wind power systems will total $27 billion between 2000 and 2005.

Power Generation in the 21st Century, Dresdner Kleinwort Wasserstein, 2001.

Speeding nowhere
According to Toyota, there were around 69 million cars and trucks worldwide in 1950. Today there are more than 10 times that number – and each year 55 million are added by new production.

TRANSPORTATION

Growing demands to move people, materials, produce, and products around the globe intensifies calls for environmentally sensitive alternatives to more cars and trucks on the roads, more and bigger airports, and deeper sea channels.

● The number of vehicles is growing fast in all regions. Transportation now accounts for one-quarter of world energy use, and about one-half of the world's oil production; motor vehicles account for nearly 80 percent of all transport-related energy. Transportation is a major contributor to greenhouse gas emissions and urban air pollution. *GEO 2000 Overview*, UNEP, 1999.

This week two nails were hammered into the coffin of the internal combustion engine... Toyota and General Motors, which between them make a quarter of the world's cars, signed a pact to develop alternatives... The second was the result of an alliance between DaimlerChrysler and Ford (another quarter of the world's car production) and Bollard Power Systems... that has been developing fuel cells for use in vehicles... "Fuel Cells Hit the Road," *The Economist*, June 24, 1999.

Worldwide growth in air passenger traffic

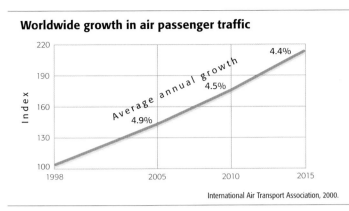

International Air Transport Association, 2000.

Increasing passenger transport
According to the International Air Transport Association, international passenger transportation will continue growing as companies and employees become more global in outlook.

Medical and Genetic Technologies

Many believe that mankind's capacity for technological innovation is fast outstripping its ability to reach ethical and societal consensus on its applications.

This is most pronounced in medical research, particularly into human genetic makeup. Gene technology will transform treatment, but not without raising huge ethical dilemmas. The increasing knowledge of our genetic inheritance and our likelihood of contracting specific diseases will have a tremendous effect on the health insurance sector: will specific illnesses be screened out of insurance benefits, and how will benefits be made available to the widest number of people? Similarly, genetically modified foods are causing great controversies. How will society judge this in 20 years' time:

> ...will we be praising the gene splicers for inventing crops that produced the first famine-free decade in human history? Or will we be prosecuting them for negligence on a global scale as we shovel genetically modified soybeans into empty missile silos, to rot safe distances away from our supermarkets? Peter Schwartz and Blair Gibb, *When Good Companies do Bad Things,* 1999.

The stage is set for a clash between those eager to apply recently acquired technical knowledge and those who fear unforeseeable consequences.

THE REVOLUTION OF MARKETS

Since the Berlin Wall came tumbling down an additional three billion people live in economies that operate on market principles, spurring a globalization of capital, knowledge, and ideas. This has been further fueled by a seemingly relentless process of privatization and liberalization.

The repercussions of that process are now being felt. The institutions of the global market economy – governments, multilateral and bilateral organizations, corporations and nongovernmental organizations – are undergoing a constant reinvention.

Inevitably, this is forcing a flux and reorientation in the relationships between institutions. Many are eager to demonstrate their legitimacy and their right to lead. Others are conscious of a blurring of what were once well-defined roles and responsibilities. The revolution of markets is by no means over, but already this global force for change has produced a complex environment in which to live, work, and play.

The Global Economy

Since the collapse of communism, the world has seen a relentless process of globalization, liberalization, and privatization. This has produced a huge daily flow of funds and global trade that to some epitomizes the spirit of a global community, but to others represents anarchy.

Approximately $1.3 trillion moves around the world every day on the foreign exchange markets – equivalent to almost one-third of the value of annual global exports.

The process of globalization has a significant effect on a growing range of goods and products.

"It is predicted that the share of the world's market that is 'globally contestable,' i.e. open to global competitors in product, service, or asset ownership markets, will rise from about $4 trillion in 1995 [one-seventh of the world's economic output] to approximately $21 trillion by the end of 2001 [one-half of the world's economic output]." Robert Atkinson and Randolph Court, quoted in John Weiser and Simon Zadek, *Conversations with Disbelievers,* 2000.

Old icons discarded
With the collapse of communism and the rejection of outdated ideologies, previously closed economies are now opening up to transnational companies and global brands.

BIG BUSINESS AND ECONOMIC INFLUENCE

Major players in the global economy are transnational companies that, individually and collectively, command significant economic influence.

- Of the world's largest economic entities, 51 are now corporations and 49 are countries. *Top 2000: The Rise of Corporate Power*, Institute for Policy Studies, 2000.
- The world's 200 largest corporations employ less than one percent of the world's population – yet control 25 percent of its economic activity. *Ibid.*
- The 500 largest transnational companies account for 70 percent of world trade and 30 percent of global GDP. Supplement for Prince of Wales International Business Leaders Forum, *Time*, June 1999.
- According to the United Nations, there were 7,000 transnational companies in 1975; 25 years later, the figure had risen to 60,000.
- When BP and Amoco merged in 2000, they became the largest single economic entity in each of 20 national economies, that together account for 20 percent of world GDP. BP spokesperson, 2000.

BUSINESS FOR GROWTH

Business is the principal motor for growth and development; it is the creator of wealth and the provider of goods and services in most parts of the world.

However, with some exceptions, notably Brazil, China, and India, investment in the developing world remains small compared with the amount invested in industrialized countries.

- Foreign direct investment (FDI) increased to over $865 billion in 1999 from only $58 billion in 1982. Cross-border mergers and acquisitions within the industrialized world largely account for the expansion. Africa received 1.2 percent of FDI flows in 1999. *Financial Times*, October 4, 2000.

This destination of investment flows is important because it represents not only the capital required to start and grow a business, but also the transfer of skills and know-how needed to operate in a competitive global economy. Without

Global economies

Comparing the annual corporate sales and GDP of certain countries highlights the growth of the multinational companies.

COUNTRY/ CORPORATION	GDP/SALES ($ MILLION)
1. USA	8,708,870
2. Japan	4,395,083
5. UK	1,373,612
11. Mexico	474,951
14. Australia	389,691
23. **General Motors**	**176,558**
24. Denmark	174,363
25. **Wal-Mart**	**166,809**
27. **Ford Motor Co**	**162,558**
28. **DaimlerChrysler**	**159,985**
29. Poland	154,146
31. Indonesia	140,964
37. **Mitsui**	**118,555**
38. **Mitsubishi**	**117,765**
40. **GE**	**111,630**
42. Portugal	107,716
43. **Royal Dutch/Shell**	**105,366**

Ranking based on corporate sales data from *Fortune*, July 31, 2000, and GDP data from the *World Bank Development Report 2000*.

The annual GDP of New Zealand is equivalent to the annual sales of Nissan Motor Co. The annual sales of IBM exceed the annual GDP of Singapore by $2.6 billion.

Based on corporate sales data from *Fortune*, July 31, 2000 and GDP data: *World Bank Development Report 2000*, World Bank.

investment, growth is negligible, living standards stagnate or fall, and the great inequalities between the industrialized and developing world remain.

The role of the public sector in investment is in decline.

"In the developing world during the 1990s, public investment fell from $60 billion to $50 billion and private investment rose from $30 billion to $300 billion." James Wolfensohn, president, World Bank, November 29, 2000.

Development aid is also in decline. Where aid is given, it is often provided for emergency relief rather than with the purpose of spurring sustainable economic growth.

● Official aid to emerging markets has fallen to record low levels. According to OECD figures, in real terms aid from the world's seven wealthiest governments dropped by 29 percent between 1992 and 1997. Supplement for Prince of Wales International Business Leaders Forum, *Time*, June 1999.

CELEBRITY CORPORATIONS

A consequence of the globalization process is that large transnational companies have become more visible. Campaigners wanting to influence social and political change often see highly visible businesses as legitimate and more accessible targets than governments.

As Naomi Klein, author of *No Logo* (1999), a book adopted as their own by critics of globalization, writes:

People are beginning to fight the big global economic battles by focusing on one or two brand-name corporations and turning them into large-scale political metaphors. They are having more luck with this strategy than they had with decades of fighting these battles on a policy level with governments.

With business regarded as the major contributor to economic development, it is no surprise it is increasingly in the spotlight. A decision by a business executive to close, or open, a factory is much more likely to receive external attention and scrutiny than in the past.

Certainly business is not shy about its ambitions:

> Our priorities are that we want to dominate North America first, then South America, and then Asia, and then Europe. **David Glass, president and CEO, Wal-Mart,** *Adbusters,* **August/September 2000.**

Today, some corporations have taken on the same status as Hollywood celebrities. Their every move is watched, analyzed, and commented upon. Every formal statement and informal comment is studied for inconsistencies. A growing movement of sophisticated nongovernmental organizations (NGOs), combined with technological developments in the media, has pushed the exposure of corporate behavior onto news channels, the pages of the popular press, and into website chat rooms. Gossip about some companies spreads as rapidly around the world today as does gossip about movie stars.

What are NGOs?

The term nongovernmental organization (NGO) is a catch-all phrase describing organizations that are outside the public sector. They may be charities or other nonprofit distributing organizations with a social or community purpose.

There is a growing diversity within the NGO community, with service organizations in areas such as health and education, those campaigning for social and economic change, and many other hybrids.

Brand Supremacy

The power of the "brand" is regarded in some business sectors as the key to commercial success.

"According to Fortune magazine, in the twenty-first century, branding will ultimately be the only unique differentiator between companies. Brand equity is now a key asset." Rita Clifton, CEO, Interbrand, September 1999.

Research carried out in 1999 by Interbrand, a branding consultancy, found that 96 percent of Coca-Cola's stock market value is in intangibles, such as reputation, knowledge, and brand. Kellogg's is estimated at 97 percent, American Express 84 percent, and IBM 83 percent. They predicted that the proportion of the intangible valuation of companies represented by brands will rise from the five percent it was in 1960 to 30 percent by 2000 and to 45 percent by 2010.

An increasingly global community of young people has significant purchasing power and shared tastes in culture, fashion, popular music, and social trends and are now, with

Global images
From Coca-Cola to Madonna, from Nike to Levi's, international brands create a global identity to which many young people aspire.

the internet and the ease of air travel, "connected." This global community can be found dancing to the same music and wearing the same global brands in the nightclubs of London, Sydney, New York, Cape Town, Buenos Aires, and Tokyo.

However, those who live by the sword, die by the sword. Just as business has benefited from popular culture and the fast spread of ideas that have made global brands more valuable, equally, business can fall prey to the same bushfire spread of ideas about unpopular corporate behavior.

Corporations now operate in many countries with different cultural conditions. They need to use brand management techniques that are responsive to local markets and that differentiate products. Skills are needed in "glocalism": the ability to sensitize global policies, brands, and corporate cultures with the needs, and within the parameters, of local markets.

"In our recent past, we succeeded because we understood and appealed to global commonalities. In our future, we'll succeed because we will also understand and appeal to local differences. The 21st century demands nothing less." Douglas Daft, chairman and CEO, Coca-Cola, *Financial Times*, March 27, 2000.

The growth of global brands brings opportunities of scale, but it also brings a greater risk to brand and corporate reputations. Corporations are held accountable for the impact of their operations through all the stages of a product life-cycle and along extended, multilevel supply chains.

Global reach of companies

Company speakers at a business conference were asked to list how many different countries they were operating in. Their answers are listed below.

COMPANY	NUMBER OF COUNTRIES
Diageo	200
Ford	200
Siemens	190
Volkswagen	150
Texaco	150
Shell	140
Citicorp	100
State Street Corp.	85
Dow	32
BT	30

Compiled from data provided by companies for the Corporate Citizenship Conference, The Conference Board, New York, 1999.

The value of company brands (June 1999)

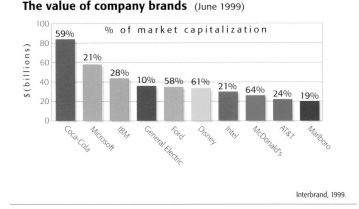

Interbrand, 1999.

Brand value

The percentage of the total stock market value of selected companies that can be attributed to the value of brands, as shown in a survey carried out by Interbrand.

*Entrepreneurialism is much in evidence in
the informal economies of those countries
whose markets are in transition. The
challenge for authorities is to turn
informal, non-tax paying businesses into
regular contributors to national economic
and human capital.*

THE INFORMAL ECONOMY

It is the large transnational organizations that capture the
headlines, but it is the small business sector that actually
employs most people around the world, and it is also where
domestic economic growth in the developing world is likely
to be focused in the near future. A growing proportion of
small businesses are outside the formal economy of
companies registered with government agencies, paying taxes,
and operating under monitored regulations.

In 1994, the National Statistical Institute of Mexico
attempted to measure the number of informal micro-
businesses in the country, and estimated that there were some
2.65 million. Another 1993 study put the number of people
in the "non-registered informal sector" at eight million, out
of a total workforce of 23 million.

Author Hernando de Soto in *The Mystery of Capital: Why
Capitalism Triumphs in the West and Fails Everywhere Else* (2000)
describes these individuals as "extra-legal," rather than
informal or illegal, on the basis that inadequate registration
systems for land, property, or business make the effort to be
"legal" simply counterproductive. For example, in a recent
investigation in Peru, it took 289 days to register a new

The shadow economy (1999)

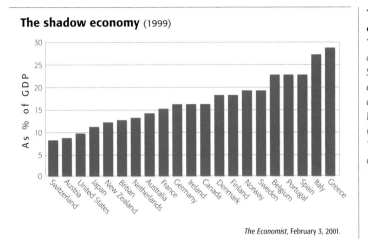

The Economist, February 3, 2001.

The growth
of the informal economy
The informal economy is not just a feature of the developing world. Dr. Friedrich Schneider of the University of Linz has estimated the informal economic activity as a percentage of GDP in Organization for Economic Cooperation and Development (OECD) countries, and concluded that the "shadow economy" as a share of national output grew in every OECD country from 1989 to 1999.

business and cost $1,231 - over 30 times the monthly minimum wage. De Soto challenges the view that this activity is marginal, "… in fact legality is marginal; extra-legality has become the norm," he says, citing evidence that 50 percent of GDP in Russia and Ukraine is underground, with 62 percent in Georgia.

PUBLIC AND PRIVATE OWNERSHIP

The 1990s saw a high volume of state-owned industries passing into private ownership via accelerated privatization programs, especially in the newly liberalized economies. An increasing proportion of the economy of almost every

The growth of privatization
According to the OECD, sales of state-owned companies equaled $145 billion in 1999, slightly below 1997's record of $157 billion.

The proceeds of privatization

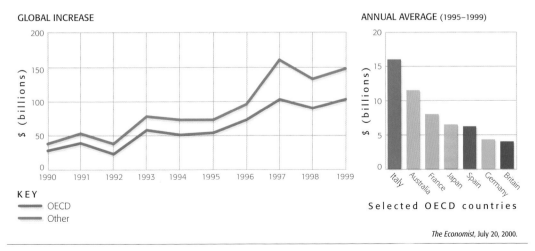

GLOBAL INCREASE

KEY
▬▬▬ OECD
▬▬▬ Other

ANNUAL AVERAGE (1995–1999)

Selected OECD countries

The Economist, July 20, 2000.

member country of the United Nations is now in the hands of the private sector.

The new companies that are started as part of the privatization process require regulatory institutions to oversee their business practices. The challenge for managers in the privatized businesses is to create a customer-focused organization and to build their relationship with the new regulatory institutions appointed to oversee their markets in an open and transparent way. For many, this requires a culture change, new management skills in building partnerships, and clear definitions of accountability.

GLOBALIZATION BACKLASH

A growing chorus of critics has developed as a result of the increase in the movement of jobs and capital flows around the world and the perceived power and influence that the private sector now commands. Global markets can bring many benefits. Business can be a powerful force for human progress, stimulating technological, medical, and economic breakthroughs that enhance people's lives, extend personal mobility and freedom, and open up life chances for many more people. But, as the benefits of globalization are not reaching everyone, voices are being raised in protest.

Questions are also being raised within the business community: "For most of us there is recognition that if globalization is so good, how come so many are being left behind?" asked one manager from management consultancy McKinsey. The "Battle of Seattle," in which anti-globalization demonstrators disrupted the proceedings of the World Trade Organization in November 1999, saw a coalition of disparate groups coming together to share their disquiet at the repercussions of the revolution of markets. Among the protesters were NGOs campaigning on a range of platforms from environmental protection to human rights.

NGO MARKET POWER

Businesses are learning how to work alongside the growing nongovernmental sector, which is growing in reach and economic significance. Also, NGOs are providing significant and growing employment opportunities.

● The nonprofit sector now accounts for an average of one in every 20 jobs in 22 developed and developing countries surveyed; that is close to 19 million full-time equivalent employees estimated as a $1.1 trillion industry. In the countries for which the change between 1990 and 1995 could be measured, nonprofits grew by 23 percent compared to 6.2 percent for the whole economy.

Global Civil Society: Dimensions of the Nonprofit Sector. The Johns Hopkins Center for Civil Society Studies, Baltimore, Md, 1999.

The Battle of Seattle
Widespread, passionate, and often inconsistent voices were raised in Seattle against the automatic progression of globalization. Such protests now regularly accompany gatherings of business and political leaders throughout the world.

● The number of international NGOs with operations in more
than one country was 26,000 as of 1999, up from just
6,000 in 1990; India has more than a million grass roots
groups; and more than 100,000 such groups sprang up in
Eastern Europe between 1988 and 1995. *The Yearbook of
International Organizations 2000*, The Union of International Associations, 2000.

International NGOs are global brands in their own right,
exercising power and authority and often commanding
greater trust and respect than governments and companies.

The majority of NGOs exist to serve a public purpose.
Others see their role, or part of their role, as being a
counterbalance to global dominance by business in general
and the transnational corporations in particular.

The revolutions that influence business also affect civil
society, and NGOs are themselves increasingly faced with
issues similar to those faced by business. They are increasingly
visible – which is regarded as a "good thing" as it increases
their influence and ability to raise resources. They are affected
by technology, sometimes having to adopt uncomfortable
shifts in work practices. And they are subject to questioning
and media scrutiny about their own accountability – in fact,
the very same issues they raise about the business sector.

NGOs as brands
*Global NGOs are now valuable brands.
Like the businesses they partner or
confront, NGOs are increasingly
facing greater pressures of
accountability and reporting.*

CHANGING RELATIONSHIPS

The relationship between the public sector, business, and society is fluid. A result of the global forces for change over the past decade has been a discernible blurring of boundaries, with each sector taking on certain characteristics of the others.

Governments and NGOs are having to learn the financial and management skills, entrepreneurialism, and customer focus of business. Businesses and NGOs are taking on roles and responsibilities previously the preserve of the public sector, and in the process learning about the challenges of balancing different stakeholders' concerns and interests. Government and business are finding ways to attract and motivate talent, encourage participation, and create the same sense of passion and adherence to values that the best NGOs manage, which enables them to excite, and be inspired by, their volunteers and staff.

One consequence of these changes includes a greater overlap between the sectors, and the potential for "creative swiping" from each other. This blurring of boundaries, however, also brings a degree of confusion about institutional roles and responsibilities and turf wars, as well as new opportunities and new expectations.

Management consultancies Bain & Co. and McKinsey have both established operations to serve the nonprofit sector.

Financial Times, February 7, 2001.

THE REVOLUTION OF DEMOGRAPHICS AND DEVELOPMENT

Demographic change, and its connection with the process of development, has a crucial bearing on business operations, future growth, and profitability.

Together, demographics and development encompass population growth and composition, as well as interrelated topics such as income distribution, access to health and education services, jobs, security, and liberty.

The interaction between these issues and business is equally complex. But it starts from a very simple premise: business does not operate in a vacuum. What happens to society matters to business. What happens to business matters to society.

Globalization has led to more companies operating in countries with limited public resources and an inadequate infrastructure, and with significant social problems that will constrain business growth or compel firms to take remedial action. Business operations are often sited next to centers of population that have little income, low skill levels, and poor prospects. As such, local people lack a stake in the system and, understandably, question the concentration of wealth in the hands of what, for them, is seen as an elite minority.

*For businesses to thrive, there needs to be a
satisfactory balance between the creation of
wealth and the needs of employees and the
environment. When these factors are
managed successfully, a business can be said
to be working successfully.*

The Needs of Business

To appreciate the link between the revolution in
demographics and development and the world of business,
it is necessary to highlight what companies require in
order to prosper.

Businesses desire economic growth and market stability. The
Resource Centre for the Social Dimensions of Business
Practice, an organization that focuses on business activity in
countries where poverty is a major issue, say they require:

- A competent, reliable, healthy, and efficient workforce so the
  company can be productive.
- An expanding market and customer base so the company
  can thrive in a competitive climate.
- A stable and safe environment so the company can operate
  effectively in the global marketplace.

However, in many parts of the world these conditions do not
prevail; and even when they do, they may be at risk because of
a range of demographic and development issues.

One of these issues is poverty, which brings into sharp relief
the connection between the well-being of business and the

well-being of humanity. Poverty, and the conditions that accompany poverty, such as deprivation, lack of access to water and sanitation, ill health, and poor education and literacy, is a threat to business.

> "The issue of poverty is an issue of peace. We can't guarantee the security of your business unless we deal with the issues of development." James Wolfenshohn, president, World Bank, November 29, 2000.

Poverty is not just the preserve of the developing world. Although abject poverty is rare in industrialized countries, the issues of social exclusion and inequality of wealth and opportunity represent real costs to business all over the world.

Lack of investment in education stifles growth and adds to the costs of industrial and commercial operations wherever it occurs. Corruption and lack of openness are not solely the preserve of developing nations – witness the financial crisis in Asia at the end of the 1990s. Breakdown in political rule and the emergence of conflict poses risks for major corporate investments in any country.

The Revolution of Markets demonstrated how business is the principal motor for growth and development. It is therefore in the enlightened self-interest of business to understand this impact on the development process, and to take on board that the revolution of demography and development is everybody's business.

The six-billionth person
Tthe United Nations symbolically declared that a baby who was born in Sarajevo in October 1999 was the six-billionth person on the planet.

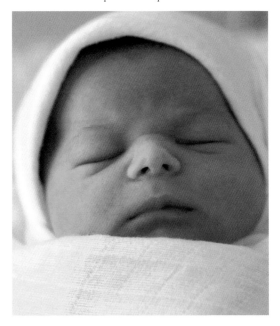

POPULATION PRESSURES

The finite natural resources of the planet are under pressure as demand for food, shelter, and space to live increases in line with the rapid growth in the world's population.

● After 3.85 billion years of evolution, the world's population had risen to 2.5 billion by 1950 and has doubled over the last 50 years to 5.9 billion. It is now set to double over the next 50 years and is estimated to reach 9.5 billion. *State of the World*, UN Population Fund, 1998.

Regional variations

The population mix in 2050 will
look very different from today,
with a population decline in the
West, explosive growth in the East,
and little change elsewhere.

Projected variations in population growth

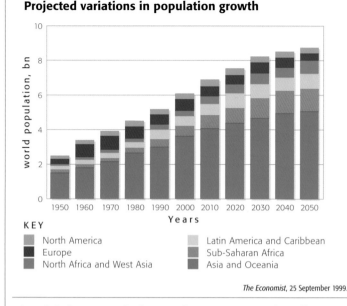

KEY

■ North America		▨ Latin America and Caribbean	
■ Europe		▨ Sub-Saharan Africa	
■ North Africa and West Asia		■ Asia and Oceania	

The Economist, 25 September 1999.

The global statistics hide significant variations in different countries. There is high growth in developing countries such as India and China, but negligible changes in some industrialized nations such as Italy and Japan.

In the developing world, high population growth causes pressure on already stretched resources and infrastructures, for example on sanitation and water systems, health and education provision, and supplies of food.

● Almost 800 million people in the developing world do not have enough to eat. *The State of Food Insecurity in the World,* Food Agricultural Organization, 1999.

Static population levels in industrialized countries can be a threat to economic growth and may lead to labour shortages, which in turn leads to the need to attract an immigrant labour workforce.

Some of the greatest challenges associated with population growth lie in urban areas. The proportion of people concentrated in cities continues to rise, producing megacities with all their associated mega-problems. According to the UN, more than half of humanity will reside in cities within a decade, most of them in less developed countries that are less able to cope with the resulting strains.

By 2015, the population of Shanghai will have grown from 14 million to 23.4 million.

CIA Global Trends 2001,
Central Intelligence Agency.

"Each year, 61 million people are added to cities worldwide, or more than one million per week. By 2025, urban areas are expected to comprise more than five billion people." Jennifer D. Mitchell, "Urban Areas Swell," *Vital Signs 1998: The Environmental Trends That Are Shaping Our Future*, 1998.

On the one hand, larger cities require investment and therefore create business for business. On the other hand, crowded and overworked transportation and utilities can equal inefficiency and added costs for business.

Population explosion
Businessmen prepare for a night's sleep in a hotel in Tokyo, the world's largest city and home to 28 million inhabitants. Is this the creative use of urban space or a frightening glimpse of an unsustainable future with teeming populations?

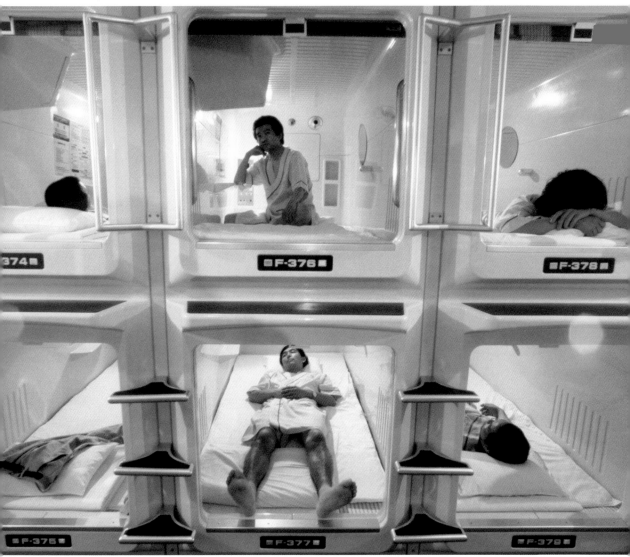

Infant mortality rates (1998)

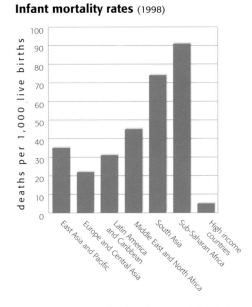

World Bank Development Report, World Bank 2000.

Variations in mortality
Across the world, infant mortality rates fell from 98 deaths per 1,000 live births in 1970 to 58 deaths per 1,000 live births by 1997. However, there are still great regional differences.

POPULATION PROFILES

The age composition of a country or region has a direct bearing on its productivity; young and older people are "heavy" users of services such as education and healthcare, whereas those of intermediate age can be net contributors to the GDP.

● Lower mortality rates in some regions are increasing the number of young people to house and feed, and who require schools and books. People are living longer because of advances in medicine and quality healthcare, resulting in the need to extend elder care provision, whether in the home or through public services. *Human Development Report,* United Nations, 1999.

Improvements in infant mortality rates are influenced by access to prenatal and postnatal medical care, availablility of clean water, a nutritional food supply, and whether there is a prevalence of opportunistic diseases. Overall, infant mortality is falling.

Aging populations of the world

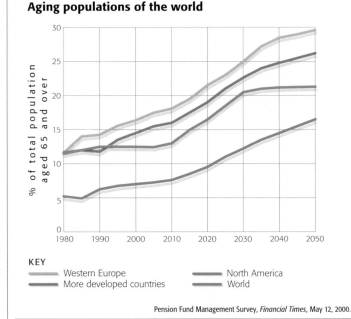

KEY

| Western Europe | North America |
| More developed countries | World |

Pension Fund Management Survey, *Financial Times*, May 12, 2000.

Global aging
The world is aging rapidly as life expectancy rises. There is pressure on the more rapidly industrializing countries to provide pensions and sophisticated social safety nets for their elder residents.

But there are still great regional variations. A country with a burgeoning youth population is potentially economically beneficial once the young people reach a productive age. In the growing urban populations, however, if there is poor supervision of attendance at school, a high incidence of poverty, and a lack of opportunity for young people to be integrated as part of society, this is likely to lead to increased youth-associated crime. In turn, this results in higher security

Youth-associated crime
Urban youth from impoverished backgrounds often face a life of reduced educational opportunities and, consequently, reduced job prospects. The subsequent frustration they experience often manifests itself in vandalism and other criminal acts.

The pensions time bomb

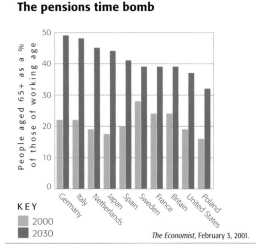

People aged 65+ as a % of those of working age

KEY
- 2000
- 2030

The Economist, February 3, 2001.

costs for business and a loss of confidence among potential investors.

"The consumption needs of children and the elderly surpass their productive capacity, while the opposite occurs for people of intermediate ages. Therefore, the capacity to save and invest in physical and human capital for any society depends on the composition of its population. Consequently, growth will be higher in societies that have an age composition that favors intermediate ages, and less in societies that are very young or very old." Development Beyond Economics 2000, Inter-American Development Bank, 2000.

Changing ratios

Across Europe there are more than four people of working age to support each person aged 65 years or more. By 2030 this will be nearer two, prompting a reassessment of the funding of pensions.

Financial security

Those who can plan for retirement can look forward to a life of ease when their working days are over. Today, however, working people will have to make much greater pension contributions to ensure a financially secure retirement.

Greater numbers of old people in the population as a whole bring their own challenges:

- By 2030, 20 percent of the US population will be over 65, and in Europe the number will be 25 percent. Ira Matathia and Marian Salzman, *Next: A Vision of Our Lives in the Future,* 1999.
- Around the world, half of all people aged 65 and over who have ever lived are alive today. *Ibid.*

There is concern among OECD countries, particularly in Western Europe, that pension program costs will be

Workers without pensions
Approximately 90 percent of the world's working population has no pension. Those without private or state pension provision can expect to have to continue working well into old age.

Living longer
Not only has average life expectancy risen, but with advances in medical technology, healthier, older people are living more active lives for longer. Conventional mores about what people still do at certain ages are also breaking down. Students in their 70s and nightclubbers in their 50s are now common.

prohibitive as the ratio of people in work contributing directly and indirectly to government funds for the retired, shrinks.

Business is feeling the pressure of these demographic changes. European governments, such as Austria, Finland, and Germany, now encourage businesses to recruit or retain older workers, and more people will be encouraged to invest in their own future financial security through the insurance and financial services sectors.

Support for elders takes on a different perspective in the developing world, where the onus is on the family. But this could change as, for example in Asia, where traditional family relationships are beginning to alter as young people become more mobile and as women, traditionally the carers, join the workforce. This is likely to put a strain on public sector safety nets.

- Ninety per cent of the world's working population who do not have a pension live in the developing world. *Social Security Pensions: Development and Reform,* International Labour Office, 2000.

Global life expectancy

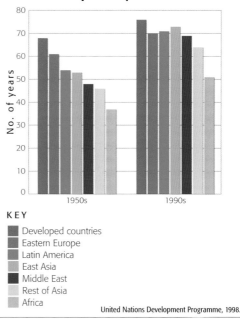

KEY
- Developed countries
- Eastern Europe
- Latin America
- East Asia
- Middle East
- Rest of Asia
- Africa

United Nations Development Programme, 1998.

POPULATION SHIFTS

Population growth is not universal. There will be a significant shift in the coming decades in the proportion of numbers of people from different ethnic origins and religious affinities. Consumer demands will change accordingly, and fashion and tastes will be affected. Corporations will need to consider their response to the projected growth of the Muslim faith:

● Muslims … constituted perhaps 18 percent of the world's population in 1980 and are likely to be over 20 percent in 2000 and 30 percent in 2025. Samuel P. Huntington, *The Clash of Civilizations and the Remaking of World Order,* 1996.

Some companies are responding to such demographic changes by introducing human resource policies that are designed to ensure that the employee base reflects the diversity of their consumers and the communities where the company operates. All-white, male, middle-aged company boards and senior management teams will find it increasingly hard to understand diverse multicultural markets.

The spread of the Muslim faith
There is a significant increase in the number of people belonging to the Muslim faith, and in the immigration of Muslims throughout the world. In Europe, for example, second-generation Muslims are better integrated than their parents and play a greater role in European social, economic, and political affairs.

Unequal Wealth

Food, shelter, health, education, jobs. These are available to some, but not all. The right to freedom of movement, of association, and of belief are rights enjoyed by some, but not all.

A key dimension of the development agenda is the unequal distribution of wealth and other resources, such as land and

The haves and the have nots
Western visitors to major cities in the developing world, who move between five-star hotels and well-stocked shopping malls, may not witness the dire poverty that lives alongside the affluence.

food, and the consequences of that inequality, i.e. extreme poverty in much of the world.

● 2.8 billion people live on less than $2 a day, some 1.2 billion live on $1 per day. *World Development Report,* World Bank, 2000.

The majority of the world's poor live in rural areas, but progress in reducing rural poverty has been stalled as aid to agriculture has fallen. There have been some changes in poverty levels: between 1965 and 1998 average incomes in developing countries more than doubled, with a drop of 78 million living in extreme poverty between 1990 and 1998. The most positive changes were recorded in Asia. But huge (some would say grotesque) inequalities also exist.

● 358 billionaires have as much wealth as the poorest 45 percent of the world's population. Malcolm McIntosh et al., *Corporate Citizenship*, 1998.

● The combined wealth of the top 200 billionaires equalled $1,135 trillion in 1999, up from $1,042 trillion in 1998. In comparison, the combined income of the 582 million people of the least developed countries totalled $146 billion. *United Nations Development Programme: Human Development Report,* United Nations, 2000.

The cost of living
Overall, the number of people living on less than $1 a day is rising, with the exception of East Asia. According to the World Bank, in European and Central Asian countries experiencing the transition to market economies, this figure rose 20 times between 1987–1998.

People living on less than $1 a day

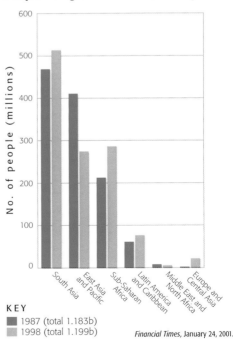

KEY
■ 1987 (total 1.183b)
■ 1998 (total 1.199b)   *Financial Times,* January 24, 2001.

Unequal wealth distribution

The unequal distribution of income throughout the world produces a disparity in wealth and life chances between the world's richest 20 percent and its poorest 20 percent. These proportions have not changed since this information was published.

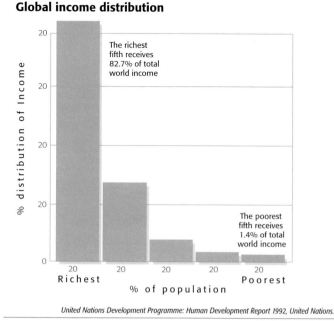

Global income distribution

% distribution of Income

The richest fifth receives 82.7% of total world income

The poorest fifth receives 1.4% of total world income

Richest   % of population   Poorest

20   20   20   20   20

United Nations Development Programme: Human Development Report 1992, United Nations.

MEASURING POVERTY

There are many views on how to measure poverty. It can differ across gender, age, and ethnic groups, and it also varies over time. The "dollar-a-day" benchmark is only one. Poverty and development studies are moving towards the view that a wider range of factors should be considered, including:
– Per capita income relative to the cost of necessities, such as food and fuel, and relative to the income of others.
– Skill and capability levels; access to safe water.
– Inclusion within a community, such as a household or government support mechanism.

In this way, it is possible to measure the relative poverty of industrialized countries and the poverty of the developing world, and consequently inform appropriate development strategies for the area.

Women and poverty

Indicators suggest that women are considerably more disadvantaged than men, particularly in poorer households. Up to 70 percent of the world's poor are women.

"Don't ask me what poverty is because you have met it outside my house. Look at the house and count the number of holes. Look at my utensils and clothes I am wearing. Look at everything and write what you see. What you see is poverty." D. Narayan et al., *World Bank Development Report,* World Bank, 2000.

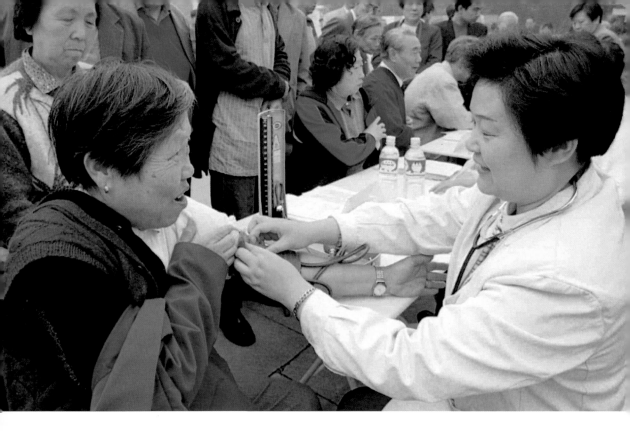

ACCESS TO HEALTHCARE AND EDUCATION

Good health and education are inexorably linked. There are two key aspects of poverty that present a barrier to development: a lack of access to healthcare and poor or nonexistent education provision. Demographic change, such as more older people requiring intensive healthcare, will cost governments more, which is why some state systems are relying on the private sector much more enthusiastically than in the past.

In Brazil, where the constitution guarantees access to free healthcare, some 44 million people have health insurance.

In the developing world, government healthcare services, which are supposed to be provided at no cost, often suffer from widespread corruption by poorly paid officials, with patients having to pay a bribe in order to receive treatment.

"A poor woman from Madaripur in Bangladesh said that the doctor in the government health center ignored them, giving preferential treatment to patients wearing good clothes and to those who could afford side payments referred to as 'visit fees'." D. Narayan, et al., quoted in *World Bank Development Report,* World Bank, 2000.

One of the major influences on poor health is ignorance of the causes – be it the dangers of dirty water, the impact of pollution from domestic fuel, or the implications of having to eat a poor diet.

- 12 million children under five years of age die each year from treatable diseases, and over 200 million of the same age group are malnourished. *State of the World's Children,* UNICEF, 1988.

- Of 2.7 million deaths related to air pollution in Asia each year, 1.8 million are caused by indoor pollution in rural areas. *Asian Development Outlook,* Asian Development Bank, 2000.

- In countries such as Cambodia, Papua New Guinea, and Vietnam, less than half of households have access to safe water, and across Asia as a whole, more than 90 percent of waste water is discharged untreated into streams, open drains, rivers, lakes, and coastal waterways. *Ibid.*

"Improvements in the health and nutrition status in individuals clearly leads to greater productivity and, in the case of students, contributes to a more regular attendance and increased learning capacity." Tadao Chino, president, Asian Development Bank, September 2000.

HIV/AIDS – personal and economic tragedy

Globally, more than 34 million people are infected with HIV. Of those, 90 percent are in the developing world, where access to medicine and availability of care is poor. In these areas, some five million people are infected each year. In African countries at the center of the world HIV/AIDS epidemic, such as Botswana and Zimbabwe, one in four adults is infected. This severely impacts on not only the workforce but also on economic performance. AIDS orphans are becoming a major burden on the traditional support mechanisms of family, community, government, and aid agencies. *World Bank Development Report,* World Bank, 2000; *State of the World Population,* United Nations Population Fund, 1999.

Life expectancy in 2010 with and without AIDS

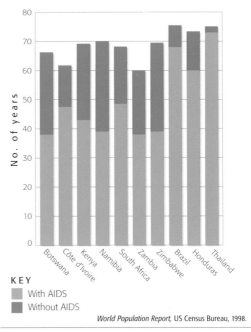

KEY
- With AIDS
- Without AIDS

World Population Report, US Census Bureau, 1998.

The spread of HIV

There are now 26 million people in Sub-Saharan Africa who are HIV positive, producing a dramatic impact on life expectancy figures. The HIV virus is also leading to a resurgence of other diseases, such as tuberculosis.

Corporations looking to sell and build markets where there are lower standards of education could have to adopt self-regulation when they market products that, if not consumed responsibly, may lead to poor health.

However, there are some positive signs. The world has a greater number of literate and better-educated people than at any other time in history. Literacy rates around the world have improved without exception (although Africa still lags behind), and enrollment rates at schools have improved.

● Enrollment at primary schools ranged from 56 percent for Sub-Saharan Africa to 99.8 percent for East Asia. *Human Development Indicators,* United Nations Development Programme, 1999.

Projections suggest a billion university graduates in 2020, compared with a few million in 1920. Overall, a better-educated population will lead to more assertive customers and employees who have the means to articulate their views. There will be several billion more sophisticated consumers by 2020. This will mean that companies will have a greater choice of locations with greater access to skilled staff.

There are great disparities in some countries between the educational progress of boys and girls (which also happens in other aspects of development). In some parts of Asia, a girl

Education for a future
For emerging economies to compete in a highly competitive global market, investment in literacy and education is vital.

Girls as carers
In poor households it is usually the girl's role to act as carer to younger siblings, sick parents, and infirm grandparents, even at the expense of receiving an education.

The growth of literacy
Worldwide, literacy rates have been growing over the past 40 years. In regions such as Latin America, where the rate of progress has been comparatively slow, this may be due to the small proportion of students finishing schooling.

who is too educated might not be considered suitable for marriage. Girls cost more to send to schools, as parents are more concerned with ensuring they have the appropriate dress. Also, if temporary care is needed in the home because of sickness, the girl will normally be the one to stay at home.

For both sexes, and for the type of skills required for jobs in the new economy, there is a danger that inequalities between the industrialized and developing countries will be exacerbated unless steps are taken to bridge the digital divide (*see* Bridging the Digital Divide, p. 58).

Levels of health and education have a direct impact on businesses, wherever in the world they operate or sell. Loss of production caused by employee sickness or family illness, and the task of remedial education when skill levels are deficient, are all direct costs to business.

It is therefore in the interests of business to help public authorities improve health and education provision. Many corporations will provide supplementary support and welfare systems for employees and their dependants, and regard it as a necessary cost of doing business in emerging markets.

Global literacy rates

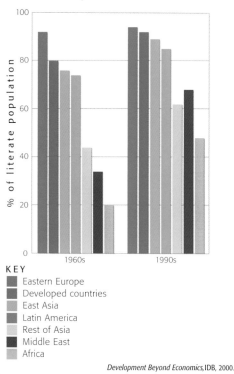

% of literate population

KEY
- Eastern Europe
- Developed countries
- East Asia
- Latin America
- Rest of Asia
- Middle East
- Africa

Development Beyond Economics, IDB, 2000.

Internet users worldwide (July 2000)

Total 359.8m

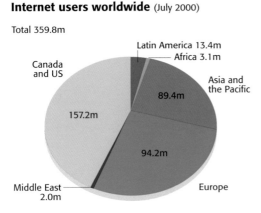

- Canada and US 157.2m
- Asia and the Pacific 89.4m
- Europe 94.2m
- Latin America 13.4m
- Africa 3.1m
- Middle East 2.0m

World Employment Report, 2000, International Labour Organization, 2000.

Development through communications

Information communication technologies are able to offer low-cost solutions to overcoming distance by facilitating communications. This in turn can help economic and market development in both urban and rural areas.

BRIDGING THE DIGITAL DIVIDE

The term "digital divide" is widely used to describe the gap between those who have access to technology and information technology developments, and those who do not. This situation creates those who are information-rich and those who are information-poor. It is feared that the economic gap between developed and developing countries will be exacerbated unless the latter gain access to new technology know-how and infrastructure.

- Half the world's population has not yet made a telephone call. *Life at Work in the Information Economy, World Employment Report,* International Labour Organization, 2001.
- Tokyo and Manhattan each have more telephone lines than the whole of Africa. *Ibid.*
- Only some six percent of the world's population uses the internet and 88 percent of them live in industrialized countries. *Ibid.*

Telecommunications companies and other businesses operating in the information communication technology sector are being called upon by political and civic leaders to help bridge the divide.

Job Creation

Business investment encourages economic growth and creates jobs, and it is these employment opportunities that help lift the poor out of poverty.

The International Labour Organization noted at the end of 2000 that as much as one-third of the world's workforce of three billion people were unemployed or underemployed.

- To accommodate new entrants to the workforce and reduce the current levels of unemployment, the global economy will have to maintain its current pace to generate some 500 million new jobs. *Life at Work in the Information Economy, World Employment Report,* International Labour Organization, 2001.

Real opportunities to increase employment and improve the productivity of existing business lie in the adoption of information communication technology.

The software sector in India has grown by 50 percent throughout the 1990s, creating not only jobs but also a talented workforce that is proving a magnet for international investment.

Software development in India
India's global reputation for software engineering was recognized when the Massachusetts Institute of Technology chose Bombay for its third Media Lab in June 2001. The other two are in Dublin and Boston.

THE JOB MARKET

The job market can be divided into the "formal" and "informal" sectors – those inside or outside the tax base and whether or not they are subject to regulatory supervision.

● Since 1990, 85 percent of all new jobs in Latin America and the Caribbean have been created in the informal sector. And in Zambia only 10 percent of the workforce is legally employed. Hernando de Soto, *The Mystery of Capital: Why Capitalism Triumphs in the West and Fails Everywhere Else*, 2000.

The informal economy provides livelihoods for those unable to break into the formal sector. But it also perpetuates poverty, seldom providing sufficient resources to live with dignity or to support children's education. It also comes with no healthcare, no pension, and no employment rights.

Children at work
It is estimated that there are some 250 million children at work. In regions of extreme poverty, children are often vital wage-earners for the family. Campaigns to end child labor must be sensitive to the dangers of forcing children out of relatively safe conditions into dangerous environments, such as the sex industry.

Corporations opening operations where there is a surplus of local labor can maximize their impact by supporting local training and raising standards among local companies through the transfer of IT skills and good operating practices.

If transnational companies do not implement good operational practices, or demand it of their suppliers, they may become the targets of activists seeking to expose the maltreatment of workers and the use of child labor. Proactive promotion of world-class standards can be used as part of communcation campaigns to differentiate goods in the retail market.

MIGRANTS AND MIGRATION

The prospect of jobs being readily available overseas has led to increased migration, a process encouraged by the policies of industrialized countries that have labor shortages. This movement of people has combined with the migration of displaced persons, due to war and conflict, infrastructure development, and natural disasters. Sudden movements to new environments result in increased vulnerability to illnesses such as pneumonia and malaria. Migration, over time, can leave home economies impoverished.

- Some countries in Sub-Saharan Africa, the Caribbean, Central America, and South Asia have lost one-third of their skilled workers ... foreign workers send home about $75 billion to their home countries each year, 50 percent more than total official development assistance. *State of the World Population,* United Nations Population Fund, 1999.
- There are some 22 million displaced people in the world. United Nations High Commission for Refugees, 1999.

Influxes of migrants create increasingly multiethnic populations in the cities of the industrialized world, bringing specific skills and culture. Some indigenous populations see the arrival of immigrants as a threat to their way of life and to their own prospects of securing jobs in a tight labor market. These pressures can combine to heighten racial tensions.

The global forces of demographic change and development have a profound effect on market conditions and business operations at home and abroad. This is becoming even more so, as companies build up their complex web of international suppliers, outlets, workers, customers, and investors.

Between 1965 and 1990, migration expanded from 70 million to 120 million people.
State of the World Population, United Nations Population Fund, 1999.

Migrant labor
Often lacking relevant language skills and institutions to formally represent them, migrant workers are open to abuse and exploitation from unscrupulous employers.

THE REVOLUTION OF VALUES

In the past century, democratic governments and large corporations commanded respect and were regarded as leaders of society. But in recent years, they have lost their gloss.

Trust in government, the political process, and business has declined. High-profile scandals, corruption, and an apparent lack of accountability have led many to question the authority vested in organizations long regarded as the Establishment.

In many parts of the world, today's public – whether as consumers, employees, health service patients, or members of local communities – is more willing and more able than ever before to question what it is being told. Information about the workings and failings of institutions is readily available, as are alternative views.

Values, the concepts people believe in, the standards they live by, and the views they hold and by which they measure others, are shifting.

Business, as the principal motor for growth and development, is now firmly center stage, bringing with it greater responsibilities and changing expectations of its conduct. As a consequence it is increasingly in the spotlight and open to the glare of public and media scrutiny. How a business acts in the light of these responsibilities, changing expectations, and intensive scrutiny is crucial to its ongoing success.

A Decline in Deference

The institutions that have held power for many years are under increased scrutiny: who is leading whom in the twenty-first century, and to what end?

All around the globe people clearly express the view that the most important source of leadership for achieving national goals will come from government (*see* Expected Sources of Leadership, at right). However, there is a split between whether national goals should be focused on economic concerns or on social and environmental issues.

- In 13 out of 23 countries, people think that their country should focus more on social and environmental goals than on economic goals in the first decade of the new millennium. *The Millennium Poll on Corporate Social Responsibility*, Environics International Ltd, 1999.

Low levels of confidence

Research shows that a low level of trust and confidence in institutions in Latin America has been recorded over many years. However, the church is ranked highly, reflecting the strength of Catholicism.

The expectation that government will provide leadership is at odds with data that suggests people have little trust in government or the political process. For example, 70 percent of the Latin American public expects their government to provide leadership, yet surveys over consecutive years on levels of trust in institutions show consistently poor scores for political institutions in Latin America (*see* Levels of Public Trust in Latin American Institutions, left). In some parts of the world, opinion pollsters have defined this trend as a decline in deference to authority, which is attributed to a loss of trust in established institutions and organizations. This loss of trust is caused by a number of converging developments:

- Traditional political parties no longer appear to reflect issues voters want tackled.
- Institutions that are slow to respond to technological and social developments, such as shifts in attitudes toward feminism and sexuality, may lose their relevance.

Levels of public trust in Latin American institutions

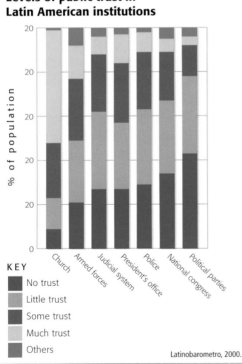

% of population

KEY
- No trust
- Little trust
- Some trust
- Much trust
- Others

Church, Armed forces, Judicial system, President's office, Police, National congress, Political parties

Latinobarometro, 2000.

Expected sources of leadership

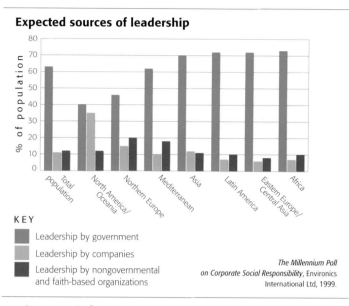

KEY

■ Leadership by government

■ Leadership by companies

■ Leadership by nongovernmental and faith-based organizations

*The Millennium Poll
on Corporate Social Responsibility*, Environics
International Ltd, 1999.

Government leadership
Despite the general trend for a fall in voter turnout in elections, people still see government as the source of leadership for fulfilling national goals.

● Values are shifting in many parts of the world in relation to the role of women in society. They are also changing with regard to discrimination against race, gender, sexual orientation, age, and so forth.

● Minorities are more assertive about their rights, and the perceived abuses of those rights.

Levels of public confidence in US institutions

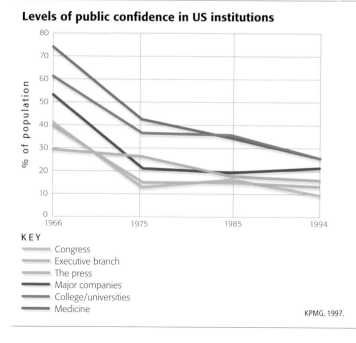

KEY

━ Congress

━ Executive branch

━ The press

━ Major companies

━ College/universities

━ Medicine

KPMG, 1997.

Decline in trust
The rapid decline in the credibility of institutions among the US population was dramatic, as shown in opinion polls from the 1960s–1990s.

Overthrow of totalitarian regime
Direct action helped anti-Ceausescu protesters, who took to the streets of Bucharest to overthrow one of the last of the old-style authoritarian East European regimes.

- Post-Cold War, the old ideological battles that kept people loyal (or nominally loyal) to their respective authorities have largely collapsed.
- The end of communism and the move to more open, democratic societies has contributed to extra information being made available to many more citizens, especially as more of the media around the world have become free to report current events more accurately and provide a plurality of views and ideas.
- As new information becomes available about the past lies, incompetence, and corruption of many totalitarian regimes, there is a backlash against authority.

- Much of the media are new and international, making them easier for individuals to search out information for themselves. The effect of this is that it reduces the old inequality between experts and the general public.
- There are now more educated people across the world who think for themselves and can access and evaluate information from different sources.
- As part of globalization, the rapid rise of a global youth culture encourages more self-expression, with people conceiving, developing, and expressing their own ideas.
- Greater affluence leads to greater choice and heightened expectations of standards of service. Once these higher standards are experienced in the private sector, expectations spread to the public sector and to newly privatized services.

CHALLENGING AUTHORITY

The internet in particular allows individuals to find out more about institutional behavior and enables them access to information previously restricted to experts and those in authority. Patients, for example, can find the latest medical research written about their condition – perhaps even ahead of their own doctors.

The result is a greater willingness of consumers to question decisions, rather than passively accept what they are told. It also makes them better equipped to argue with establishment figures and institutions. In Asia, for example, the internet is used to expose corruption and promote alternative political views, even in societies more used to deferential politics.

Governments used to keeping a tight control on traditional media have generally been almost powerless to prevent dissenting views from being spread via websites and emails.

An old lopsidedness in democracy – big business and big government are better informed than individuals, so win most of the big arguments – is suddenly corrected. It used to be that executives and bureaucrats could assure small-fry citizens that problems had been analyzed, scientists consulted, safeguards put in place. Now citizens no longer need to accept those assurances helplessly. They can log on to the internet and check them with a few clicks of a mouse.

"www. democracy.com," *The Economist*, April 3, 1999.

Countries like the US and the UK have shown dramatic reductions in the proportions of the public expressing trust in each other.

Robert Putnam, professor of Public Policy, Harvard University, speaking in Copenhagen, June 29, 2001.

TWENTY-FIRST CENTURY LEADERS

In the new world order, NGOs have emerged as the institutions the public feel they can trust. After the Battle of Seattle, a survey was carried out by Edelman PR in 2000 on attitudes among opinion leaders in Australia, France, Germany, the UK, and US. They found that:

● NGOs are trusted nearly two to one to "do what is right," compared to governments, media, or corporations. Nearly two-thirds of the respondents said that corporations only care about

Growing activism
For the first time in history, large numbers of people across the globe are free to express their own values, and often do so in unpredictable and spontaneous ways. For example, lack of consultation with the public over the growing of genetically modified crops led to NGOs orchestrating protesters to rip up test crops grown in secret locations.

profits, while well over half said that NGOs "represent values I believe in".

- NGOs ranked significantly higher as a source of credible information than media outlets or companies on issues including: labor and human rights, genetically modified food, and environmental and health issues.
- NGO influence has increased significantly over the past decade, according to 64 percent of those surveyed.
- In times of corporate crisis, for example the recall of defective Bridgestone/Firestone tires in the US in 2000, at least twice as many respondents turn to NGOs for information than to the media and corporations.
- NGOs such as Amnesty International, Greenpeace, Sierra Club, and World Wildlife Fund have greater credibility with the public than corporations such as Exxon, Ford, Microsoft, Monsanto, and Nike. Greenpeace is viewed by 80 percent of US respondents as highly effective, and the figure is 78 percent for Amnesty International.
- In Germany, Greenpeace and Amnesty International had higher favorability opinion ratings (59 per cent and 72 percent respectively) than Deutsche Telecom and the Ford Motor Company (30 percent and 22 percent respectively). Local government in general received a 38 percent favorability rating from respondents.
- In France, The World Wildlife Fund and Amnesty International had higher favorability opinion ratings (60 percent and 73 percent respectively) than Air France and Microsoft (37 percent and 34 percent respectively). Local government in general received a 17 percent favorability opinion rating. NGOs are five and a half times more favorably viewed than business, nine times more so than the media, and three times more than government in general.

The consequence of a loss of standing for institutions – including business institutions – is that they can no longer expect automatic deference and trust. Trust and authority have to be constantly earned and re-earned, which requires a higher degree of accountability compared to that demonstrated by most today.

> On the big issues like environment, human rights, and health, an international survey of opinion leaders found that NGOs are trusted by nearly 60 percent versus 15 percent for government and media and only 10 percent for business.
>
> StrategyOne, Edelman PR Worldwide, 2000.

THE BUSINESS OF BUSINESS

Concerns about the accountability of business run parallel to questioning of the purpose of business and its role in society. Expectations are running high that business, as the principal motor for growth and development, will play a more active leadership role in helping to address a wide range of issues. There is a greater questioning of the role of business in society.

Promoting responsibility
Leading international statesmen such as Nelson Mandela are promoting the value of partnerships between governments, business, and NGOs to help achieve sustainable development.

"The spread of markets far outpaces the ability of societies and their political systems to adjust to them, let alone to guide the course they take...history teaches us that such an imbalance between the economic, social, and political realms can never be sustained for very long. Without your active commitment and support there is a danger that universal values will remain little more than fine words. Unless those values are really seen to be taking hold, I fear we may find it increasingly difficult to make a persuasive case for the open global market." Kofi Annan, secretary-general, United Nations, at the Davos World Economic Forum, January 1999.

Keeping pace with the market
UN Secretary-General Kofi Annan has championed the argument that in order to maintain support for globalization and continued market liberalization, business needs to be more active in tackling the problems of inequality and social exclusion.

Development can no longer be regarded as the responsibility of government alone. It requires...partnership...with [the] private sector, labor, and nongovernmental organizations...There are many ways in which the special skills and know-how of the business community can help achieve development objectives. Nelson Mandela, quoted in Peter Schwartz and Blair Gibb, *When Good Companies do Bad Things*, 1999.

Hopes for business are high. And yet regard for their past and present contributions is low, with a widespread belief that corporations have too much unchecked power. Polling firm MORI has been asking the British public for more than a quarter of a century whether they agree or disagree with this statement: "The profits of large companies help to make things better for everyone who uses their products and services." By 2000, the earlier majorities in favor of the statement were reversed: 28 percent agreed and 51 percent disagreed.

● A Harris-Business Week poll of the US public in mid-2000 found that 72 percent of Americans say that business has too

Confidence in the benefits of profits

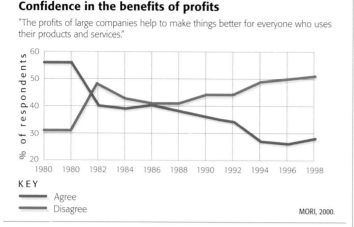

"The profits of large companies help to make things better for everyone who uses their products and services."

KEY

━━━ Agree
━━━ Disagree

MORI, 2000.

Hostility toward large profits
UK pollsters MORI annually ask a cross-section of the British public for their views on the profits of large companies. There has been a marked reversal of popular views over the past two decades, and polls now show that a significant majority are hostile to large company profits.

much power over too many aspects of American life; and less than half (47 percent) agree that "in general what is good for business is good for most citizens" (versus 71 percent in 1996). *Business Week*, September 11, 2000.

On the one hand business is called upon by some to have a greater role in society, while on the other hand it has alienated many, such as the "victims" of corporate downsizing:

> Few top executives can even imagine the hatred, contempt, and fury that has been created not primarily among blue-collar workers who never had an exalted opinion of the bosses – but among their middle management and professional people. I don't know what form it will take, but the envy developing from their enormous wealth will cause trouble. Peter Drucker, quoted in Peter Schwartz and Blair Gibb, *When Good Companies do Bad Things,* 1998.

Negative impacts of liberalization and globalization grab the headlines. The results of the processes of globalization, such as privatization, led to the UN Development Programme questioning how privatization in Europe's former communist states could, in the 1990s, lead to misery:

> Attempts to transform the state economies of Eastern Europe and the former Soviet Union into a market system may prove to be the biggest mistake of this millennium, according to a report by the UN Development Programme (which)...is sure to provoke huge

controversy. It claims that the social and economic upheavals of the 1990s have been calamitous for a vast swathe of Eastern Europe and central Asia, leading to widespread poverty, alarming falls in life expectancy, widening inequalities between the sexes, falling investment in education, the collapse of public health, and the spread of disease, crime, nationalist violence, and suicide. Michael Binyon, "Maimed by Embracing the Market," *The Times,* August 23, 1999.

Some high-profile events have put the spotlight on the relationship between corporations and external groups. Dissension over the proposed disposal of an oil storage and loading buoy by Shell in 1995 led to a fierce debate in the media, in the political corridors of power, and, in Europe, in the streets. The Brent Spar episode, as it became known, focused attention on the apparent shift in power from corporations to a wider stakeholder constituency. Shell was forced to change its disposal plans.

"We have listened very closely to our customers. We have listened very closely to our government and to our staff. They, after all, were the institutions we had always dealt with. Of course, we also dealt with environmentalist groups, consumer groups and so on, but we tended to let the public affairs department deal with them. They were important, but they were not as important as government, industry organizations and so on.

"In essence, we were somewhat slow in understanding that these groups were tending to acquire authority. Meanwhile those institutions we were used to dealing with were tending to lose authority." Cor Herkstroter, then CEO of Shell International, 1996.

Global review
Cor Herkstroter, CEO of Shell at the time of the Brent Spar episode, was faced with a volatile situation in which the logic of scientific argument was challenged by the passion of emotion. Shell subsequently undertook a major global review of the changing expectations of business.

And in Shell's *Profits and Principles* report for 1998, the following comment appeared: "Faced with uncertainty, people are withdrawing their trust in traditional institutions unless in can be demonstrated that such faith is warranted."

After the Brent Spar incident, Shell instituted a global consultation exercise to find out about the company and its role in society. The results of the survey highlighted a broad interest in the company's impact on communities and the environment.

Shell's findings are echoed in many other research studies. There is an increased awareness of environmental and sustainable development issues and an understanding that corporations can act to minimize the negative effects they cause and, if they choose, that they can make a positive contribution in many areas.

ENDURING VALUES?

Automatic deference to the Establishment is in decline in many parts of the world. Instead, there is an increased questioning of the behavior of institutions, coinciding with more people becoming connected to a common, global, more popular culture.

This does not mean that all values are changing. Considerable research evidence backs the claim that core moral values are universal across different cultures, religions, and nations. If you had a giant wall painted with the key tenets of each of the great faiths, there would be a remarkable consistency in the so-called Golden Rule – of treating people as you would like them to treat you.

> Small groups identify the five most important values they would like to carve above the door of a new school in the community. With uncanny regularity, participants from all around the world identify five values – compassion, honesty, fairness, respect, and responsibility.
> Rushworth M. Kidder and Sheila Bloom, quoted in *Winning with Integrity: Guiding Principles,* 2000.

Universal values
In the Philippines, hundreds of thousands of protesters took to the streets in January 2001, to oust the scandal-tainted president Joseph Estrada. The protesters were able to unite in their common aim to oust the president and gather at short notice by sending text messages to each other on their mobile phones.

The Rising Expectations of Stakeholders

The shifts in values described above are leading to changing expectations of business that are being articulated by various categories of stakeholders.

All institutions or organizations have an effect on a range of people as a result of their actions. These are the stakeholders – those who have an interest in the outcome of the actions. For business, the stakeholders include those who are considered to affect business success, such as shareholders, employees, customers, business partners, suppliers, communities, governments and regulators, and increasingly, special interest groups such as environmental activists. Their expectations of business are changing, and their capacity to make their views heard is increasing.

Understanding how to respond to these changing expectations is key to business success.

● In a survey of the most respected companies, 750 CEOs were asked their views on the most important business challenges for companies in 2000. Ranked second was "increased pressure from stakeholder groups." *World's Most Respected Companies, Financial Times* and PricewaterhouseCoopers, 1999.

Consumer activism

Canadian polling organization Environics coordinated the first ever global survey of popular attitudes toward corporate social responsibility. Approximately 25,000 people in 23 countries were asked a series of questions about business. Significant numbers reported that they had "punished" (for example, by boycotting products) corporations whose behavior they had disapproved of in the past year.

EXPECTATIONS OF CONSUMERS

In a connected, global information economy, consumers (who are now generally better informed and more affluent than ever before) will be loyal to brands and organizations that they are consistently given reasons to trust. According to *The Millennium Poll on Corporate Social Responsibility* conducted by Environics International in 1999, when forming impressions of companies, people around the world focus on its contributions to social causes and its environmental performance ahead of either brand reputation or financial factors. Half the

Consumer responses to perceived corporate irresponsibility

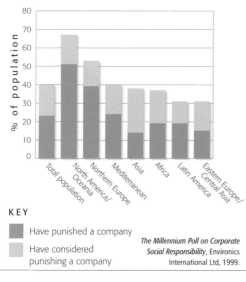

KEY

■ Have punished a company

□ Have considered punishing a company

The Millennium Poll on Corporate Social Responsibility, Environics International Ltd, 1999.

population in the 23 countries surveyed are paying attention to the social behavior of companies – one in five consumers reporting that they had either rewarded or punished companies in the previous year based on their perceived social performance, and almost as many have considered doing so.

- Two-thirds of Americans report having greater trust in those companies aligned with a social issue. *Cone/Roper Cause Related Trends Report: The Evolution of Cause Branding,* 1999.

Europeans expect business to act responsibly and are more likely to buy from companies that they perceive as being trustworthy. The Fleishman-Hillard/Ipsos Report on *European Attitudes Toward Corporate Community Investment* surveyed more than 4,000 people in France, Germany, Italy, and the UK in May, 1999. It found that:

- 88 percent of respondents felt large companies should use some of their resources to help solve societal problems.
- 84 percent felt companies should contribute resources to help solve societal problems in countries where they sell products.
- 86 percent would be more likely to buy from a company that supports and engages in activities to improve society.

Ethical stance
The Body Shop International cosmetics retailer, founded by Anita Roddick, led the way in corporate ethics. Its success is based on ethical standards of product sourcing and its stance against the use of animals for testing cosmetics and beauty products.

Consumer protest

"Which of the following have discouraged you from buying a brand in the last six months?"

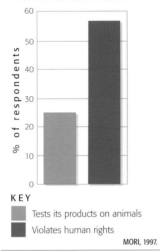

KEY

Tests its products on animals

Violates human rights

MORI, 1997.

Vigilante consumers
Increasing numbers of consumers are scrutinizing the behavior of companies on issues such as human rights, animal testing, and environmental performance, and taking boycott action if their performance is found lacking.

● 87 percent felt their job loyalty would increase if their company supported activities that improved society.
● Just 8 percent were most likely to believe corporations regarding issues such as public health, the environment, or human rights; a significant 49 percent would most likely believe charities on such topics.

EXPECTATIONS OF EMPLOYEES

Increasingly, motivation is based on values rather than purely on financial reward. Historically, loyalty was bought. The employer offered gradual progression up the hierarchy, a decent salary, and job security. In return, the employee offered unwavering loyalty and a hard day's work.

Today, values also determine motivation and loyalty. "Every organization needs values, but a lean organization needs them even more." Jack Welch, CEO, GE, quoted in Jonas Ridderstrale and Kjell Nordstrom, Funky Business, 2000.

As we move into the twenty-first century, companies will need to draw on the full creative energy and talent of their people. But why should people give this help of commitment and devotion? As Peter Drucker has pointed out, the best and most dedicated people are ultimately volunteers, for they have the opportunity to do something else with their lives. With an increasingly mobile society, cynicism about corporate life and an expanding entrepreneurial segment of the economy, companies need more than ever to have a clear understanding of their purpose in order to make work meaningful and, thereby, attract, retain, and motivate outstanding people. James Collins and Jerry Porras, Built to Last, 2000.

Many more employees are prepared to go to court nowadays when they become dissatisfied with corporate behavior. For example, companies allowing bad practices that could cause work/life balance problems, such as increased stress, and RSI-related injuries, are increasingly finding themselves the target of lawsuits.
● In Europe, employment-related cases have almost doubled in the past 10 years, according to insurance company AIG.
Reputation Management, Institute of Directors, 1999.

EXPECTATIONS OF INVESTORS

As the ultimate owners of the business, the views and expectations of investors are particularly important. Senior management is obliged to respond to their concerns efficiently and effectively. The profile of investors is changing with the popularization of stock ownership, and that is opening the gates for shareholder activism.

Investor boycott

The investment managers of 15 US mutual funds joined a boycott of Mitsubishi over the company's plans to build a new salt evaporation plant near a prime gray whale habitat in San Ignacio Lagoon, Mexico.

Mitsubishi operates the world's largest salt evaporation plant at the lagoon in Baja California and wanted to build a $150 million expansion facility. Environmental groups, led by the International Fund for Animal Welfare and the Natural Resources Defense Council, launched global efforts to deter the new one from being built. *Associated Press/Billings Gazette*, September 24, 1999.

Mitsubishi update

Mitsubishi announced it would not proceed with the program, despite a favorable environmental impact assessment report, after over a million people wrote in to protest. According to a report in the *San Jose Mercury News* (March 3, 1999), company spokesman James Brumm said, "There was a lot of public pressure, and we certainly felt the brunt of that. Although there was no real basis for their fears, we were not able to convince the general public that this was an environmentally sound project."

Collective action
Institutional investors, NGOs, and concerned citizen activists successfully joined forces to block the expansion of a major desalination plant in San Ignacio Lagoon, Mexico, which had already received government approval and support.

Three major institutional investors sent a letter in January 2000 to companies in the FTSE 350, stating that they expected to see the companies participate in the Environmental Index run by the *Financial Times* and Business in the Environment:

"We regard the Index as a valuable indicator of environmental engagement and risk management, and it is a factor in our understanding and assessment of management performance in the companies in which we invest. We encourage you to participate in the Survey in your interests and our own as shareholders."
Signatories: Prudential, Merrill Lynch Mercury Asset Management, CGU.

- Prudential will screen all its shareholdings for environmental and social impact. *The Times* (UK), November 24, 1999.
- A new UK regulation on pension funds requires trustees to state the extent to which they have taken environmental and ethical considerations into account during fund management.
- Companies that fail to meet basic social, environmental, and ethical standards run the risk of damaging their reputation and financial well-being, according to the Association of British Insurers (ABI), whose members control $1.4 trillion of assets and one quarter of the UK stock market. According to an ABI statement, "failure to take these risks into account can head to a long-term loss, not just in a company's reputation, but also in its value..." *Financial Times*, March 30, 2001.

Socially responsible mutual funds have "Hit the Big Time"

The $520 billion Vanguard Group and the $250 billion Teachers Insurance and Annuity Association-College Retirement Equities Fund, known as TIAA-CREF, announced plans for socially responsible mutual funds. Over $1 trillion of investments are now said to be managed with some socially responsible screens, though the exact amount fluctuates considerably depending on whether funds that use religious criteria are included, and how "socially responsible" is defined.

Bloomberg Financial News, December 21,

Ethical funds database

The UK Ethical Investment Research Service maintains a database of ethical funds and researches more than 1,000 companies. Among the issues that investors can screen for are:

Alcohol

Animals (meat production and sale, leather/fur manufacture and sale)

Arms and sales to military purchasers

Community involvement

Corporate governance

Directors' pay

Environmental issues

Equal opportunities

Gambling

Greenhouse gases

Health and safety convictions

Human rights

Intensive farming

Military contracts

Newspaper production and television

Nuclear power (fuel, components, and construction of plants)

Overseas interests
(wages exploitation in emerging markets, deriving profits from countries with poor human rights' records)

Ozone-depleting chemicals

Pesticides

Political contributions

Pornography

Third World involvement

Tobacco

Waste disposal

Water pollution

Religious groups stand up for God's creation

A multifaith coalition is flexing its financial muscle to press big business over the environment.

"Using their pension funds as leverage, religious shareholder activists are backing resolutions, funding public campaigns, and meeting corporate representatives to demand protection for God's green earth."

Financial Times, January 12, 2000.

The Association of British Insurers is to issue new disclosure guidelines detailing the type of information large investors expect to see in company annual reports on environmental and social impacts.

The InterFaith Center on Corporate Social Responsibility, a US NGO, keeps a running brief on shareholder resolutions concerning social responsibility issues. Examples of shareholder resolutions that they have recorded in *Human Rights, Is It Any of Your Business?* (Peter Frankental and Frances House, 2000) include:

− A resolution asking Boeing to adopt "basic human rights criteria for its business operations in and/or with the People's Republic of China" and to describe how it intended to implement them.

− A resolution asking Exxon, in relation to an exploration venture in China, to review its "code of conduct with the view to including it in an explicit commitment to human rights, social justice, and environmental responsibility" toward the communities in which the company operates.

− Resolutions asking General Motors and Lucent Technologies to adopt "policies for dealing at all levels with China," including that it will not: accept goods or services produced by slave or forced labor, not sell any facility using slave or forced labor, will pursue the right to on-site inspection to determine the existence of slave or forced labor.

Sumitomo to ease loan terms for green firms

Sumitomo Bank announced Friday it would introduce a system to grade companies according to their willingness to help protect the environment as a condition for receiving loans from the bank.

The more enthusiastic enterprises are about tackling environmental problems, the better the terms of loans offered by the bank will be, according to the bank. The bank reportedly aims to avoid the risk of companies defaulting if an environmental problem, such as the need to clean up contaminated soil, drained the company's funds. The system would also encourage enterprises to develop environmentally friendly products, bank officials said. *The Daily Yomiuri*, Japan, October 25, 1999.

EXPECTATIONS OF GOVERNMENT AND REGULATORS

Responding to pressure from interest groups, civil servants and governments, often through regulatory bodies, are now expressing their changed expectations of business behavior. This varies from "pronouncements" by officials to taking concrete action:

- In the final communiqué of their summit in Lisbon in March 2000, the heads of government of the European Union declared: "The European Council makes a special appeal to companies' corporate sense of social responsibility regarding best practices on life-long learning, work organization, equal opportunities, social exclusion, and sustainable development."

- Danish Prime Minister Poul Rasmussen, speaking at the first Europe-wide conference on the social responsibilities of corporations in November 2000, said "the business of business is no longer just business: it is becoming sustainable business… public-private partnership as well as corporate social responsibility is both a precondition for adapting to changes [in the new economy] and a result of a knowledge-driven economy…"

Concrete measures include:

- Under Directive 94/62/EC, member states of the EU have been set targets for the recycling and recovery of packaging waste. By the year 2001 each member state must:
  – recover between 50 and 65 percent of packaging waste.

Debating social responsibility
The Danish government under Prime Minister Poul Rasmussen has championed European debates on the social responsibilities of business, establishing The Copenhagen Centre as a debate facilitator.

Better recycling
Governments are seeking to impose higher standards on business for more efficient recycling, not only by using the law but also by encouraging business-led self-regulation.

– recycle between 25 percent and 45 percent of packaging waste, with a minimum of 15 percent by weight of each packaging material recyclable. *Croner's Environmental Management,* July 1999.

According to the 1998/1999 World Bank Development Report, environment officials in Indonesia, frustrated by weak enforcement of water pollution standards, hit upon the idea of collecting information on compliance and disclosing it to the public. Even before the information was made public, firms hurried to improve their ratings. After publication, citizens' groups used the ratings to put pressure on underperforming factories to clean up. Regulators, meanwhile, could focus their limited enforcement resources on the worst offenders.

In the first 15 months of the program, roughly a third of the unsatisfactory performers came into compliance with the regulators. The pilot program spurred a 40 percent drop in water pollution in just 18 months. The program has since been expanded, and similar efforts are being contemplated in the Philippines, China, India, and Mexico.

● The European Union Amsterdam Treaty of May 1999 created a power for EU institutions to enact legislation tackling discrimination in areas such as disability and sexual orientation, creating a new avenue of potential litigation for the business community.

● The US Customs Service ordered that all clothing manufactured by a Chinese-owned company in Mongolia be stopped at the US border:

The US Customs Service is committed to ensuring that products entering the country were not made by exploiting those least able to fend for themselves," read a statement issued by the service following an investigation which allegedly found the company using forced child labor. Miami Herald, November 29, 2000.

● The Canadian government announced in 1997 that civil servants on government business could only use domestic hotels with sound environmental performance – forcing Canadian hotels that valued public service contracts to adopt new environmental programs.

EXPECTATIONS OF
INTERGOVERNMENTAL INSTITUTIONS

The institutions responsible for overseeing governance issues at a regional or global level are increasingly expressing their expectations of business, both through mandatory mechanisms, such as intergovernmental agreements and treaties, and voluntarily by encouraging the adoption of sets of guidelines and codes of practice.

● OECD has published new guidelines for transnational companies to address public concern about the activities of transnationals, with new standards proposed for corporate governance, workplace conditions, environmental safeguards, bribery, and protection for whistleblowers.

Financial Times, January 12, 2000.

Environmental protection
The industrialized country grouping of the OECD published a landmark analysis of environmental problems in April 2001, which called for urgent action to prevent irreversible environmental damage, such as river pollution. The OECD called for a robust regulatory framework, as well as strong pricing mechanisms, tradeable emission permits, and land use regulation.

At the 2000 World Economic Forum in Davos, Switzerland, an annual gathering of the world's top business and political leaders, UN Secretary-General Kofi Annan called on business to join a Global Compact, a voluntary pact in which signatories embrace nine principles derived from international conventions. These address labor standards, human rights, and environmental practices. Since its launch, the UN Global Compact has announced what it calls "complementary strategic goals." Businesses supporting the compact are expected to:

– Issue a clear statement in support of the compact and its principles.

– Annually post on the Global Compact website an example of progress made or a lesson learned in implementing the principles.

– Engage in partnership with UN organizations by undertaking activities that further the application of the principles, or by entering strategic partnerships in support of broad UN goals.

Building partnerships

The UN Global Compact aims to involve companies in partnerships to develop social infrastructure and reduce poverty in the developing world on the basis that "If we cannot make globalization work for all, in the end it will work for no one."

Norwegian-based Statoil signed an agreement in March 2001 with the International Federation of Chemical, Energy, Mine, and General Workers Union based on the principles of the Global Compact, including respect for labor rights, health and safety, and environmental standards. The agreement covers 16,000 workers within 23 countries. Gier Westgaard, Statoil vice-president, said that the pact, "makes good business sense". Complying with and furthering the Global Compact is "part of securing our license to operate internationally."

"... Let's choose to unite the powers of markets with the authority of universal ideas. Let us choose to reconcile the creative forces of private entrepreneurship with the needs of the disadvantaged and the requirements of the future generations." **Kofi Annan, UN secretary-general, Davos World Economic Forum, January 1999.**

EXPECTATIONS OF NONGOVERNMENTAL ORGANIZATIONS

A wide range of roles are fulfilled by NGOs, from exclusive service provision through to those that campaign on single issues – with variations between the two. Inevitably, with such diversity of NGOs, they have no single view of the role of business, and that in itself is a challenge for companies.

For those that are campaigning to change corporate behavior, developments in information technology have allowed individuals and organizations to find out about corporate behavior, share this information with people who think similarly, and coordinate campaigns to persuade companies to change. Well-known examples include animal activists at the Huntingdon Life Sciences laboratory; street attacks on symbols of Western capitalism such as McDonald's; and the Greenpeace campaigns against Shell's Brent Spar oil platform, and Home Depot for the sourcing of their wood.

NGOs are among the most trusted institutions, even though some managers on the receiving end of critical NGO campaigns might find this ironic.

"The only organizations now capable of global thought and action – the ones who will conduct the most important dialogues of the twenty-first century – are the transnational corporations and the NGOs." **Peter Sutherland, then director-general of GATT.**

NGOs have developed highly effective communication skills and are using modern information technology to express their expectations to business. Control Risks Group, the international business risk consultants, has identified three ways in which changes in international communications have influenced business via NGO campaigning:
– Lighter cameras and sophisticated satellite technology make filming and transmission easier, enabling accusations and conflict to reach newsdesks and living rooms almost instantly.
– Western-based NGOs can communicate

Global perspective
Peter Sutherland has viewed the world as a national politician, a European commissioner, as head of an international institution, and now as a global businessman.

more effectively with their operations or partners in developing countries, providing access to information and images from the field to be deployed against global corporations and institutions based in the West.

– The internet provides a cheap and fast means to organize mass protests and boycotts. NGOs now have power and are both a challenge and a potential magnet for business:

...the more interesting development to watch will be the relations between NGOs and business. Here lies the greatest rivalry and attractions. As brands become more important to companies, NGOs' power grows accordingly... the clever businesses will attempt to co-opt NGOs.
"NGOs: New Gods Overseas" by Adam Roberts *The Economist Yearbook 2000*, 2001.

However, expectations can work both ways. NGOs themselves are faced with increased media scrutiny as they play a more prominent role with governments and business. NGOs that have questioned corporations on issues of accountability and transparency are now facing similar inquiries about their own operations.

Popular media and business

Movies, television, and other media are both a reflector of popular moods and a shaper of them. They have helped to stoke up and reflect this growing questioning of business and of business values and behavior.

Many of today's popular movies feature stories based on an individual's fight against bureaucracy, greed, and autocratic behavior by those who represent a commercial operation. For example, one of the main villains in *Mission Impossible II* was the CEO of a bio-tech company; and in three major Hollywood movies released in 1999–2000 – *A Civil Action*, *The Insider*, and *Erin Brockovich* – each featured a US company as the villain.

Global information
With the proliferation of media channels and the use by NGOs of sophisticated communications technology, the stories behind world events such as war and conflict are portrayed from a variety of viewpoints, allowing viewers to form their own opinions about what is happening in the world.

BUSINESS EXPECTATIONS OF BUSINESS

To secure new contracts, and sometimes not lose existing business, companies have to demonstrate to their business customers that they meet certain standards of performance in areas such as the environment, employment practices, and community relations.

> As companies increasingly play hopscotch across national boundaries and run into widely differing laws and regulations, one corporate concern – responsibility to the environment and the community – seems to take on an importance unmatched in our domestic survey."
> "Global Most Admired Companies Report," *Fortune*, 1997.

- The most renowned advantage of obtaining international certification (such as quality mark ISO-9000 and environmental mark ISO-14001) is the access it permits to international markets. *Business Mexico*, Special Edition, 1999.
- General Motors has declared that all its suppliers must, by 2002, have achieved ISO-14001 to continue to provide supplies.
- The cities of Los Angeles and Seattle have passed laws requiring city contractors to offer all domestic partners – including same sex partners – health benefits. A similar ordinance passed in 1997 by San Francisco led to 2,100 new employers instituting domestic partner benefits. *Black Book*, January 2000.
- The American Bar Association, the biggest purchaser of conferences globally, now distributes a questionnaire to potential venues enquiring about environmental policies.

Swarming

The changing expectations of stakeholders do not impact individually. One phenomenon is "swarming" – when there is a sudden, intense critical mass of attention focused on a particular organization or issue from the media and sections of the public. This can be hard to predict and hard to manage. It can lead to an issue shooting up the political and popular agenda, demanding attention that may be out of all proportion to its long-term significance and possibly leading to rushed and poor decisions, in the heat of the moment, to divert the swarm. The popular protests against high fuel prices in Europe in Autumn 2000 were a classic example. Arguably, swarming is encouraged by the combination of global media, vigilante consumers, and activists, a short time-span society, and the decline of the predictable, old-style ideologies.

Conflict of stakeholder interests

Stakeholders' expectations may be diametrically opposed to each other, forcing businesses to choose between them. Sara Lee has made awards to honor women who have made a difference to society and who inspire other women to excel. There are four categories: the arts, business, government, and the humanities. A $50,000 grant is given in each frontrunner's name to a nonprofit organization that addresses the interests and concerns of women.

The group Women Against Gun Control (WAGC) has urged its members and gun rights supporters to participate in a worldwide boycott of Sara Lee products. This boycott is in protest at Sara Lee's presentation, in November 1997, of its humanities award to Sarah Brady, a leading gun control campaigner, as well as its donation of $50,000 to the Center to Prevent Handgun Violence. The WAGC is protesting against this award, because the Center to Prevent Handgun Violence is calling for bans on the private ownership of defensive weapons. The WAGC believes that this is a violation of the Constitution and will make law-abiding citizens easy targets for criminals.

Making Sense of the Big Picture

The expectations of how business should run its own affairs and how it should contribute to tackling the problems of a wider society are being heightened – just as the bar that athletes have to jump over is raised in successive rounds of a high jump competition.

Simultaneously, the perception is growing that business behavior in many parts of the world is declining. The gap between expectations and perceived standards of behavior is both fueled by and reflected in the ways in which the popular media portray business.

Managers today have to face the extra challenges from these heightened expectations and the greater willingness and capacity of stakeholders to push for their expectations.

A new struggle is appearing in a number of different societies, which might be described as traditional family values versus individual choice and personal freedom.

Furthermore, the expectations of one set of stakeholders are not always compatible with those of other stakeholders.

A broad range of issues related to a company's corporate responsibility is gaining currency, whether concerning equality, diversity, equity, transparency, governance, or accountability.

The old left–right struggles have become far less significant with the collapse of communism. A new struggle is appearing in a number of different societies, which might be described as traditional family values versus individual choice and personal freedom.

Further conflict is evolving as advances in science lead to often polarizing ethical dilemmas. An example of this is the debate about the use of stem cells extracted from human embryos for medical research. The forces of organized religion seek to stop such studies, but they are opposed by a range of disparate groups that have been brought together by a desire that such research be allowed.

It is in this increasingly complex environment that managers are making decisions on a daily basis, without the knowledge or tools to consider how the many complex topics raised by the global forces for change might be impacted by, or impacting upon, their work.

SIGNPOSTS

THE REVOLUTION OF TECHNOLOGY

For more in-depth explanations of the impacts of the revolution in technology and communications, particularly for business and the world of work, dip into Bill Gates's *Business at the Speed of Thought* (Penguin, 1999), *High Tech, High Touch: Technology and Our Search for Meaning* by John Nesbitt (Nicholas Brealey, 1999), *Blur* by Stan Davis and Chris Meyer (Addison Wesley, 1998), *Living on Thin Air* by Charles Leadbeater (Penguin, 1999), and *The Death of Distance* by Francis Cairncross (*The Economist*, 1997). Esther Dyson's *Release 2.1* (Broadway Books, 1998) includes consideration of ethical issues.

A number of gurus on the subject have personal websites, such as Nicholas Negroponte, founder of the Massachusetts Institute of Technology's Media Lab (www.media.mit.edu/people/nicholas/).

THE REVOLUTION OF MARKETS

Pro-globalization arguments can be found in *A Future Perfect: The Challenge and Hidden Promise of Globalization* by John Micklethwait and Adrian Woolridge (William Heinemann, 2000) and *Runaway World: How Globalization Is Reshaping Our Lives* by Anthony Giddens (Profile Books, 1999). For a counterview, try *False Dawn* by John Gray (Granta, 1998).

Works questioning the power of corporations include: *When Corporations Rule the World* by David Korten (Kumarian Press, 1995); *Corporate Nation: How Corporations Are Taking Over Our Lives and What We Can Do About It* by Charles Derber (First St. Martin's Griffin, 2000); and *No Logo: Taking Aim at the Brand Bullies* by Naomi Klein (Picador, 1999).

The implications of globalization on brand and corporate strategy are given a refreshing treatment in *Funky Business* by Jonas Ridderstrale and Kjell Nordstrom (ft.com, 2000), and *Leading the Revolution* by Gary Hamel (Harvard Business School Press, 2000), and in the monthly magazine Fast Company.

The important, but often overlooked, informal economy is explored in *The Mystery of Capitalism: Why Capitalism Triumphs in the West and Fails Everywhere Else* by Hernando de Soto (Basic Books, 2000).

Many of the principal business associations – such as the three million-strong corporate member US Chamber of Commerce (www.uschamber. org) and the International Chamber of Commerce (www. iccwbo.org) have websites with arguments for the benefits of continuing trade liberalization. NGOs questioning these views are listed below under *The Revolution of Values*.

For information on trends within civil society, go to The Johns Hopkins Center for Civil Society Studies, The Johns Hopkins University, Baltimore, Md. (www.jhu.edu).

THE REVOLUTION OF DEMOGRAPHICS AND DEVELOPMENT

Key sources are the multilateral institutions, which regularly publish indicators and specialized publications. Many are available in on-line formats and several languages. The gateway portal to the UN agencies, which deal with development, refugees, human rights, and so forth is www.un.org. The World Bank (www.worldbank.org) is also very useful. Regional information is available from the African Development Bank Group (www.afdb.org), the Asian Development Bank (www. adb.org), and the Inter-American Development Bank (www. iadb.org).

For information on employment trends and conditions, visit the International Labour Organization (www.ilo.org).

For data on the link between business and poverty, visit The Resource Centre for the Social Dimension of Business Practice (www.rc-sdbp.org). For access to a list of the major humanitarian NGOs, such as Oxfam and Save the Children, visit www.reliefweb.int

THE REVOLUTION OF VALUES

Opinion-polling companies regularly share headlines from their privately commissioned research into political and social issues, including the role of business in society. Visit www. mori.com and www.environics.net. Publications such as *Fortune, Time, Business Week, Financial Times*, and *The Economist* commission and publish surveys that measure business and societal values and attitude shifts, for example, *The Economist's* report of the 2001 Latinobarometro survey of attitudes to authority in Latin America (*An Alarm Call for Latin America's Democrats*, 26 July 2001). NGOs research, track, and report on particular issues, such as poverty, children's rights, labor rights, refugees, and so on. Visit www.reliefweb.int to see an organizational listing. Peter Schwartz and Blair Gibb report on changing expectations in *When Good Companies Do Bad Things* (John Wiley & Sons Inc., 1999).

Robert Putnam's *Bowling Alone* (Simon & Schuster, 2000) describes the decline of civic and social engagement in the United States.

Stakeholder interest sites include:

Consumers:
www.ethicalconsumer.org
Shareholders:
www.shareholderaction.org
www.asyousow.org; www.ethicalinvestor.com
www.socialfunds.com
Intergovernmental Institutions:
www.europa.eu.int/
www.unglobalcompact.org
Nongovernmental Institutions:
www.corpwatch.org
www.humanrightswatch.org
www.globalwitness.org

Dr. Oliver Sparrow, founding director of The Chatham House Forum, has produced a series of illuminating reports and scenarios on the future, including *Open Horizons* (1999), which encompass various elements of the global forces for change (www.chforum.org).

All websites active at the time of writing.

THE EMERGING
MANAGEMENT ISSUES

"They [corporate executives] understand that big corporations have to behave differently if they want to build a reputation that enhances their brand and makes them attractive not just to customers but to the best workers."

Jeffery Gartner, Dean, Yale School of Management, quoted in *International Herald Tribune*, October 2, 2000.

THE EMERGING MANAGEMENT ISSUES DEFINED

The implications for business of the multidimensional and interconnecting global forces for change are distilled down to four emerging management issues:

ECOLOGY AND ENVIRONMENT
HEALTH AND WELL-BEING
DIVERSITY AND HUMAN RIGHTS
COMMUNITIES.

There are varying components within each of these issues, and they will have both individual and cumulative effects on business decisions and corporate responsibility. The significance of each component will differ depending on a range of interdependent variables such as the physical location of business operations, local cultural norms, and the industrial or commercial sector. They are also likely to be influenced by the increased questioning of corporate activity. Managers need to gain a clear understanding of these issues in order to avoid an inappropriate response that could expose their company to unnecessary risk.

THE EMERGING MANAGEMENT ISSUE
Ecology and Environment

Managers need to be sensitive to environmental factors since they are increasingly affecting business decisions and commercial practice.

This is not "new" news, and managers in many companies will have a basic knowledge of environmental concerns, such as energy conservation, recycling, and waste management. However, in most cases, managers will assume that the job of being alert to environmental risks and opportunities is not theirs, but the task of specialists in the company. This is an outdated assumption.

As the environment becomes an emerging management issue for managers with a range of responsibilities, there is a need to broaden the scope of issues that fall under its traditional heading. Thus, the inclusion of "ecology."

This wider scope is necessary. The technology revolution has enabled accurate measuring and monitoring of pollutants, such as emissions, and the development of cleaner technologies. The revolution of markets has spurred more companies to invest in newly liberalized and developing countries with ineffective environmental regulatory regimes. The revolution of demographics and development has highlighted populations at risk from environmental degradation. And the revolution of values has led to demands by interest groups for tougher environmental controls and standards in order to protect the planet. Ecological and environmental concerns may impact negatively or positively across a wide range of operational areas. Consequently, in a company, they are everybody's business.

Deforestation and destruction
Rising world population levels have led to an increased demand for natural resources. Land clearing and other environmentally destructive activities are putting the delicate balance that exists between humanity and the planet at risk.

CONSPICUOUS CONSUMPTION

There are now more than six billion people in the world. This number of inhabitants puts the planet's ecosystems at risk, principally because of heavy rates of consumption in industrialized countries. In 1999, the World Resources Institute estimated that 80 percent of natural resources were consumed by the 16 percent of the world's population who lived in the US, Europe, and Japan.

High rates of consumption encourage unsustainable production methods to satisfy the high demand. For example, intensive farming methods can result in deforestation, loss of biodiversity, soil degradation, and desertification, which in turn have significant effects on the global ecosystem.

It is estimated that over the past 150 years, deforestation, partly the result of intensive farming and commercial logging, has contributed 30 percent of the atmospheric buildup of carbon dioxide (EarthTrends, World Resources Institute).

Population growth and higher consumption increase the demand for finite natural resources, and create pressure for greater levels of extraction of nonrenewable resources, such as coal, gas, and oil.

About one-third of the original recoverable oil endowment of the Earth has already been produced and consumed. If unconstrained modern oil exploitation continues around the world, the remaining two-thirds of the Earth's natural oil will not be able to sustain world output at its

Worldwide energy crisis
The massive consumption of energy by city populations is contributing to the development of a worldwide energy crisis, with over-rapid exploitation of the finite supply of natural gas, oil, and coal.

Destructive demand
Demand for timber products has led to uncontrolled commercial logging in areas such as the Amazon. This has contributed to global warming, and threatens the survival of many animal and plant species.

current rate for much longer than the middle of this century. Then, a declining resource base will finally force down production. During the twenty-first century, a world oil supply crisis, while not imminent, appears likely sooner rather than later. *Survey of Energy Resources*, World Energy Council, 1998.

An increasing proportion of the world's inhabitants have high expectations as consumers, affecting the rate at which energy and materials are consumed. Furthermore, more people have the wherewithal to pay for ever higher levels of consumption. In his report, *Open Horizons – The 1998 Report of the Chatham House Forum*, Dr. Oliver Sparrow states that 200 million inhabitants of India now have purchasing power equivalent to the average income in the European Union.

Images portraying lifestyles based on high levels of consumption are available to many viewers through global media and information technology, again fueling demand.

Technological advances mean that natural resources in the more remote areas of the world are less expensive to extract, and easier to reach. Whether this is a beneficial development or not depends on one's perspective. Some argue that the result is a threat to affected communities or natural habitats. Others think that it brings benefits such as investment, employment, and infrastructure development to the communities where resources are located.

One of the world's natural resources that appears most at risk from these advances is forest. Trees are regarded as the world's lungs, absorbing carbon dioxide from the atmosphere and producing oxygen.

● Just one-fifth of the earth's original forests remain in large, relatively natural ecosystems, or frontier forests. Seventy-six countries have lost all their frontier forests, and 70 percent of what is left is found in three countries: Brazil, Canada, and Russia. *World Development Report*, World Bank, 1999/2000.

● Nearly 80 percent of the Earth's ancient forests have already been either destroyed or degraded. In the Amazon alone, criminal timber exports have contributed to destroying a section of the forest that is nearly the size of Texas; and each year an area half the size of the state of Maryland disappears. EarthTrends, World Resources Institute.

> **If present growth rates continue, energy consumption will double by 2035 relative to 1988, and triple by 2055.**
>
> *The World Energy Assessment*, United Nations Development Programme, 2000.

REGULATING WASTE DISPOSAL

Greater consumption produces more waste. In emerged economies, regulations are in place to ensure that waste disposal is carried out in a manner acceptable to society. The cost of disposal borne by business and government, and therefore ultimately taxpayers, is increasing as landfill charges rise and as higher disposal standards are imposed.

● In 1999, the EU adopted a Directive on the Landfill of Waste, designed to make waste disposal environmentally safer and more efficient. The UK government has estimated that the cost to waste producers of additional waste treatment required by the directive is between $189m and $1,28b (£135m–£915m) per year.

As a consequence of rising costs, companies are avoiding creating waste. This is being encouraged by regulations that force companies to take responsibility for the environmental impacts of products, from manufacture to disposal. The EU is passing legislation requiring any company doing business in member countries to conform to standards of "extended product responsibility." The amount of environmental legislation for companies to respond to is rapidly increasing.

● Twenty-eight countries have legislated to encourage recycling, and further extended product life-cycle laws are planned in Japan, Taiwan, Korea, Brazil, Peru, and Canada. **Business for Social Responsibility (BSR).**

● According to the World Trade Organization, in 1999 there were 216 multilateral environmental agreements worldwide.

● The 1999 *Handbook on Environmental Legislation* produced by the European Commission lists 83 directives and regulations.

Mountains of waste
One consequence of the throwaway society is growing landfills and garbage dumps. In emerging economies, scavenging from dumps is commonplace, despite the health risks posed by the rotting refuse.

Water shortages
In many countries, water is already scarce and difficult to obtain. Innovative solutions to growing water shortages will be required in the coming decades.

More than 90 percent of the natural flow of the Nile River is used by irrigation or evaporation, primarily from reservoirs.
World Water Council.

WATER WARS

Once regarded as free and plentiful by many, water is now a scarce resource. It is estimated that if the consumption of water grows in line with present conditions, two-thirds of the world's population will live in "water-stressed conditions by 2025" (*GEO Overview*, United Nations Environment Programme, 1999). There are significant implications for the use of water by industry and in agriculture.

Though the problems are most acute in Africa and West Asia, a lack of water is already a major constraint to industrial and socioeconomic growth in many other areas, including China, India, and Indonesia.
Kofi Annan, UN secretary–general, *Civilization*, October/November 2000.

- On the basis of conservative estimates, the International Water Management Institute predicts an increase in demand for water for irrigation of 17 percent by 2025. The World Water Council predicts that this increase is likely to be matched by increases in demand for water for industrial and municipal use of 20 percent and 70 percent respectively.

"Water wars" are predicted within decades, as water availability and quality issues result in conflicts between nations. There will be severe cost implications for business from disruptions to supply and distribution chains. Water issues are already causing massive human displacement.
- The land and water crisis in river basins contributed to the total of 25 million environmental refugees in 2000, which for the first time exceeded the number of war-related refugees. By 2025, the number of environmental refugees could quadruple. *A Water Secure World: Vision for Water, Life and the Environment*, World Commission on Water for the 21st Century, 1999.

THE TWO SIDES OF TOURISM

Areas of outstanding natural beauty and regions rich in animal and plant species are threatened by the growth in tourism. Advances in air travel and other transportation methods have opened up remote areas to visitors. Tourists bring on the one hand welcome local economic development, and on the other, a threat to local communities and the environment.

As well as the potential damage to natural habitats, poorly planned development in the hotel, tourism, and associated sectors can adversely affect local resources. For example, scarce water sources may be depleted, and pollution created.

However, growth in eco-tourism is leading to the development of vacation destinations planned with sensitivity to ecological and environmental concerns, and is providing a means to educate visitors on conservation topics.

THE THREAT FROM GLOBAL WARMING

New technologies have allowed greater accuracy in the measurement of ecological and environmental degradation. NGOs and environmentalists can access this information and publicize it through the media. Governments and business can no longer hide behind a "monopoly" on technical expertise or information. This is particularly true of the global warming issue, the threat of which has been exposed by better measurement techniques. The UN *Global Environmental Outlook 2000* report stated:

Over the past 50 years, carbon dioxide emissions have more than quadrupled from 1.6 billion to seven billion tons per annum. These emissions are created mainly from man's burning of non-renewable fossil fuels, so contributing to nonrenewable resource depletion and causing global warming. Global warming will raise temperatures by up to 5.8°F, triggering a "devastating" rise in sea levels and more severe natural disasters.

One year later, the estimated temperature rise was revised to 2.5°F–9.7°F (1.5°C–5.8°C).

The predicted effects of global warming will have an impact on business, either as a direct result of the changed weather patterns and the rising sea levels, or because of the effect of measures taken to reduce emissions of greenhouse gases.

> Developing countries would bear the physical brunt of the effects of climatic change, and yet the EU and the US produce 40 percent of greenhouse gas emissions.
>
> *Second Assessment – Climate Change*, Intergovernmental Panel on Climate Change, 1995.

Rising sea levels
El Nino (a warm current in the Pacific Ocean) heats the ocean, and, in some areas, (shown in white) raises the sea level 5.5–12.5 in (14–32 cm) above normal. The warming has become more severe in recent years, possibly because of global warming.

Business leaders at the 2000 meeting of the World Economic Forum in Davos agreed with the UN and listed global warming as the most pressing issue for world business. The insurance sector stands to be particularly affected.

Given the role that insurance companies play on the global capital markets, and the importance of insurers in underwriting commercial development, the calls of the insurance industry are not likely to go unheard by other industry sectors (P. Newell and M. Paterson, "A climate for business: global warming, the state and capital," *Review of International Political Economy*, 5 (4), 2000).

Insurance companies should adapt their predictive models to ensure that their prices are accurate and to prevent large financial losses due to payouts after unexpectedly severe storms. To value waterfront properties correctly, real estate companies have to keep up on changes in flood patterns. Agriculture companies may have to invest heavily in areas where the climate is warmed enough to make farming viable; and, at the same time, abandon some investments in regions that have become too warm. Kimberly O'Neill Packard and Forest Reinhardt, "What Every Executive Needs to Know About Global Warming," *Harvard Business Review*, July/August 2000.

The response of companies in other industries to global warming can be illustrated with a few examples:

- DuPont, the largest transnational in the chemicals sector, has committed to cut its emissions by nearly two-thirds (compared with its 1990 level) within a decade, while holding its total energy consumption level, and using renewable resources for one tenth of its energy worldwide. "Beyond The Hague," *The Economist*, December 2, 2000.
- BP has established an internal emissions trading system among its national divisions, and is committed to investing in the development of clean and renewable energy sources.
- The Royal Dutch/Shell Group has decreed that all large projects must take into account the likely future cost of carbon emissions. This is adding to cost calculations a figure of $5 per ton of carbon between 2005 and 2009, rising to $20 per ton from 2010. Shell reports that this "is not altruism," but is "giving us a competitive advantage."

Some of the predicted effects of global warming worldwide

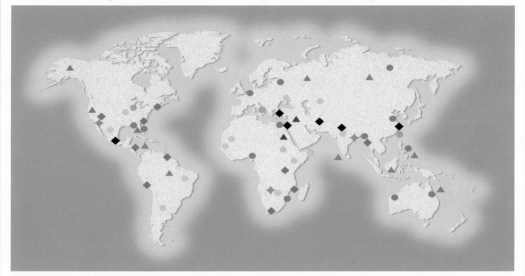

Key

▲ **Coral bleaching:**
Warmer water could
bleach coral reefs,
leading to their
destruction. This may
deplete fisheries,
disrupting food
supplies and tourism.

○ **Crops:**
Drought and high
temperatures could
cause crop failure
and malnutrition.

◆ **Disease:**
Warmer, wetter
weather may aid
insect-borne diseases,
such as malaria;
flooding could spawn
more waterborne
illnesses.

▲ **Fires:**
Drier summers and
higher temperatures
are ideal conditions
for wildfires. In 1997,
some 40,000 people
were treated for
smoke inhalation in
southeast Asia.

● **Floods:**
Sea levels will rise
in the next century,
leaving people more
vulnerable to storm
surges. Snow melting
earlier than usual
could cause rivers
to overflow.

○ **Heat wave:**
Deaths from
heatstroke worldwide
may double by 2020.

◆ **Pollution:**
Sunlight breaks
pollution into noxious
substances, causing
more respiratory
problems.

◆ **Refugees:**
Floods displaced
230 million people in
China in 1998. Future
floods could have
similar effects –
submerging homes
and contaminating
water.

▲ **Water wars:**
Droughts may bring
on conflicts over
scarce water
resources, pitting
upstream nations
against downstream
neighbors.

Adapted from *US News
and World Report*,
February 5, 2001.

CONCERNS ABOUT GENETIC ENGINEERING

It was perhaps only in the later years of the last century that
the potential ecological and environmental consequences of
genetic engineering advances became an issue of concern.
One of the main questions is whether "gene flow" from
targeted species (those species that have been genetically
modified) to other species is likely.

Champions of genetically modified crops point to the
potential of increased yields from disease resistant plants.

Planning for global warming
*Global warming may have many different
effects in different regions, such as flooding,
droughts, increases in diseases, and mass
movements of refugees. Companies sourcing
goods, operating, or selling in affected areas
must plan to compensate for the effects of
these adverse events.*

Critics argue that the impacts of genetic engineering have not been well researched, and that there is a possibility of an ecological catastrophe, as modified plants may be able to harbor new viruses.

PRESSURE FROM ENVIRONMENTAL ACTIVISTS

A shift in values has led to the more environmentally aware citizens regarding themselves as "tenants with a full repair and maintenance lease, rather than owners of the planet," to quote former British Prime Minister Margaret Thatcher.

This shift is enhanced by the revolution of markets. In the old Communist bloc, citizens did not have the freedom or the technical capacity to complain about environmental problems. It is in these ex-Communist countries, where businesses have taken over the old state enterprises, that some of the worst environmental degradation now exists.

Three billion new consumers have entered the global market in the last 10 years, and if even a small percentage of them has environmental concerns, they can add significantly to the number of environmental activists, some of whom are called "eco-warriors."

Controversy about genetically modified crops joins other long-standing concerns, such as the use of herbicides in intensive farming, as the basis for campaigns by environmental NGOs. Campaigns are targeted at businesses directly, and at consumers by encouraging changes in purchasing behavior. Activists call for greater disclosure by companies of the impact of their activities on the environment, and for comprehensive product labeling, covering themes such as farming techniques and the origin of ingredients.

Increased scrutiny has led some corporations to sign up to management standards, such as the (ISO) 14000 series from the International Organization for Standardization, which encompasses policies and processes for a company's environmental management system. There is also a growing number of certification programs tailored for specific industry sectors (see Measuring and Reporting pp. 288–301).

Deadly crops?
Genetically modified crops have attracted a great deal of negative press. Environmental activists feel that the crops may have deadly consequences for the environment and for people.

THE EMERGING MANAGEMENT ISSUE
Health and Well-Being

Globalization, the speed of communications, and the efficiency of new technology have all combined to alter the nature of work, and consequently the nature of the relationship between corporations and citizens.

These alterations are most evident in the changing nature of the responsibility corporations have for the health and safety of their workforce, consumers, and local communities. The corporate health and safety agenda was traditionally centered on protecting people from the harmful effects of business operations or products. The global forces for change are now stretching this issue to encompass a broader set of criteria more accurately labeled as "health and well-being."

The emergent management issue of health and well-being incorporates not just physical health and safety concerns, but also external influences such as stress, dependant care, the need for continuous learning and developing new skills, and issues of work/life balance.

This issue is further complicated for managers in emerging markets, who must also deal directly with a variety of medical and health-related concerns that are handled by government agencies in industrialized countries.

Stress and depression
Managers responsible for health and well-being have to take into account the growth in the incidence of stress and depression in today's high-pressured and rapidly changing corporate environment.

Introducing worldwide standards
Evidence of the link between unregulated waste discharge from operating plants and incidences of ill health among local people has led to calls for companies to introduce worldwide standards of pollution control.

The organic food sector has seen a 40 percent annual growth in the UK since 1998.
Soil Association, 1999.

HEALTH AND SAFETY

Traditionally, this topic concerned the health and safety of employees (such as miners and builders) and those living near a plant who might be affected by physical discharges, such as poisons into a river or the sea, or dangerous fumes into the atmosphere. Health and safety also involved responsibility for ensuring that a company's products were safe for consumers.

There is a need for continuing vigilance on these core issues, especially as the speed and extent of technological innovation makes a whole range of new products and ingredients possible. However, the revolution of values means that there is greater questioning of the safety of new products.

This questioning may occur irrespective of what the "experts" say. Indeed, in some societies, these experts will be under suspicion from consumer activists and NGOs. Also, the revolution of information and communications technology means that such groups can access more information and share it quickly. Even if a business is convinced about its products' safety, the public may not be. One example is the case of genetically modified organisms (GMOs).

The public's resistance to GMOs has already had a significant impact. After rapid adoption of the technology by the food industry, controversy over the safety of genetically engineered foods led the majority of European food manufacturers, retailers, and caterers to phase out the use of GMOs in food production (Economic Impacts of Genetically Modified Crops on the Agri-Food Sector, The European Commission, 2000).

There are consumer concerns that genetic modification may result in genes for antibiotic resistance being taken up by bacteria, or harmful proteins appearing in crops. These worries come at a time when consumers are showing more interest in modern food production methods, with a large move toward organic farming.

Like NGOs, consumer groups are now more able to turn the spotlight on corporations that they feel have fallen short of expected standards. The global reach of the media makes it difficult for the damage done by a product shortfall to be limited by geography, as US tire company Bridgestone/Firestone found to its cost when the possibility that its tires were defective was publicized in 2000.

Ensuring sound risk management drills and adequate insurance coverage is imperative, as is the need to sensitize management to be alert to issues before they become crises. If appropriate, companies also need to engage in education campaigns and dialogue in order to inform and address fears. This did not happen adequately on the genetically engineered foods issue, when negative media comment, implying that the industry was putting potential profits before safety, led to a major retrenchment in the industry.

"I believe that the irresponsible speed to introduce advances of genetic engineering is inspired by the greed of economic globalization."
Brazilian Judge Antonio Sourza Prudente, quoted in Jack Epstein, "A Seedy Business," *Latin Trade*, October 1999.

Transnational companies may switch production to industrializing countries and open up new markets where health and safety standards may be lower and supervision less thorough. Yet, with the global information network, details of a company's inferior product content or its lower safety standards can be broadcast around the world.

Commercial interests and disease
Foot and mouth disease broke out in Europe and South America in 2001. Suggested causes included a shift to intensive farming and transportation of livestock over long distances.

FROM SAFETY TO WELL-BEING

A number of elements are influencing the stretch to health and well-being:

- There is an increased interest in personal health and physical fitness, especially in the West.
- Individuals can log on to the internet and interrogate medical databases for the latest research about medical conditions. This, combined with the decline in deference to those in authority, means that people are prepared to challenge medical diagnoses.
- As government provision for healthcare is reduced due to the increasing costs, individuals are encouraged to take greater personal responsibility for their well-being, spurring business to promote good health.
- There is growing recognition that health is both physical and mental, leading to the acknowledgment of stress as a business issue.
- People are now less reluctant to talk about depression and mental health problems (although there is still a stigma about doing so in many societies) and the often associated substance abuse problems, such as alcoholism and drug addiction.
- Greater affluence and the ability to telecommute and work from home is producing a greater interest in work/life balance. There is also a greater emphasis on new patterns of work, especially for knowledge workers.
- There are a greater number of single households, single parents, and households in which both partners are working. Add to this increasing longevity, and childcare concerns are now broadened to include care of the elderly.

STRESSED-OUT EMPLOYEES

"Downsizing," "job-loading," "flatter structures," "the 24-hour day": all are buzzwords and phrases that result in greater stress for those both in and out of work.

For employees, the nature of the employment contract is changing, with a move toward short-term or freelance contracts. For managers, this can result in greater levels of direct responsibility, with flatter organizations, often on an international basis. However, these changes also lead to

The German company Siemens is offering no-smoking bonuses to those who stop smoking, worth approximately $100 per month for up to two years.

Financial Times, November 24, 2000

employees fearing a loss of job security. *Fortune* magazine once satirized the dilemma that is felt by many managers in a mock memo from employer to employee:

> *You're expendable. We don't want to fire you, but we will if we have to. Competition is brutal, so we must redesign the way we work to do more with less. Sorry, that's just the way it is.*
>
> *And one more thing — you're invaluable. Your devotion to our customers is the salvation of this company. We're depending on you to be innovative, risk-taking, and committed to our goals. OK?* Brian O'Reilly and John Wyatt, "What Companies and Employees Owe One Another," *Fortune*, June 13, 1997.

Stress at work is magnified by the pressure from society to be highly paid and productive. Dual careers for husbands and wives are now common. This reinforces the demand for childcare provision by governments and business and for the right to parental leave. Mobile phones, laptop computers, and emails result in the intrusion of work into personal time.

Stress created in the workplace can have serious effects on home life. If both partners in a relationship are stressed from work, this can cause problems in the relationship. And because the traditional levels of home support no longer exist, a vicious circle of still more stress is created.

> "You're expendable. We don't want to fire you, but we will if we have to. Competition is brutal, so we must redesign the way we work to do more with less. Sorry, that's just the way it is."

An epidemic of stress

As many as one in 10 workers in Europe and North America is suffering from depression, anxiety, stress, or burn-out, according to a report by the International Labour Office (*A 12-Point Program for Business to Combat Depression in the Workplace – Mental Health in the Workplace*, ILO, 2001). The ILO suggests that in the EU, spending on mental health problems may be the equivalent of 3–4 percent of GDP. The World Federation for Mental Health says depressed employees may be costing US and European businesses some $120 billion a year in absenteeism, low productivity, and sick pay. Stress is now the most common work-related disability. The rising incidence of stress in the workplace reflects the 24-hour society, economic globalization, information technology overload, and the loss of job security.

HSBC nursery partnership
After opening its first nursery in 1989, HSBC has found that providing flexible, inexpensive childcare options helps with the recruitment and retention of talented female staff, who might otherwise delay returning to work after having children.

WORK/LIFE BALANCE

It can be argued that we are seeing a small, but economically significant, minority of knowledge workers shifting their values and priorities toward a greater sense of work/life balance. This situation will challenge companies to become more creative in responding to work/life aspirations if they want to attract and retain such employees. Alternatively, companies will find themselves in a bidding war for talent that is motivated purely by the size of the pay package.

Businesses are finding that ignoring work/life balance issues can lead to recruitment difficulties: persistent sickness and lateness for work; poor staff retention; high rates of non-return after maternity leave; low or inconsistent morale and commitment; and declining continuity in important customer relationships. A corporation's reputation can be threatened if employees take out stress-related litigation; casting doubts on whether a company operates good employee practices.

Some work/life balance solutions include: job-sharing; individualized contracts; annualized hours contracts; working from home and telecommuting; sabbaticals; school-term working; and hours built around the school day for those with young children. Companies are offering extended parental leave, study leave, and compassionate or emergency leave to fulfill care-giving responsibilities. For example, the UK supermarket chain Sainsbury's offers special leave of up to one year for study or care-giving.

Companies may sponsor care-giving facilities, or offer loans or allowances. HSBC Bank in the UK opened its first nursery partnership in 1989, and now has over 100 such partnerships with 900 places for the children of employees, including 300 places at five nurseries on bank premises. The company also provides "LifeWorks," a confidential advice helpline that helps employees to manage the dual demands of home and work effectively, and offers online mentors.

- Forty percent of all US companies offer assistance with care of the elderly, double that of five years ago, according to a survey by Hewitt Associates. Anne Fisher, "Finding a Job That Lets You Care for an Aging Parent," *Fortune*, February 21, 2000.
- The annual "100 Best Companies" survey by Robert Levering and Miton Moskowitz, quoted in *Fortune* magazine (January 10, 2000), noted how some companies were attempting to help with work/life balance by creating self-contained communities. Forty-six of the 100 offered take-home meals for employees; 26 (up from 15 the year before) offered personal concierge services.
- KPMG offers mobile dental and general medical services at their corporate HQ so that staff do not have to take time off for appointments.
- The right to take "parental leave and leave for family reasons" became national law in 15 EU member states in 1999. *Agreement on social policy, Article 138*, The European Commission, 1999.

The perceived benefits to business of providing support packages for employees include greater staff loyalty, greater productivity and flexibility, and greater receptivity to change. By developing work/life programs, companies are signaling to their employees that it is, "OK to talk," about previously taboo issues, such as stress, and are trying to stop the long hours culture from being a constant way of life.

Generation X

The gap between the need to balance the demands of work and family or personal life and workers' perception of how well they are able to achieve this balance, is at its widest among the under 35s – the so called Generation X. Nearly a third say balance is very important, but less than a sixth manage to achieve it, according to a survey across 13 industrialized countries by consulting group Cap Gemini Ernst & Young (*International Workforce Management Study: Capitalizing on the Workforce Revolution*, Yankelovitch Partners Inc., 2000). Workers in every country surveyed, except Russia, rate work/life balance higher than a good salary. Workers want quality time to spend their earnings.

Lack of balance has a clear effect on mobility and job satisfaction. A third of workers worldwide would leave their current jobs for one that provides more flexibility. Gemini concluded that the workforce is a fluid growth investment that can affect productivity, reputation, service levels, the development of intellectual capital, and in so doing, is the bottom line of businesses everywhere.

SECURITY OF EMPLOYABILITY

One cause of stress at work may be the pressure to balance the conflicting pressures of a job at a time of rapid technological change, which may result in people's skills becoming obsolete very quickly. Hence, there is a growing emphasis on the use of corporate universities, virtual learning programs, and peer group mentoring to enable employees to keep re-skilling themselves – thereby gaining a feeling of security of employability, if not of security of employment.

Competition among companies for the best talent is fierce. Talented people choose from potential employers, not just on the pay and prospects offered, but also on whether the organization has flexible work conditions and has a learning culture in its core values.

Security of employment can be said to be giving way to security of employability. That is, an organization should have a culture of learning and training so that, if made redundant, individuals have a head start in the job market.

Skandia, a Scandinavian insurance group, helps employees amass learning funds, and Ford Motor Company runs an Employee Development Action Program to fund personal learning. In 2000, after discussion with the United Auto Workers, Ford announced that it would provide all employees with a home computer for a small monthly fee. Bill Ford, the Chairman of Ford Motor Company, stated in 2000:

> "Like the $5-a-day wage Henry Ford pioneered in the last century, the $5-a-month internet connection is an affirmation that the only sustainable advantage a company has is its people."

Re-skilling employees
Learning at the Unipart Corporate University (the "U") in Oxford, England, takes a number of forms and is open to any Unipart employee who takes a minimum of 10 days training a year. Unipart believes that this provides customer benefit, and a highly trained and motivated workforce.

HEALTH AND WELL-BEING IN EMERGING MARKETS

This section has focused on health and well-being issues for people and organizations where basic nutrition and treatment of life-threatening diseases are taken for granted. However, the globalization of business means that, within a workforce, there are varied cultural and ethnic groups with different healthcare needs. For international companies, a larger proportion of their workforce is likely to be located in societies with poor standards of public health care.

As more firms extend operations into other parts of the world, the "health and well-being" agenda there is likely to look very different. There is increasing demand for healthcare resources, especially in the emerging markets. These are precisely the markets where governments are least able, organizationally and financially, to meet the growing scale of demand. Yet these are the same societies most at risk from global pandemics such as TB, malaria, and HIV.

Public health inefficiencies can result in substantial costs to business, which often justifies direct business provision of healthcare for workers. For example, DHL Worldwide Express in Mexico have an on-site doctor to reduce workplace absence caused by the long waiting times at public health facilities.

Healthcare provision for employees and their families – and sometimes for local communities – may extend to using the company's communication channels to spread health messages, such as information on HIV-prevention, or, via marketing channels, to the public. The Toy Manufacturers Association in Brazil, for example, encouraged its member companies to carry messages on its packaging for parents about how to prevent dehydration in children.

The threat from HIV
The HIV virus invades immune cells in the body and reproduces, with thousands of new virus particles budding from infected cells. By 2010, HIV will have caused more deaths than any disease outbreak in history.

THE EMERGING MANAGEMENT ISSUE
Diversity and Human Rights

The global forces for change are bringing to the fore issues once regarded as tangential to the business world, but that are now relevant to mainstream management.

Such is the case in the emergence of the issue of diversity and human rights, which if not managed sensitively can result in significant exposure to risk. Conversely, it offers opportunities that can add value and earn competitive advantage.

The parameters for this issue are set by a series of international agreements, such as the United Nations Universal Declaration of Human Rights, and the conventions of bodies such as the International Labour Organization. These agreements address common principles and set standards in human rights. They establish that an individual is entitled to fundamental and inalienable rights, including the right to freedom to lead a dignified and independent life, free from abuse and violations.

Over time, the range of human rights and diversity issues covered in international and national law and convention has grown, and the implications for managers and for business have increased accordingly.

It means that those with whom a business has contact or who are affected by its operations (its stakeholders) have the right to be treated justly and fairly, equally and consistently, irrespective of their gender, ethnic origin, creed, color, sexual orientation, or disability. Furthermore, individuals have the right of redress against a business through internal and external mechanisms if they consider that any of these rights have been infringed.

But the human rights and diversity issue is not only about taking care not to cause offense. It is also about recognizing the opportunity for innovation, creativity, and insight that lies in bringing together peoples of different backgrounds and cultural traditions, and varied histories and experiences.

Integration through technology

Developments in technology, such as computer printouts in Braille and voice recognition software, allow people with disabilities to be fully integrated into the workplace.

IN THE WORKPLACE

Globalization is resulting in companies operating in many markets, bringing them into contact with different demographic profiles, religions, races, customs, and traditions. Workforces are now drawn from a more diverse pool of potential employees, making recruitment, employee retention, and personnel management more complex matters.

Both the revolution of technology and the revolution of values compound the issue, further increasing the diversity and complexity of the workforce.

The growth in the knowledge-driven economy puts a premium on talented staff, and leads companies to draw upon a wider population in order to find the best. Technological innovations such as the internet open up a pool of workers across national borders. Technology also enables disabled employees to be integrated into the workplace, or allows them to contribute fully through telecommuting.

More women are entering the workforce. With the increase in the number of families where both parents are working, issues of care of the elderly and of children are brought firmly onto the business agenda.

> "Long-term, I believe eldercare will outweigh childcare as a business issue — and the profile of men in eldercare will emerge — because all have parents but not all have kids." Anne Watts, head of Diversity and Employee Support, HSBC Bank, March 2001.

Companies are serving or selling into diverse markets with different needs, preferences, and sensibilities. Some business leaders have adopted strategies to ensure that the diversity of their workforces reflects the diversity of their customers, seeing it as a source of competitive advantage. As Alan Lafley, chief executive of Procter & Gamble, says:

> "Our success depends entirely on our ability to understand these [its diverse customer base] diverse consumers' needs. A diverse organization will outthink and outperform a homogeneous organization every single time. I am putting particular importance on increasing the representation of women and minorities in leadership at all levels." Alan Lafley, quoted in *Financial Times*, February 6, 2001.

"A diverse organization will outthink and outperform a homogeneous organization every single time."

WORKING CONDITIONS

Companies face increased pressure from organized labor and consumers (via NGOs and the media) on the labor conditions of their direct workforce, and the conditions of employees in suppliers and subcontractors.

Scrutiny falls on workplace practices such as a living wage, use of child, prison, or bonded labor, freedom of association and the right to collective bargaining, and discrimination.

There have been many reported allegations of employees working under sweatshop conditions at suppliers, particularly those in Southeast Asia, for global brands such as Nike and Adidas, and for retailers such as Gap and Wal-Mart. Child labor has been identified in the footwear and toy sectors in Asia and South America. While these alleged or proven abuses may be committed by suppliers, it is the big brands that suffer the damage to reputation in the public eye.

Differences in working conditions and the wages for comparable work in countries around the world have led to demonstrations, boycotts, and shareholder resolutions attacking corporate offenders. These have prompted many companies to change their workplace practices, and demand the same changes from their suppliers and subcontractors.

Companies such as Nike and Adidas are tackling labor-related issues by introducing codes of conduct, independent auditing and verification of workplace standards among suppliers, and transparent reporting. For auditing and verification, some companies employ recognized firms such as PriceWaterhouseCoopers and KPMG. Others, recognizing that NGOs are the most trusted institutions by much of the public, hire specialized NGOs such as Verité or Corveco, or work directly with NGOs such as the Rainforest Alliance.

In industrialized countries, the relationship between employer and employee is also under the microscope. There is an increasing body of law relating to employment rights, and the growth of "no win, no fee" legal services has led to an increase in legal action being taken against employers. In the US in 2000,

Microsoft, Lockheed Martin, and Nextel were all the subject of filed lawsuits alleging discrimination.

A number of companies have initiated plans to embrace and manage diversity. Texaco has established an independent task force to monitor employment practices, and Coca-Cola has launched a Procurement Advisory Council to advise on spending with businesses owned by minorities and women.

SENSITIVE MARKETS

Because of their economic power and influence, corporations find themselves involved in wider human rights issues and dilemmas. Transnational companies often operate in markets with a weak rule of law, or in countries governed by repressive regimes, such as Myanmar (formerly Burma). They are under pressure to ensure that human rights abuses do not happen because of their investment, and should ask some basic questions:

● Companies operating in conflict zones need to consider their interaction with the players in the conflict: are their actions contributing to a solution, or perpetuating, or even worsening, the conflict? For example, what is the conduct of local security forces subcontracted to protect company sites?

Responding to human rights issues
Companies with investments in Myanmar have made different decisions about how to respond to problematic human rights issues in the country, such as bonded labor and harsh treatment of protesters against the Myanmar regime. Heineken, Hewlett Packard, and Texaco withdrew operations in response to protests by campaigners. Unocal and Premium Oil have remained.

Countries in which transnationals may face human rights issues

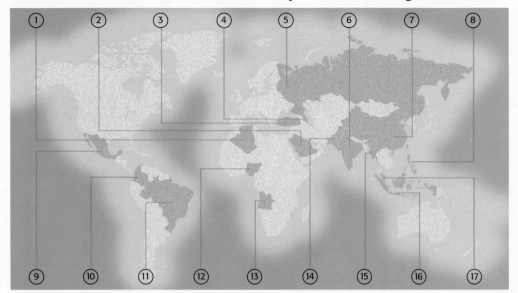

Key

1 ALGERIA
Torture, "disappearances," extrajudicial executions, harassment of human rights defenders, prisoners of conscience.

2 SAUDI ARABIA
Torture, denial of freedom of association, forcible relocation, systematic denial of women's rights, prisoners of conscience.

3 TURKEY
Torture, "disappearances," extrajudicial executions, harassment of human rights defenders, denial of freedom of association, forcible relocation, prisoners of conscience.

4 AZERBAIJAN
Torture, hostage-taking, prisoners of conscience.

5 RUSSIAN FEDERATION
Torture, hostage-taking.

6 INDIA
Torture, "disappearances," extrajudicial executions, harassment of human rights defenders, bonded labor, systematic denial of women's rights, prisoners of conscience.

7 CHINA
Torture, denial of freedom of association, forced labor, prisoners of conscience.

8 PHILIPPINES
Torture, "disappearances," extrajudicial executions, hostage-taking, forcible relocation, prisoners of conscience.

9 MEXICO
Torture, "disappearances," extrajudicial executions, hostage-taking, harassment of human rights defenders, prisoners of conscience.

10 COLOMBIA
Torture, "disappearances," extrajudicial executions, hostage-taking, harassment of human rights defenders, denial of freedom of association.

11 BRAZIL
Torture, extrajudicial executions, harassment of human rights defenders.

12 NIGERIA
Torture, extrajudicial executions, harassment of human rights defenders, denial of freedom of association, prisoners of conscience.

13 ANGOLA
Torture, "disappearances," extrajudicial executions, hostage-taking, harassment of human rights defenders, prisoners of conscience.

14 PAKISTAN
Torture, extrajudicial executions, denial of freedom of association, systematic denial of women's rights, prisoners of conscience.

15 MYANMAR
Torture, extrajudicial executions, harassment of human rights defenders, denial of freedom of association, forced labor, bonded labor, forcible relocation, prisoners of conscience.

16 INDONESIA
Torture, "disappearances," extrajudicial executions, hostage-taking, harassment of human rights defenders, denial of freedom of association, prisoners of conscience.

17 MALAYSIA
Forcible relocation, prisoners of conscience.

Adapted from *A Geography of Corporate Risk: UK Transnational Companies*, Amnesty International UK, 2000.

- Companies with operations that require them to operate in territory subject to disputed land claims and/or occupied by indigenous peoples should ask how their operations are affecting or affected by claimants to the land, and if they are respecting the rights of indigenous peoples.
- Companies engaged in construction projects requiring movements of people should consider if their actions are respectful of the rights of the displaced population, what steps are being taken to support the rehabilitation of those people, and what the company's role in that process is.
- Companies that operate in markets prone to corruption should consider whether the company is clear about its stance on bribery, and if it has training and systems in place that enable reporting of incidents.

When a business commits to a joint venture, or acquires or merges with another business, the due diligence process, which traditionally focused only on issues of finance, must now take into account the potential of exposure to risks associated with diversity and human rights.

A GLOBAL PERSPECTIVE WITH LOCAL RESPECT

Those responsible for human resource policies and practices within a business must be sensitive to both local norms and standards set by other companies. However, what is regarded as acceptable behavior in one part of the world and what is normal in another is sometimes hard to determine.

- Reebok, reported *The Economist* ("Best Foot Forward," October 21, 1999), is aware of the "difficulty of introducing industrial-world values into industrializing-world plants." In one report into efforts to help raise workplace standards, Reebok reported that no workers knew of any sexual harassment incidents. In fact, many did not understand the term for it. As a result, there are now gender awareness sessions run by an Indonesian NGO.

Companies' reputations are at risk through their own core business, the activities of their partners, and through their supply chains. Some companies are setting clear operating standards for their own and their suppliers' operations by

> Human rights activists call for the promotion of higher labor standards. Their critics say such measures will add costs, deter investors, and dampen economic growth.
>
> Prince of Wales International Business Leaders Forum, June 2001.

> "An already worrying gap is widening between the international norms and declarations on human rights, such as the UN Charter, and current societal and business realities. Big companies need to step into the breach to ensure that globalization delivers more than a litany of dashed hopes. We must act as co-guarantors of human rights."
>
> Goran Lindahl, "A New Role for Global Businesses", *Time*, January 31, 2000.

introducing new global policies for people to follow, some of which are aligned with those of international organizations such as the ILO.

● Telefónica, the Spanish-owned telecommunications business, signed an agreement early in 2000 with Union Networks International that commits it to guarantee core labor standards in employment practices worldwide. As part of the agreement, the company commits to never using indentured or child labor and, "…will reject forms of gender and racial discrimination in its employment practices". *Financial Times*, April 13, 2000.

● Phillips-Van Heusen Corporation, in the apparel and footwear sectors, has published guidelines in a statement of "A Shared Commitment" that encompass expectations of conduct related to discrimination, child and forced labor, harassment and abuse, health and safety, wages and benefits, hours of work, freedom of association, environmental requirements, and community commitment. The company states, "we have not established business relationships, and have suspended our association, with companies that were found to abuse the rights of employees."

PART OF THE SOLUTION

There is increasing pressure for transnational corporations to play a proactive role in promoting and addressing broader human rights issues that may be affecting a country or region. This challenge for business to take a role in promoting human rights has been accepted by some business leaders, who see it in a wider context of business retaining its "license to operate" in an age of globalization.

Business principles in practice

A survey of Fortune 500 companies' approaches toward human rights by the Ashridge Centre for Business and Society (UK), quoted in *Winning with Integrity*, Business in the Community, 2000, reported that 98 percent of respondents had a code of ethics, business principles, or similar guidelines, and 96 percent applied those codes to subsidiary companies. Some 39 percent of the companies surveyed had decided not to proceed with investment projects in certain countries because of human rights concerns, and 19 percent had divested for these reasons.

THE EMERGING MANAGEMENT ISSUE
Communities

The quality of the relationship between a business and the communities with which it interacts is set to become a crucial determinate of business success.

This is because the global forces for change are producing an environment in which business and other sections of society are highly interconnected, and because communities are being redefined, producing better organized, more vocal, and more powerful constituents. The result is a shift in the nature of the dynamic between business and community.

Communities today have the power to influence business operations in a positive or in a negative way. They have demonstrated that they are willing and able to use that power. Consequently, the notion of community relations, once a term used to describe a limited relationship between a business and the local community, and usually built on the charitable largess of the company, has a new importance.

The emerging management issue of communities describes how the nature of community relations is changing, and how what was considered by many executives and managers as a "nice to" has now become a "have to."

Innovative partnerships
Even a rich and technologically connected area such as California's Silicon Valley has recognized that poverty and poor schools are a threat to business, and has formed a series of innovative community business partnerships such as Joint Venture Silicon Valley and the Community Foundation of Silicon Valley.

Categories of community

The revolutions of technology and markets that have so influenced the nature of business have also affected the dynamic between business and the community. Communities that interact with business today include not only those defined by geography, but those defined by other characteristics as well. Work by Edmund M. Burke and Raymond V. Gilmartin (*Corporate Community Relations: The Principles of the Neighbor of Choice*, 1999) and others, suggests that it is possible to identify three key types of community (listed below).

COMMUNITY	CHARACTERISTICS
Communities of geography	Defined by a community's geographical location, such as a village, town, or city. These communities can be subdivided into three areas: ● The "fenceholder" community – the immediate neighborhood, the other side of the fence physically adjoining the company's property. ● The locality – where this property is situated. ● The impact community – the physical area that is affected by the business. Localities have ongoing needs such as good housing, good schools, good leisure and sports facilities, cultural activities, protection from crime and violence, jobs, and positive activities for local residents to do.

Community complexity

A geographical community can contain complex subcategories. In the case of those living close to an airport, there are residents concerned with noise, pollution, and congested local traffic. There is also a subset of residents who have a vested commercial interest in the airport because they are employees or local businesspeople who supply goods and services.

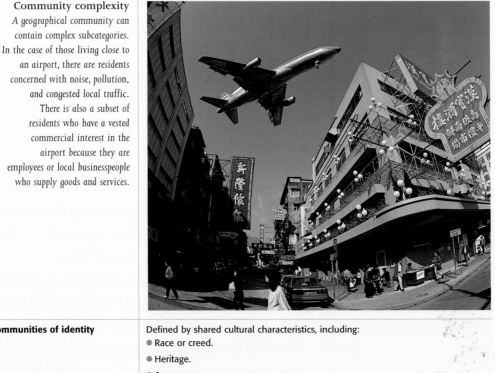

COMMUNITY	CHARACTERISTICS
Communities of identity	Defined by shared cultural characteristics, including: ● Race or creed. ● Heritage. ● Age group.
Communities of interest	Defined by shared interest in a topic, such as: ● Clubs and societies organized to exchange information. ● Shared concern for societal issues. ● Shared beliefs and needs.

CORPORATE WELFARE?

Transnational companies, operating in many countries, have relationships with different types of these communities, all of which have various needs.

In more developed countries, the government may be the major provider of social services and welfare. In the less developed countries, government provision may not exist or may be insufficient and social problems more pronounced.

Corporations may choose to help meet community need as a way of ensuring social cohesion and a stable community, facilitating the recruitment of employees and the safe passage of goods and people to and from company operations.

The pressure for corporations to supplement and, in some cases, replace government provision is increasing. As a result of globalization, governments have less ability to set tax levels out of line with other countries competing for limited sources of foreign investment. Consequently, their ability to raise or even maintain government spending levels on social programs is restricted.

In the absence of adequate provision, communities are playing roles that were traditionally played by governments:

- In Chihuahua, a northern state of Mexico, 20,000 businesses contribute voluntary taxes to a business coalition called FECHAC to run social programs to combat poverty, homelessness, and unemployment.
- "When regulatory environments do not function, community-led monitoring can be effective: for example, in the group lending programs such as Bangladesh's Grameen Bank and Bolivia's Banco Solidario. Loans go to individuals, but if someone defaults, lenders understand that none will receive subsequent loans. This gives an incentive to monitor performance." *World Bank Development Report*, World Bank, 1998/1999.

Expanding businesses
Projects such as the Grameen Bank's group credit program have helped to grow micro-enterprises. Companies in the financial services sector, such as Citigroup and Deutsche Bank, offer similar programs.

NGO support for Amazon tribe

Amazon Watch, an NGO, gave a video camera to U'Wa Indians opposed to drilling on lands they claimed as theirs. They filmed their own gassing by the Colombian army, and the NGO then distributed the video to the media.
Financial Times, February 21, 2001.

CORPORATIONS: COMMUNITY FRIEND OR FOE?

If a company is making a significant change in the scale of its operations in a community – for example, by cutting back or closing down an operation – this may create local opposition. Alternatively, opening a new plant may be met enthusiastically with tax breaks or other forms of incentive.

Through the increased scrutiny and monitoring of corporate behavior and greater access to information identified in Global Forces for Change, a company's reputation, viewed as either a "dangerous intruder" or good corporate citizen, can precede it, either hindering or positively helping its future development plans.

Western NGOs may influence the attitude of remote communities that are influenced by business operations – such as those of a mining company. As a result of contact with these institutions, communities now have access to telecommunications technology that enables them to organize themselves, communicate their views widely, and negotiate from a position of strength.

Managers within affected companies are changing the way they interact with remote communities, increasing consultation and dialogue in order to understand community concerns, and to present better the view of the corporation.

PROSPEROUS COMPANIES REQUIRE PROSPEROUS COMMUNITIES

One element of the heightened expectations of business that communities have is that businesses will put something back into the communities from which they make their profits.

Many companies now support the homeless or those with inadequate shelter, provide access to food and water, and support education, sports, and the arts. Corporations are responding to community expectations and helping meet social needs through methods such as direct company provision, providing healthcare for staff, supporting community groups or NGOs, and lobbying public authorities for improvements in public provision. Corporations can also get involved with the social issues of local communities by providing management or project expertise to make existing public services more effective. They can also contribute to the public policy debate about new ways of tackling social issues.

Prosperous and strong communities can be a source of business benefit; poor and weak communities can be a cost. Where educational standards are low, many businesses are investing in education initiatives to avoid remedial education programs or the cost of transferring operations.

PARTNERSHIPS

The contributions that business can make to problems that communities experience is often achieved best by the corporation working with other businesses or with the government and NGOs. This helps to pool resources, cut costs, and share skills and risks among the partners.

● The Caribbean Tourism, Health, Safety, and Resource Conservation Program is a response to episodes of ill-health among visitors to the Caribbean, which resulted in negative publicity, loss of revenue, and costly lawsuits. The Caribbean Hotel Association teamed up with the Caribbean Epidemiology Center, the Pan-American Health Organization, and the Caribbean Action for Sustainable Tourism in a joint initiative to improve health and hygiene conditions for guests and staff at hotels across the region. International Hotels Environment Initiative.

Partnerships between business and community groups enable business to gain credibility. Because

Positive Caribbean initiative
Environmental health and resource conservation standards are under development by a cross-sector partnership of Caribbean hotels, tourism facilities, and other bodies to encourage good practice in sustainable development.

NGOs are some of the most trusted institutions in many markets, some businesses are attempting to associate themselves with these positive values of trust by linking with community issues and NGOs. This also helps with the pressure to differentiate their brand.

BARRICADES AND BOUNDARIES

The ability of communities of shared interest to come together rapidly and campaign to change the behavior of business brings dilemmas for business and, some say, is a challenge to democracy.

Just as corporations have been targeted by some NGOs for lack of transparency and accountability for their behavior and impact, so too NGOs are now being questioned about their legitimacy to represent the views of their constituents. This is another example of blurring of roles and boundaries.

There is pressure for business to engage with communities, and a business case argument to be made for it. However, there are critics of business involvement in the community. Some of the main arguments for and against business involvement are summarized in the table below.

Evaluating business involvement in the community

ARGUMENTS AGAINST	ARGUMENTS FOR
● Solving the problems of communities is not the job of businesses: the proper business of business is business, not social welfare.	● Tackling problems in the community that restrict business potential is a normal part of doing business. Ignoring the problem may threaten the community's stability and increase the cost of business.
● Getting business involved in the community is akin to putting Dracula in charge of the blood bank. According to these critics, business is the cause of many of the social ills it is trying to help. And even if it is not, it is undemocratic to give such a role to unelected businesspeople.	● Support from business in tackling community problems should be complementary to, not a supplement for, government provision. The support should be transparent, and subject to checks and balances. In some developing countries, corporate engagement in the community may provide the foundations on which a democratic system can be built.
● It would be nice if businesses did play a large part in improving the lives of communities, but most of their involvement is just a token gesture and self-serving. Often it is carried out for publicity, or, at best, is well-meaning but marginal.	● Business has a lot to learn about what is good practice in engaging with communities and addressing their development needs. The challenge is to recognize good practice where it is happening, share it widely, and scale up programs.

WHERE ARE THE LIMITS?

Even businesses that believe that it is legitimate and beneficial to be involved in communities are often confused about where to draw the line on their involvement. There are no neat, predictable guidelines. The major needs of business and communities vary greatly around the world. Cultural and societal norms about the role of business in the community also vary in different regions.

As a rough guide, managers may want to focus on those community issues where:

- There is a direct link to business needs. For example, it makes sense for a book publisher or bookseller to be supporting literacy campaigns.
- There is interest among employees – especially where they may become directly involved in community work.
- There is relevant corporate expertise and other resources that can be deployed.

Generally, businesses that focus their activities, maintain the activity over time, systematically learn well from their involvement, and look to leverage their involvement with that of other businesses, NGOs, and the public sector, ultimately see the best results.

"Greening" industrial land
The ash mound outside this coal-fired power station in India was regenerated and developed to provide a pleasant "green" area for the local community's use.

THE IMPACT ON BUSINESS STRATEGY

A greater understanding of the risks and opportunities provided by the emerging management issues can be achieved by considering how they affect some major elements of business strategy.

Operations in emerging markets are increasing because of globalization, and more managers are having to deal sensitively with the challenges of dealing with overseas customers, suppliers, and operational locations. Brands and corporate reputation, which are now crucial components of a business's market capitalization, have been made more vulnerable by the emerging management issues. Protecting a brand's reputation has become the responsibility of every manager and employee. The commercial environment is also demanding constant corporate reinvention and reorganization, leading to a constant process of business restructuring.

Some companies have taken advantage of the opportunities presented by the emerging management issues in these areas. Others have fallen foul of the risks and incurred costs.

Operating in an Emerging Economy

Many managers who work for a company based in an OECD country will work in an emerging economy during their careers. Many more, while not overseas themselves, will liaise with a manufacturer, business unit, partner, subcontractor, or supplier who is.

The emerging economies are becoming increasingly important to business. Rapid industrialization has led to a growth in consumer markets in places such as Brazil, China, and India. Cheap labor there gives a competitive advantage, and improvements in international transportation make moving raw materials and finished goods more economical. It is now easier to extract the untapped raw materials that lie underground, even in remote locations.

Privatization in the 1980s and 1990s accelerated business interests overseas. Public sector concerns such as railroads, water, electricity, and telecommunications were transferred to the private sector to form major international firms. What were public utilities in one country are now international companies with global aspirations. An example is the New Zealand Post Office, which is managing the reorganization of postal services in South Africa and South America.

New opportunities
With the opening of the Chinese economy, the most populous nation on the planet has the potential to become a huge new marketplace for transnationals, as long as obstacles such as poor transparency, heavy bureaucracy, and protection of intellectual property are overcome.

The technology revolution means that it is easier to transmit data and work to offices and subcontractors in lower-wage economies. For example, Bangalore, in southern India, has a thriving software industry sector carrying out work for European and North American transnationals. Service sector businesses have followed to back up the growth in international operations.

Managing reputations

In some emerging economies, regulations on labor, health, safety, and the environment are less stringent or less strictly enforced than in the parent company's country of origin. However, NGOs and consumer activist groups in OECD countries are linking up with local NGOs overseas to track the performance of transnational companies.

If a company's conditions are exposed as poor, this can quickly impact its reputation at home. Companies that state that they are operating to certain norms and standards of behavior are expected to meet those standards wherever they do business, not just in developed economies. In order to demonstrate their performance and improve their reputation, companies may request verification and monitoring by a third-party.

Managing a culturally diverse workforce or marketing to culturally diverse customers requires sensitivity to different cultural perspectives. Insensitivity over marketing or other business practices can lead to accusations of corporate colonialism, and a backlash from consumers and authorities.

There may be differences of opinion between host governments that want fast-track industrialization, and environmentalists and NGOs concerned about possible damage to the environment, local cultures, and communities.

Demonstrating added value

Transnational companies may be operating in areas where there is poor welfare provision, and where managers may have to deal with the basic health-care and nutrition of staff.

Although they are attractive as a potential employer, companies may have to demonstrate the added value of their presence in order to do business in these areas. Companies

Of 44 North American manufacturing companies surveyed, 90 percent believe that they maintain higher health and safety standards than national manufacturing companies in the developing country in which they operate.

US Manufacturing Industry's Impact on Ethical, Labor, and Environmental Standards in Developing Countries. A Survey of Current Practices, Manufacturers' Alliance/MAPI and National Association of Manufacturers, April 2001.

Demonstrating added value in emerging economies

AREA OF ADDED VALUE	METHODS OF DEMONSTRATING VALUE
Building human capital	● Investing in the education, training, health, and safety of employees. ● Exposing local nationals to international contacts and practices. ● Paying taxes for the government to spend on social services. ● Investing in education, training, health, and nutrition projects.
Encouraging good governance	● Adopting and sharing internationally accepted standards and management practices. ● Supporting local and national governments to achieve efficient public administration and service delivery. ● Having fair and transparent regulations. ● Respecting human rights. ● Eliminating bribery and corruption.
Assisting social cohesion	● Helping to raise the quality of life and providing social services in some situations. ● Minimizing conflict resulting from the company's activities and tackling crime. ● Supporting social entrepreneurs and community-based capacity building. ● Encouraging cultural tolerance and diversity and supporting the arts and heritage projects.
Strengthening economies	● Creating jobs and generating export revenues and taxes. ● Expanding local infrastructure. ● Transferring technology and international standards. ● Releasing more disposable income into the economy. ● Investing in local financial markets. ● Building supplier and distribution networks. ● Supporting local business developments.
Protecting the environment	● Introducing cleaner production systems and developing environmentally sound products and services. ● Promoting the concept of product stewardship and life-cycle analysis. ● Sharing best practices in environmental management. ● Promoting energy and other natural resource efficiency. ● Addressing environmental policies with governments.

Adapted from Jane Nelson, *Building Competitiveness and Communities*, Prince of Wales Business Leaders Forum, in collaboration with the World Bank and the United Nations Development Program, 1988.

can show this in many ways, such as the seniority of jobs open to local candidates, the transfer of skills to the local economy, improvements in the local environment, supporting local heritage, and contributions to the broader community.

De facto leaders

The Western transnationals are often attractive potential employers for talented local graduates in the emerging economies. Local units become standard bearers for corporate behavior in a host of areas, from community involvement to transparency and responsible advertising. This is especially true in markets where there have been few private sector role-models.

Managers may also find themselves confronting bribery and corruption. If they make a stand, they may *de facto* help to set new standards. The World Bank has created a blacklist of companies known to use bribes, and has barred them from tender lists.

Transnationals may be operating in areas in which the public sector is fragile, there is armed conflict, and in which tax revenue from transnationals (often the government's main source of income) is used to prolong the conflict. Alternatively, tax revenue may be helping to perpetuate an undemocratic regime.

Managers may also face unrealistic expectations of how much their company can lessen a country's social and economic problems. This requires a sensitive dialogue with external stakeholders in the media, civil society organizations, and public institutions.

Making a contribution
A large number of transnational firms are contributing to the emerging economies where they operate by training local people in international methods and practices. The UK-based transnational Thames Water has taken its skills in water management and conservation to 44 countries, including Chile and China.

ECOLOGY AND ENVIRONMENT

The likely environmental impact of a company's investment can now be rigorously assessed. There are also procedures for monitoring environmental impact once operations have started. Increasingly, corporations are being held responsible for environmental impacts at all stages of the product or service life-cycle, and along an extended supply chain, wherever in the world they do business. And suppliers are having to demonstrate their compliance to corporations. However, industrializing countries fear that importing Western environmental standards will also delay much needed economic development.

Capitalizing on opportunities

● Through a partnership with the Indian Market Research Bureau, Swiss company Novartis undertakes research and training for safe and effective use of crop protection agents. The application of these agents has been controversial because of their use in areas of poor literacy, the health and environmental costs of improper usage, and aggressive marketing by the transnational chemical companies. Studies in Mexico, Zimbabwe, and India led to the production of information, education, and communication programs to be implemented in specific regions. One motivation for this was to learn about use of the agents in different cultural conditions, in order to adapt marketing campaigns and encourage safer application. **Prince of Wales International Business Leaders Forum.**

- Siemens sees environmental issues as part of its corporate commitment to the sustainable development of all of the countries in which it operates. It is one of the leading companies in developing technologies that are capable of minimizing the environmental impact of industrial processes, and in finding innovative solutions for problems that would otherwise lead to pollution and waste. Siemens Brazil was one of the first companies in São Paulo to adhere to the Tiete Project, which aims to clean the city's most important river. Its waste disposal complies with current legislation, and disposal of solid wastes is carried out via companies licensed by environmental agencies.

Perhaps one sector of industry that has most to gain from sound ecological and environmental management practices, and the most to lose from poor practices, is tourism.

- For more than 10 years, British Airways has supported the Tourism for Tomorrow Awards, in association with the World Conservation Union and tourism bodies. One winner was the Central Region Project of Conservation International in Ghana, which improved the environment in and around Kakum National Park. A spokesman for British Airways said:

> "This has seen the installation of a visitor center, canopy walkway, and forest trails in the park, along with the sympathetic restoration of buildings and castles along the historic Cape coast reflecting the rich cultural history of the area. The local community has benefited from the increase in visitor numbers by providing an alternative to logging and hunting endangered species which include Diana monkeys and Bongos."

Positive effects of ecotourism

Ecotourism is a source of increasing income and an improved reputation for travel companies. By supporting awards for ecotourism, British Airways has helped to raise the profile of the Kakum National Park and contributed to the Diana monkey's chance of survival.

As the BA website says:

> Remember that without an environment which is properly cared for, there will be no tourism for tomorrow.

And, one might add, fewer passengers for the airlines!

Exposure to risks

- An Argentine subsidiary of the Belgian firm Solvay has experienced protests and blockades at its PVC plant near Bahia Blanca, after an escape of chlorine gas. Local residents are demanding appropriate safety measures. Greenpeace.
- French firm Lapeyre (part of the Saint Gobain group that owns Brazilian logging company Eldorado) has been targeted by Greenpeace for its involvement in production and trade in timber from the Brazilian Amazon region. To publicize its accusations, Greenpeace created an "alternative" website about Lapeyre's involvement in the timber trade.

  Shortly afterward, Lapeyre announced its intention for Eldorado to join the Forestry Stewardship Council's (FSC) Buyers Group in Brazil. This group ensures that timber is sourced from legal and sustainable sources.

Effective direct action
Companies accused of being involved in activities that are harmful to the environment in one part of the world are often targeted in their home territory by campaigners. Campaigns, such as the Greenpeace protest against the trade in timber by French firm Lapeyre, can seriously damage a company's reputation and force changes in procedures.

HEALTH AND WELL-BEING

Increasingly, when investors establish operations in emerging economies, they are expected to run them with the same standards of health and safety and other workplace practices as they would be required to have in their home country.

Data from pollster MORI shows that a significant proportion of the general public polled in the UK expect businesses not just to apply legal minimum standards to their operations in developing countries, but also expect that best practice should be applied throughout their operations anywhere in the world. The people polled were asked about health and safety matters:

Profiting from poor quality?
Some transnationals have been accused of marketing products to a lower standard, such as cigarettes made from poor quality tobacco, in order to boost profits in emerging markets.

> "There has been much discussion about how companies should behave in other countries where they operate, especially in developing countries or the Third World. Should companies ensure high standards, or comply with their legal obligations? Which comes closest to your views? MORI question on Business Ethics Overseas from BITC, 1998.

Seventy percent of respondents said that companies should ensure high standards. Only 27 percent said that companies should just comply with legal obligations.

Some transnationals face allegations of selling inferior products in emerging markets. The tobacco industry faces criticism for intense marketing efforts in emerging economies, and allegations that cigarettes sold in these markets have a higher tar content, and, therefore, have more serious health risks.

Companies must respond to different expectations from host governments as to their responsibilities to the workforce. Firms may be hit by unexpected costs as they are urged to play a greater role in social and economic activity when government resources come under pressure.

Capitalizing on opportunities

● The US airbag manufacturer TRW started operations in Mexico in 1992, and has 1440 employees. When TRW management realized the high degree of muscle injuries among its employees, they investigated and found that employees were doing their laundry on washboards. The company therefore introduced a laundry service for employees, with workers leaving their washing in the morning and collecting it that evening. After this service started, repetitive strain injuries fell by 60 percent.

- Placer Dome, a transnational mining firm, has set up a program in Papua New Guinea aimed at improving healthcare in the area around one of its mines. It is estimated that one in 10 Papua New Guinea children under five die of malnutrition, pneumonia, meningitis, and other ailments. Placer Dome is a member of the World Alliance for Community Health. With the WHO's help, this alliance is helping companies to find local partners for health projects, and work out their budgets and performance measures. Placer Dome will work in 10 villages on the Strickland River, training villagers to issue antimalaria drugs, practice better midwifery, and improve local healthcare. The company will benefit from healthier employees, improved recruitment and productivity, and lower medical costs and absenteeism. "Corporate Hospitality," *The Economist,* November 27, 1999.

- BMW has been in South Africa for 25 years. As part of its ongoing involvement, it has built a community clinic, provided housing for employees, and is to use its dealer network to provide local health support, offering information, contacts, and condoms to help tackle the spread of AIDS and other sexually transmitted diseases. *The Times* (UK), February 24, 2001.

- In India, carmaker Fiat (through its local operator, Magneti Marelli) has worked with the United Nations Industrial Development Association (UNIDA), local public agencies, trade associations, and the Prince of Wales International Business Leaders Forum (PWIBLF), to develop the capacity of 20 local car component producers. This has improved their efficiency and health and safety standards. *A Decade of Difference 1990–2000,* Prince of Wales International Business Leaders Forum, 2000.

Sharing responsibilities
By supporting state and community initiatives in areas such as health of the local workforce, companies can increase production and improve community relations. BMW built this health clinic to support efforts in its South African plant in a bid to combat the spread of communicable diseases such as AIDS.

Exposure to risks

● Pharmaceutical companies came under pressure in 2000 and 2001 to make large price reductions in antiretroviral drugs for HIV/AIDS treatment in developing countries. Investors concerned about the risks to the pharmaceutical companies' reputations pushed for preferential pricing of drugs for poor countries. Many of the companies responded by offering heavily discounted drugs and a commitment to review current pricing policies. *Financial Times*, April 20, 2001.

HUMAN RIGHTS AND DIVERSITY

When considering a location for investment or when monitoring ongoing performance, risk assessment needs to include the complex issues of human rights and diversity.

Local cultural considerations need to be taken into account alongside central corporate policies. For example, a transnational company may have a standard policy toward women in the workforce. How does that policy translate in Muslim countries where the cultural norms are different?

It is possible that managers will be faced with cases of labor practices or work conditions that fall short of company standards, for example, the use of child labor in supplier factories, or substandard health and safety procedures. These situations may not be easy to change, and may require long-term measures for gaining trust among employee representatives, and for enlisting the support of international NGOs working in the country.

Capitalizing on opportunities

● In a move to show transparency and to learn from its critics, Levi Strauss opened up its international workplace monitoring program in the Dominican Republic. Four NGOs were invited to comment on Levi Strauss's monitoring efforts. Their feedback included the need for Levi Strauss to be more explicit on the subject of the workers' right to organize, and the use of local idiomatic language on paperwork. This process led to one of the NGOs working on a long-term basis with a supplier to help them understand women's health issues. **"Levi's Open House,"** *Business Ethics*, January/February 1999.

Monitoring self-regulation

The traditional relationship between big companies and interest groups is changing all the time. To become more accountable, Levi Strauss recently invited a number of NGOs to inspect its self-regulatory program in the Dominican Republic.

- In November 1997, toymaker Mattel announced a global code of conduct for its production facilities and contract manufacturers. These Global Manufacturing Principles (GMP) cover issues such as wages and hours, child labor, forced labor, discrimination, freedom of association, legal and ethical business practices, product safety and quality, and respect for local culture, values, and traditions. An independent monitoring group, the Mattel Independent Monitoring Council for Global Manufacturing Principles (MIMCO), was established. Managers and technical experts from Mattel worked with MIMCO to develop standards that could be used to measure compliance. Over three years, the standards were implemented and passed down the supply chain to include all companies from whom Mattel buys more than 40 percent of its output. All auditing is undertaken by independent organizations.

Exposure to risks
- The chair of the UK's Ethical Trading Initiative (ETI), businesswoman Yves Newbold (who has served on the boards of transnationals such as Hanson plc), described to an international conference in March 2001 what happened when the ETI sent Western male inspectors into a vegetable processing plant in Zimbabwe. They found no problems, but when a local woman who spoke the dialect of the predominantly female workforce checked with the workers, she uncovered widespread tales of sexual harassment. **The Conference Board Global Corporate Citizenship Conference, New York, March 2001.**

COMMUNITIES
The acceptance of a company's operations by a local community cannot be taken for granted. If a community is supportive, it can make a positive contribution to an operation's success; just as an antagonistic community can add to costs such as insurance, or even force closure. Being able to demonstrate the direct and indirect impact on the economy is helpful in gaining local goodwill.

When operating in a region affected by conflict, dilemmas are common, such as the use of corporate security forces linked to state police forces, or problems with disputed land rights.

> The UK and US governments have worked with leading oil and other extractive companies to agree good practice guidelines when working in conflict zones.
>
> Prince of Wales International Business Leaders Forum, July 2001.

Capitalizing on opportunities

- ABB in eastern Europe, and South African Breweries provided low-cost loans and mentoring to help truckers start a business, and to develop a quality local supply base.
- In South Africa, there have been substantial requirements for community involvement as an integral part of the tendering process for government licenses, in the third round of mobile phone licenses, and for running casinos.
- Texaco has developed a program for training the CEOs of NGOs, which they have introduced in Nigeria.
- Cisco is establishing its Network Training Academies in 24 of the 48 poorest countries in the world to help address issues of the digital divide.

Exposure to risks

- The Canadian mining company Gabriel Resources would like to mine Europe's largest known high-quality gold deposit in Transylvania, Romania. It has to persuade almost 600 homeowners to relocate to newly built, better accommodation, and has engaged a specialized community planning company to consult the local residents and manage their move. However, the Romanians are suspicious of the company, and associate the plans with the brutal forced relocations of the Ceausescu regime. The Canadian company has had to build a model house in the center of the village and engage in a long, slow exercise to win the villagers' trust and prepare them for the sudden influx of a large number of outsiders.

Financial Times,
March 9, 2001.

Network training
Companies are discovering that programs such as computer education and training help to gain trust and build valuable links with the community.

Building a Brand and Protecting Corporate Reputation

In a crowded and competitive global market, companies are seeking ways to increase their market share, secure customer loyalty, and differentiate their product offer from that of their competitors.

Several factors influence the methods used by companies to develop strategic brands:

- Brands are valuable assets and are becoming even more so.
- Brands are becoming more vulnerable because of the speed at which negative information can be communicated.
- The global market is divided into the "haves," those who are able to buy brands, and the "have-nots," whose desire to possess branded goods is fueled by media images.
- Companies and their brands are subject to high scrutiny from consumers and campaigning NGOs.

The emerging management issues have affected brand development and the management of corporate reputation in two key areas. One is the alignment of a product or service with a cause. The other is the increasing number of ways in which brand or corporate reputation can be affected by corporate activities that are out of the direct control of the marketing or communications departments.

The draw of brands
The power of a brand as a symbol of aspiration to a particular lifestyle affects even the poorest. A young boy called Eric living in a Tanzanian refugee camp had seen people wearing Nike shoes, so he drew the Nike logo on his old and battered sneakers.

Alignment with a cause

In the last decades of the 1900s, some entrepreneurs were farsighted enough to link their companies and products with topics embraced by the emerging management issues. They recognized the potential of developing niche markets for their brands by associating them with specific causes.

Examples of such companies include UK cosmetics firm The Body Shop International, which built its brand and reputation by stressing its policy of no animal testing on its products, developing a community trade progam, and actively expressing concern for the environment. Natura, a Brazilian cosmetics company, promotes its use of natural ingredients in its products.

Some companies decided to run cause-related marketing promotions in order to make consumers link their brand with a particular worthy cause.

For many years, a small number of companies pioneered the development of brands associated with the environment, health, well-being, communities, and human rights. They were then the exception. The growth in consumer interest in these issues suggests that they may soon become the norm.

> "The brands that will be big in the future will be those that tap into the social changes that are taking place." Sir Michael Perry, chairman Centrica plc, quoted in Rita Clifton and Esther Maughan (eds), *The Future of Brands: Interbrand*, 2000.

Out of control?

The characteristics that traditionally defined a brand: its benefits, pricing, distribution, and personality, are now joined by a wide range of factors that are difficult for brand managers to influence or monitor. These factors include the sourcing and manufacturing conditions and the product's impact on the environment. A brand's image can be affected in a negative or in a positive way by events at any stage in the life-cycle of the product or service, or at any place in the business process. For example, the supply chain can affect a brand's reputation.

"The brands that will be big in the future will be those that tap into the social changes that are taking place."

- Toymakers Mattel invested in a program to inspect suppliers' factories in response to concerns about the possible use of child labor. Mattel regarded the costs of the inspection program as small compared to the potential sales loss from a consumer boycott. "Sweatshop Wars," *The Economist*, February 27, 1999.

The internet and organizations that report on corporate behavior allow consumers to become more informed about the actions of a corporation.

"People are going to want, and be able, to find out a lot about the citizenship of a brand, whether it is doing the right things socially, economically, environmentally." Mike Clasper, president of Global Home Care and New Business Development, Proctor & Gamble (Europe), quoted in Rita Clifton and Esther Maughan (eds), *The Future of Brands: Interbrand*, 2000.

ECOLOGY AND ENVIRONMENT

There is growing consumer interest in the impact that goods have on the environment during manufacture and after disposal. There is concern about how food is produced, how materials are sourced, and how products are manufactured, packaged, and recycled.

Manufacturers, food producers, and retailers are responding to this interest by changing their practices, and informing consumers through labeling and certification programs.

Capitalizing on opportunities

- Companies in Michigan receive fewer regulatory checks and have some flexibility about meeting environmental guidelines when they participate in The Clean Corporate Citizenship program, and demonstrate good environmental practice. Address by Robert Zoellick, president and CEO Center for Strategic and International Studies (CSIS), Geneva, May 27, 1999.
- UK supermarket firm J Sainsbury plc has introduced biodegradable packaging for its organic food line. The packaging is designed to degrade within two weeks of disposal in a landfill site.

"People are going to want, and be able, to find out a lot about the citizenship of a brand, whether it is doing the right things socially, economically, environmentally."

- Nabisco responded to consumer interest in environmental issues by forming a partnership between their Animal Crackers cookies and the World Wildlife Fund (WWF). Changing the cookies' shapes to represent endangered species, and redesigning the packaging contributed to a 20 percent sales increase over a two-year period. Five cents from each sale up to a ceiling of $100,000 were donated to the WWF. Richard Steckel et al., *Making Money While Making a Difference*, 1999.

Exposure to risks

- In 1999, Home Depot, the largest chain of home improvement warehouses in the US and Canada, announced that they would stop selling wood products from "environmentally sensitive areas" by the end of 2002. The move followed a campaign by Greenpeace and questions raised by shareholders. Home Depot denied that they were responding to pressure from "extreme groups."
  Lowe's, one of Home Depot's competitors, has told suppliers that they will have to certify that lumber has been harvested responsibly, and that Lowe's will be issuing an environmental policy for lumber sales soon. *Greenpeace Business, October/November 1999.*

- In 1991, Brent Spar, a floating oil storage unit for crude oil produced by the Brent platform in the North Sea, was taken out of operation. Its owners, the Royal Dutch/Shell Group, planned (with government approval) to dispose of it at sea as the Best Practical Environmental Option.

Cause-related marketing

Nabisco's partnership with the WWF is an example of a cause-related marketing campaign. Business in the Community defines cause-related marketing as "a commercial activity by which business and charities or causes form a partnership with each other to market an image, product, or service to mutual benefit." Tim Mason, director of Tesco supermarkets in the UK, says: "The increasing importance of building customer loyalty, enhancing brand, and providing added value as a differentiator, and the benefit that can be gained through cause-related marketing, increasingly validates it as a core part of the marketing mix."

Sue Adkins, *Cause Related Marketing: Who Cares Wins*, 1999.

In 1995, Greenpeace activists occupied Brent Spar in an attempt to prevent it from being dumped offshore, sending dramatic reports to the international media on a daily basis. This sparked controversy over Shell's plans, and public opinion turned against the business. In Germany, several Shell service stations were bombed, and one was raked with gunfire. Several northern governments voiced their disapproval of the disposal plan, and Shell capitulated, eventually selecting an alternative, more expensive, decommissioning option.

Shell had underestimated the ability of Greenpeace to stir up controversy, and the strength of public opinion on an emotive environmental issue. In a later publication, *Profits and Principles – Does There Have to Be a Choice?* (1998), Shell commented, "we have learned that we must change the way we identify and address issues, and interact with the societies we serve."

A seminal campaign

The campaign against the disposal of Brent Spar is regarded as a seminal moment in the relationship between business and society, and not just for companies. Greenpeace was subjected to increased scrutiny after disclosures that claims made about aspects of Brent Spar were incorrect, and the media were criticized for their willingness to show images provided by Greenpeace.

HEALTH AND WELL-BEING

Consumers assume that products they buy and use meet tough health and safety standards. They may stop purchasing products and brands that are said by the media to be potentially defective or harmful. Consumers are especially vigilant when it comes to products and services that are designed to improve their health and well-being, such as food, medicine, and cosmetics.

Because of these factors, marketers often promote health and safety features of their products as part of the brand offer.

Capitalizing on opportunities

● The Japanese company Honda Motor Corporation introduced traffic safety education programs for its customers in response to public appeals for improved traffic safety. Honda regards the programs as a complement to its improved vehicle safety technology.

Bean boom
Consumers are likely to boycott products if they feel their health or well-being is at risk. In the furore over genetically modified seeds, Brazil, which is officially a GM-free country, has the opportunity to become the world's biggest soybean exporter.

Honda dealers run the programs, which give them the opportunity to visit customers. In 2001, the program was running in 35 countries, with 22 training centers worldwide. The number of participants has increased over the years, and this has created positive images and improved the company's reputation.

Exposure to risks

● Monsanto Corporation developed genetically modified seeds that are resistant to bugs, viruses, and fungi. Some countries, including Brazil, have banned the sale of these seeds and growth of experimental crops, until tests prove that they are safe.

DIVERSITY AND HUMAN RIGHTS

Brand and corporate reputation are vulnerable to accusations that a company is not committed to promoting diversity in the workplace and among its suppliers. Reputations can also be affected by the use of inappropriate cultural images for marketing purposes. For example, sexism and racism in advertising is now the subject of regulatory codes.

Consumer interest in the conditions under which goods are sourced and produced has been stimulated by journalists and NGOs reporting on the alleged use of child labor or sweatshop conditions. These reports have led to boycotts, the introduction of rigorous monitoring practices by famous brands, and to disinvestments.

Capitalizing on opportunities

● Starbucks Coffee has an independently verified program that monitors and identifies ways of improving the workplace conditions of its coffee suppliers. The monitoring is carried out by the Commission for Verification of Codes of Conduct (Coverco), a Guatemalan NGO. Coverco literature states:

Coverco is independent of all national and multinational corporations, unions, and governments. Because we are independent, Coverco gains the confidence of all relevant parties: management, workers, NGOs, community and advocacy groups, unions, and government.

Recognizing that levels of trust in corporations are low, some companies, such as the coffee company Starbucks, are turning to independent third-party organizations to verify working conditions or sourcing practices. Starbucks has appointed Coverco to monitor the working conditions of its coffee suppliers.

Chiquita has formed a successful partnership with the Rainforest Alliance for ongoing, independent inspection of conditions on its Latin American farms growing bananas.

Chiquita Brands International.

● In 1993, Levi Strauss announced that it would defer any direct investment in China and began to withdraw its existing manufacturing contracts. This decision was made because of the human rights climate in China at the time. Levi Strauss believed that it could not ensure that its employees, or those working on its behalf, would not be subjected to human rights violations. The company also believed that doing business in China would risk the reputation of its brands. Production of Levi Strauss products in China decreased by about 70 percent.

The decision was reversed in April 1998, when Levi Strauss decided to end its restrictions after evaluating the business opportunities and the country's political climate.

● The nonprofit Abrinq Foundation in Brazil offers a logo, through its Child Friendly Companies program, to companies that are committed to fight the use of child labor. Over 400 companies have been certified, after checks from unions, employees, and NGOs. Companies use the logo to communicate their values. Malcolm McIntosh et al., *Corporate Citizenship: Successful Strategies of Responsible Companies,* 1998.

Exposure to risks

● In 1992, sporting goods company Nike adopted a code of conduct on health, safety, and working practices worldwide. Despite this, poor working conditions in factories producing Nike products have frequently made headlines over the past 10 years. Nike hired a former US ambassador to the UN to review factory conditions in Asia. His positive report was undermined when a leaked internal report detailed unsafe working conditions at a plant in Vietnam, and excessive hours, with low wages, in Korea. In 1997, 28 US states and 13 countries participated in a day of protest centered on Nike's labor practices, followed by a "boycott Nike" campaign. These actions are believed to have caused slower sales. Nike embarked on an extensive program of education and monitoring, and has since become an industry leader in efforts to monitor and influence supplier practices. *Seminar Paper: Managing Social and Environmental Risks*, Prince of Wales International Business Leaders Forum and KPMG, 1999.

For a company so used to being a step ahead of its market, Nike was caught flat-footed. There are several lessons in this. The status quo is never fixed. Not long ago the concerns of ecologists were as irrelevant to business planners as those of ethicists are today. "Green" has gone from being a disparagement to becoming a badge that no smart company would risk being without. Ethics are similarly en route to becoming a strategic imperative. John Dalla Costa, *Ethical Imperative*, 1998.

Controlling working conditions
When operations are outsourced to subcontractors around the world, it can be difficult for transnational companies to maintain high standards. Nike has drawn up a worldwide code of conduct in order to communicate the standards it requires from the suppliers who make its athletic shoes.

COMMUNITIES

The support of communities can contribute to a brand's value in the eyes of consumers. Conversely, if a corporation has poor community relations, its brands' reputations may be damaged.

The opinion pollsters MORI report that the percentage of the British public responding "very important" in answer to the question, "When forming an opinion about a particular company or organization, how important is it for you to know about their activities in society and the community?" rose from 28 percent in 1998 to 36 percent in the 1999 survey. The percentage answering "important" remained steady at 48 percent in 1999, versus 49 percent in 1998.

Capitalizing on opportunities

● In 1990, Eli Lilly and Co. angered neighbors when it tore down houses and businesses to expand its Indianapolis operations without prior consultation with the local community. After this debacle, the company worked for more than nine years to improve community relations by

Building relationships
Supporting employees who carry out volunteer work in the community pays well, as Eli Lilley and Co. demonstrated.

The cost of complaints

Poor community relations can cost companies more than just a good reputation. Complaints about Broken Hill Proprietary's mine in Papua New Guinea led to legal cases and large payments for scientific assessments.

supporting employee volunteers and providing cash to improve local houses and parks. A subsequent expansion was supported by the local community. *Trend Alert,* The Center for Corporate Citizenship at Boston College, July 1999.

Exposure to risks

● Broken Hill Proprietary (BHP), an Australian mining company, holds a major stake in a mine in Papua New Guinea's remote Western Province. The mine has received complaints for years about its waste disposal operation. A 1996 legal case resulted in BHP paying for an independent scientific assessment of the mine, which showed that none of the cleaning-up options available, from dredging waste from the nearby river, to closing the mine, were environmentally suitable. BHP's chief executive, Paul Anderson, said, "The easy conclusion to reach with the benefits of the reports and with 20/20 hindsight, is that the mine is not compatible with our environmental values and the company should never have become involved." *The Economist* ("Mea copper mea culpa," August 21, 1999) reported that there were many reasons why the mine should be kept open: it generated $25 million in profits in 1998; it was considered the mainstay of the local economy, supporting 50,000 people; and it generated a fifth of Papua New Guinea's exports. It was felt that closing the mine would push the already unstable economy of Papua New Guinea into bankruptcy.

A LIFE-CYCLE APPROACH

Revolutions in technology and the market have resulted in greater visibility for international business and branded products. This has brought more consumers within reach, but has also made companies more vulnerable. Interest groups and an inquisitive media have shown that corporate behavior has no hiding place from a raised level of scrutiny.

There is now greater risk of a damaged reputation for a corporate or product brand. Consequently, managers from all parts of a business, not just marketing, need to develop an awareness of corporate and product brand issues, based on a wide definition of risk and opportunity.

For many years, companies have used environmental management systems that incorporate a life-cycle approach to understand the environmental impact of particular products. This involves assessment of the environmental impact of various stages in production. This widely used technique can be applied to the protection of brand and corporate reputation.

A Life-Cycle Approach to Building and Protecting Brand and Corporate Reputation

Monitoring each stage of the business process cycle helps identify risks and opportunities to corporate or brand reputation in light of the emerging management issues and stakeholder expectations. Stages will vary from company to company.

OPPORTUNITIES TO BUILD REPUTATION	STAGE IN BUSINESS PROCESS	RISKS TO REPUTATION
The B&Q home improvement business in the UK is committed to using wood from certified sustainable forests only, and has made this part of its brand differentiation.	**Sourcing** ● Under what conditions (labor, sustainability, etc.) are materials or goods sourced? ● Could sourcing be open to criticism or could it be turned to market advantage?	Some sportswear companies have been the subject of a campaign by interest groups accusing them of buying from suppliers with poor workplace conditions. Many of these companies now have programs to monitor suppliers.
The Body Shop International, cosmetics retailer, has a policy of not using animal testing in the manufacture of its cosmetics, supporting differentiation of the brand in the market place.	**Manufacturing** ● Are the ingredients and the processes used in manufacture open to question? ● Could they be adapted to help appeal to a segment of the market?	Taco Bell had to recall its taco shells from across the US due to their apparent manufacture with genetically modified corn not approved for human consumption.
The Coca-Cola company teamed up with Wal-Mart and contributed a proportion of sales on Coke products to the Mothers Against Drunk Driving. US sales increased by 490% during the promotion.	**Marketing** ● Have sensitivities of marketing promotions been considered against a diverse consumer base? ● Or have the topics in which consumers are interested provided direction for cause-related marketing activity?	US company General Mills organized a promotional tie between a cereal brand and the Bible. The company failed to consider their diverse consumer base, and had to pull the promotion after complaints from non-Christians.
US company ABB Electrolux runs a functional sales program, in which the function of the appliance is sold rather than the appliance. The firm takes back the appliance at the end of its useful life and recycles it. The program has increased the firm's market share and reduced environmental impact.	**Selling** ● Is the sales team practicing ethical sales techniques, and who is monitoring them? ● Is there a way of redefining the offer to make the product or service more attractive to the buyer?	The British insurance industry paid heavily for mis-selling personal pensions in the mid 1990s. Sales teams, who were working largely on commission, sold large numbers of inappropriate pensions. Fines were imposed and retraining of sales teams was undertaken.

30,000 jobs were saved from termination when Volkswagen A. G. of Germany negotiated with trade unions to reduce the working week from 36 to 28.8 hours, with a loss of proportionate earnings. Employers, employees, and the local community saw this as preferable to large layoffs.	**Disposal/retrenchment Re-use/recycle** ● Are management expectations about waste disposal adequately communicated? ● Are there creative ways to avoid waste of human capital as well as material goods?	Cruise liners sailing off Alaska have been accused of discharging untreated waste, polluting the very environment they are promoting to their customers. Several operators have been fined and their actions are now being subjected to intensive media scrutiny.
In the mid 1990s, the British Airports Authority won the bid to run Melbourne's international airport in Australia. One reason for securing the contract was its proactive public affairs record in the UK, where it is seen as a good corporate citizen concerned about the effect of its operations on the environment.	**Expansion** ● Does permission for expansion or building a new plant require research into the impacts on a range of stakeholders, and stakeholder dialogue? ● Are the systems and processes in place to achieve this?	After protests from environmental activists and a boycott from investment managers, Mitsubishi abandoned plans to build a major salt evaporation plant near an environmentally sensitive site in Mexico in 2000.
Unilever has introduced an innovative distribution system in Tanzania that creates employment and markets its brands, such as Key Soap. Salesmen are given bicycles with branded boxes loaded with product packs to take to local stores for onward sale. Sales increased fivefold in five months.	**Distribution** ● Are there sufficient safeguards placed on distribution systems to ensure good safety and security? ● How are these monitored? Have opportunities to contribute to social need through distribution been considered?	The Brazilian subsidiary of German pharmaceutical company Schering was fined $2.5 million in 1998 after being found responsible for unintentionally distributing fake contraceptive pills made of flour.

OPPORTUNITIES TO BUILD REPUTATION	**STAGE IN BUSINESS PROCESS**	**RISKS TO REPUTATION**

Business Restructuring

Global forces for change are driving a relentless process of business restructuring, as companies adjust to the impacts of technology and global markets.

Companies are making these adjustments by moving toward e-commerce platforms, outsourcing all but core activities, merging with competitors, reducing the size of the workforce and transferring operations overseas to reduce costs, or breaking up and restructuring. Major restructuring may take a number of forms:

● Mergers and acquisitions.

● Downsizing.

● Buying or selling a major business unit.

● Joint ventures and marketing alliances.

● A dramatic "reinvention" of the business, which is often heralded by rebranding of the company with a new name and a more dynamic image.

Any business restructuring will be a time of significant risk and opportunity for the corporations involved. The main potential risks are:

● Through a merger or acquisition, a company may inherit assets and liabilities that are less visible than financial liabilities, such as poor employee or community relations, and inadequate environmental management systems.

- Restructuring is often associated with downsizing, and a loss of jobs. In the high-pressure atmosphere of the closing stages of a deal, in which events move quickly and are commercially sensitive, it is difficult to keep employees and other stakeholders informed. However, their goodwill may be vital to the future success of the business.

Between 1990 and 2000, 67 companies on the FTSE top 100 list disappeared, radically changed, or were displaced from the list.

Greg Dyke, BBC Director General, CBI Conference, London, November 6, 2000.

- Closure, or substantial job reductions, in places where unemployment levels are high is hard to handle sensitively.

By contrast, sensitivity to the emerging management issues at a time of restructuring may provide opportunities to gain a competitive advantage. A strong statement from the business leadership of the "values" that the new entity will adhere to may, in a period of inevitable uncertainty and instability, help retain talented staff. Gerry Levin, AOL TimeWarner' s CEO, asked for a strategy on environmental and social performance for the new company before the final merger was agreed.

When combining or committing to work with another business, deal-makers should be looking for policies at least as good as the best of those of the predecessor organizations, with action plans to bring all parts of the new organization up to this standard.

The emerging management issues present specific risks and opportunities for managers who are overseeing or affected by a restructuring program.

ECOLOGY AND ENVIRONMENT

When a business undergoes restructuring, managers need to consider the environmental impact of downgrading operations and closing the plant or site. What will happen to the land, premises, or machinery? Who is responsible, and who will pay for cleaning up?

If a merger or an acquisition is taking place, environmental liabilities, such as landfill, have to be taken into account. One partner may have a reputation as a leader in environmental performance, while the other may be a laggard – facing regulatory investigations or boycotts from campaigners.

Capitalizing on opportunities

● The Bamburi Cement Company was established in 1954 to quarry limestone and produce cement on the Kenyan coast. When the quarries were exhausted, the company started an environmental and economic rehabilitation program. The core elements of this included: reforestation; an integrated aquaculture system; agricultural activities; tourism; and education, research, and consulting. The program has led to the formation of Baobab Farm, with over 200 hectares of forest. Trees can be cut for firewood, charcoal, and timber. The land is later reforested. The farm has a wood-fuel business with local communities, provides retail opportunities, and generates employment.

Exposure to risks

● Companies in traditional heavy industries may bear the burden of responsibility for cleaning up brown field sites (old industrial sites that may be polluted). Many of these sites are in potentially valuable inner city locations, often close to disadvantaged communities where jobs are needed. But the costs or potential liability for cleaning up can be prohibitive and may deter potential investors and partners.

Closures provide opportunities
The closure of commercial operations provides an opportunity to produce environmental or social benefits. A success story is the former Bamburi cement works in Kenya that have been extensively redeveloped with reforestation and agricultural plans to form Baobab farm.

HEALTH AND WELL-BEING

In their study "Loyalty in the Age of Downsizing" (*Sloan Management Review*, 1997), Linda Stroh and Anne Reilly confirm that the way in which layoffs are made affects the pride and commitment of those workers who survive the cuts. The loss of a significant employer or of a significant number of jobs in an area has an impact on many in the community.

Discord may occur if one partner in a restructuring has good workplace practices in relation to work/life balance and family-friendly practices, and the other sees employees as a burden. The chances of keeping good employees through an unsettling merger process can be improved by transferring good employee practices from one firm to the other.

Capitalizing on opportunities

● ALKA Forsikring, a European insurance company, has developed policies to improve work/life balance, including flexitime and time off to take care of sick relatives. When downsizing in the mid-1990s, ALKA used an external consultancy firm to set up financial and job-seeking courses for laid off employees. Part-time employees were given full-time status for payments from the unemployment fund. CSR Europe.

● Before merging with BankBoston, Fleet Bank in the US was not recognized as a family-friendly employer. Today, the company is known for its ability to meet the needs of its workforce while achieving high marks for client service.

Barbara Frankel, "WorkLife Initiatives Benefit Companies as Well as Employees," DiversityInc.com, October 24, 2000.

Far-reaching effects
Environmental damage, such as that caused by the lignite industry near Leipzig in Germany, can affect many lives. Industrial pollution in urban areas can be detrimental to the health of local inhabitants, and the cost of cleaning may later deter redevelopment and new job opportunities.

Exposure to risks

● When the consumer electronics firm Pioneer fired some managers in Tokyo in 1993, local shoppers organized a boycott of its products in protest. *"Gang Sackings," The Economist,* November 14, 1998.

● During 2000, the international companies BMW, Corus, Danone, and Michelin all provoked controversy in Europe when they annnounced major closures and layoffs. The companies were subjected to a mixture of government pressure, labor criticism, and threats of consumer boycotts, which took considerable time to respond to.

DIVERSITY AND HUMAN RIGHTS

Companies involved in a merger or takeover may have differing policies or approaches to diversity and human rights. The policies of the dominant company will prevail.

One partner may have implemented a program to tackle human rights abuses and improve workplace practices in its overseas factories and among its developing world suppliers. The other may have taken no such measures, leaving the new entity open to accusations of human rights abuses.

Shifts by the dominant company away from more liberal policies, such as same-sex partner benefits and paternity leave, may cause a backlash from employees.

Capitalizing on opportunities

● A quarter of the total workforce of A G Petzetakis, which is based in South Africa, are over 50. There is no bias in this organization against the training and promotion of older people, and workers aged over 60 are protected from unemployment. Older workers are awarded payments toward their insurance contributions on top of a bonus payment. **CSR Europe.**

Exposure to risks

● The Bank of Scotland initiated a joint venture with the organization of American evangelical preacher Pat Robertson. However, this fell apart after opposition from the bank's investors concerned about the televangelist's attitudes on diversity and human rights issues.

Vulnerable alliances
Corporate alliances with individuals who hold very strong opinions, such as Pat Robertson, the right-wing fundamentalist, seen here campaigning for nomination to the US presidency, can become the focus for consumer and activist pressure.

COMMUNITIES

Restructuring may bring new jobs and economic benefits to a community, or it may increase the strain on the local infrastructure through higher levels of traffic, noise, or pollution. Downsizing may have a negative domino effect on local suppliers and the local service sector.

News of a proposed merger may result in expressions of goodwill, or raise protests from communities of interest, who will highlight possible negative impacts of the merger.

Capitalizing on opportunities

- When Procter & Gamble restructured a chemical plant in the former Soviet Union, in the city of Novomoskovsk, they offered large severance packages, and established a private labor foundation and job center for retraining. About 10 percent of those affected later started their own businesses. **Prince of Wales International Business Leaders Forum.**
- International Paper and Union Camp merged their companies with the theme, "Strength of Two, Value of One." The message, meant to reinforce the company's commitment to the community, was repeated in newspaper advertisements, internal publications, and a videotape mailed to every new employee. The company received letters, including some from public officials, thanking it for continuing its commitment to the community through the merger process.

Exposure to risks

- In 1987, the Minnesota legislature blocked the hostile takeover of Dayton-Hudson, citing the company's outstanding record of corporate citizenship. **Address by Robert Zoellick, president, Center for Strategic and International Studies, Geneva, 1999.**
- A coalition of public interest organizations, including Friends of the Earth, challenged the $186 billion merger of Exxon and Mobil, claiming that it would create a company with power to: "skew critical debates over matters such as global warming." **Corporate Watch.**

Corporate citizenship builds trust

Good corporate citizenship is key to maintaining relations during mergers. This was the finding of a report by The Conference Board (*The Impact of Mergers and Acquisitions on Corporate Citizenship*, The Conference Board, 2000), based on a survey of leading US corporations that had recently experienced a merger and acquired another business. The report suggests that community relations are a factor in a merger's success. Companies make commitments through corporate citizenship programs that help reaffirm long-standing relationships.

MERGER MANIA

There is evidence that mergers and acquisitions are not generally successful. McKinsey found that only 23 percent of acquiring companies recouped their acquisition costs within 10 years. Other studies set the rates of failure at between 50 and 75 percent. In a recent study of 116 deals of $1 billion and over in the past 15 years, the US investment bank J P Morgan found that only 56 percent had created value for the bidders.

In 2001, The International Labour Organization (ILO) published a report on the banking and financial services sector (*The Employment Impact of Mergers and Acquisitions in the Banking and Financial Services Sector*, ILO, February 2001). Their report states that two-thirds of mergers and acquisitions fail to achieve their objectives, despite the often massive job losses and restructuring that they entail.

All too often, the report says, the sought-after benefits of greater size and efficiency risk being "nullified by increased complexity and losses related to top-heavy organizations, while the difficulties of adequately blending cultural and other human factors in the integration of combined enterprises are often underestimated."

The report attributes much of the foundering of mergers and acquisitions expectations to shortcomings in dealing with the fallout of layoffs, which may seriously undermine operational capabilities and employee morale. Among the consequences of heightened merger activity for the financial sector workforce that survives the restructuring, the report cites: "reduced job security, increased workloads, anxiety and stress," all of which can impinge negatively on performance in an intensely competitive work climate.

In some previous mergers and acquisitions, it would appear that there was insufficient attention paid to the emerging management issues, and to the enduring values and strong corporate culture that have produced sustainable successful businesses over the long-term. Other reasons that mergers and acquisitions fail include:

- Plummeting morale as staff wait for downsizing.
- Customers defecting.
- The purchase price was too high.
- Expectations of cost-savings were overestimated.
- Unforeseen opposition from one or more stakeholders.
- A clash of cultures between merging companies.
- Synergies are not present or are not exploited.
- Dislocations from the merger were underestimated.

Downsizing

Downsizing is never *per se* good for a company. There are diseconomies from:

- Lost institutional memory and expertise.
- Employee burnout if the pressure of the job on remaining staff is too intense.
- Loss of flexibility if investment with suppliers is not made.
- Loss of staff morale and loyalty.

Mitigating the negative effects of restructuring

Significant restructuring of companies can produce many negative effects, such as loss of employee morale and adverse publicity. These effects can be mitigated by introducing sound business practices. Listed below are recommended actions to take towards employees and those who have been made redundant.

ACTIONS TOWARD EMPLOYEES	ACTIONS TOWARD LAID OFF EMPLOYEES
<ul><li>Constant upskilling of employees.</li><li>Putting together "career resilience consortiums" where groups of local employers work together to understand changes in their industry, the skills implications, the best methods of training for these skills, and then provide up-to-date training.</li><li>Involving employees in examining alternative strategies to downsizing, such as taking temporary job cuts, or considering part-time working.</li><li>Providing two-way debate of issues and prospects.</li><li>Active outplacement by approaching other employers.</li><li>Providing opportunities to taper off work as an alternative to the shift from full-time work to no work.</li></ul>	<ul><li>Helping laid off workers to become self-employed, including some initial, guaranteed work from the company, and the provision of surplus premises as incubators for new business starts.</li><li>Making "surplus" business ideas available to laid off employees to exploit for themselves in their new business ventures.</li><li>Supporting local business advice services so that they are better able to offer a customized service to the firm's laid off workers.</li><li>Making reassignments to the community as part of the severance package.</li></ul>

THE IMPACT ON COMPANY FUNCTIONS

The emerging management issues will have different repercussions for company managers depending on their functional responsibilities.

The key corporate functions include human resources, purchasing and supply, marketing and sales, plant and unit management, and corporate communications. Managers in each of these functions have the challenge of meeting their differing overall purposes and needs, while responding in the appropriate way to the emerging management issues. Getting it right brings benefits to the company, but costs and damaged reputation may be the result of inappropriate actions.

Emerging management issues can no longer just be the responsibility of specialists within a company. Any manager may have to deal with some or all of these issues and will need the help of other business functions to manage them. The example of an ideal interconnected management team (*see* p.174) illustrates the implications of the actions of one manager on a manager in another department and the importance of cross-functional coordination.

The Human Resource Manager's Challenge

The challenge for a human resource manager is to recruit, retain, and motivate the most talented and dedicated workforce possible for the company.

The HR manager will need to set guidelines and policies on expectations of conduct, which all of the company's employees understand and honor, and which are not compromised by the conduct of any of the company's suppliers. The HR manager also needs to ensure that line managers fulfill their human resource responsibilities.

THE BENEFITS OF GETTING IT RIGHT

Setting and communicating clear guidelines on employee behavior, while respecting employee's circumstances, may increase costs at first, but can pay dividends in terms of loyalty and staff retention and in reducing time lost due to sickness, as Aarhus Dockyard Ltd. in Denmark discovered.

The human resource manager's response

ACTIONS IN RESPONSE TO CHALLENGE	WHO GAINS
• Ensure that the company is an attractive place to work, with flexible workplace policies and practices that allow work/life balance. • Draw up clear guidelines on expectations of employee conduct and make sure employees are aware of them. • Provide counseling services, information and advice on health options, and support mechanisms for childcare and care for the elderly. • Ensure that recruitment practices and employees reflect the diversity of customers and local communities. • Ensure that the emerging management issues are reflected in internal and external training provision and in employee target setting, incentive, and appraisal processes. • Provide mechanisms for employees to register concerns of misconduct. • Support employee volunteering efforts with corporate resources such as cash, time, equipment, and use of company premises.	**Your employees** • Feeling valued and appreciating the help in managing their sometimes stressful lives. • Motivated by the opportunity to put something back into the community and by the chance to attract company resources for causes important to them. **Your company** • A more stable and productive workforce. • Recruitment and training costs kept down. • Improved informal communications channels and greater PR opportunities through volunteering. • Business development needs helped by good community relations with local opinion-formers and authorities. **Your community** • Appreciative of a supportive local employer. • Benefiting from the efforts of employees to help meet community needs and improve the local environment.

- Aarhus Dockyard Ltd. is a Danish manufacturing company that builds ships and other steel constructions. The company experienced high levels of sick leave until a new policy for sick employees was introduced. At first, a letter is sent. After four weeks a meeting is held with the employee to discuss the matter. If the employee is still not fit to return to work, another meeting is set up between the employee, the shop steward, an adviser from the workers' union, and a social adviser from the local authorities, in order to find ways in which the sick employee can return to work quickly. Sick leave has been reduced to 3.5 percent from 8.5 percent in 1995. CSR Europe.

THE COST WHEN IT GOES WRONG

Guidelines and policies on employee conduct apply to all employees, including managers. Failure to honor company policy can cost a company reputation and cash.

- In 1994, six African-American employees, on behalf of 1,400 others, filed against Texaco, alleging systematic discrimination against the firm's minority employees. In November 1996, Texaco announced that it had agreed to a $176 million legal settlement for the suit.

    After the settlement, Texaco's Chairman and CEO Peter Bijur told the firm's employees, "We will not tolerate disrespect or prejudice in this company." Risk seminar paper, Prince of Wales International Business Leaders Forum and KPMG, 1999.

Improving employee relations
Texaco took steps to improve its policy toward employees from ethnic minorities when, in 1994, it was taken to court by members of its own staff. Since then it has established an Equality and Fairness task force, which has successfully met its targets during 1999 and 2000.

The Purchasing and Supply Manager's Challenge

The challenge for a purchasing and supply manager is to source suppliers who produce quality goods to the company's specification at a competitive price and deliver the goods at the right time and place.

The manager also needs to ensure that all suppliers run their workplaces and treat their workforces in ways that will not compromise the reputation of his or her corporation.

THE BENEFITS OF GETTING IT RIGHT

Investment in suppliers helps to ensure that a company's products are of the highest possible quality.

- In the 1970s, the cream for Baileys (a cream-based liqueur owned by UK drinks company Diageo) was provided by the surplus of the domestic milk market in Dublin, Ireland. But by 1998, sales of Baileys reached 4.2 million cases, which required about the same amount of milk as the annual need of Dublin. The fragmented Irish dairy industry could not cope with this demand. Instead of looking overseas for

Meeting strict standards
Suppliers are increasingly having to meet stringent standards, such as in environmental practices, in order to satisfy contract conditions. These conditions include the use where possible of environmentally friendly packaging.

imports, Baileys provided technical and management expertise to Irish dairy farmers to bring them up to EU standards. As a result, the cream for Baileys is still supplied by Irish farmers, and Diageo enjoy the support of the Irish community. *Diageo Corporate Citizenship 2001 Guide*, Diageo, 2001.

THE COST WHEN IT GOES WRONG

If clear codes of conduct are not set or are not monitored, poor conduct by suppliers can lead to increased costs, negative press coverage, and even damaging lawsuits for the purchasing company.

● In January 1999, the international NGO Global Exchange, along with the garment workers union (UNITE), Sweatshop Watch, and the Asian Law Caucus, filed a $1 billion class action lawsuit on behalf of 20,000 sweatshop workers on the Pacific island of Saipan. The lawsuit charged 17 US retailers of using indentured labor and violating human rights laws.

In Autumn 1999, four of the targeted companies (Nordstrom, J. Crew, Gymboree, and Cutter & Buck) agreed to an out-of-court settlement, paying into a $1.25 million fund to set up an independent monitoring program that guarantees that the workers' basic rights are honored, that they are paid overtime, and that they have access to clean food and water. *Global Exchange Newsletter*, Issue 40, Fall 1999.

The purchasing and supply manager's response

ACTIONS IN RESPONSE TO CHALLENGE	WHO GAINS
● Help suppliers to understand your expectations through clear and regular communications, with training and capacity-building if necessary, to ensure that standards are met. ● Build the capacity of local NGOs to undertake independent verification and support the development of an effective regulatory environment by public authorities as ways of helping to raise the standards of local suppliers. ● Establish links with minority-owned suppliers and build a diverse supply base to reflect the community, workforce, and customer base.	**Your company** ● A guaranteed regular supply of product made to your specification because of partnerships with suppliers. **Your suppliers** ● Chance of increased business because of higher operational standards. ● Reduced reliance on your company if you have to shift to alternative sources in the future. ● A more contented and motivated workforce because of better workplace standards. **Your supplier's community** ● Having a standard set for local businesses.

The Marketing and Sales Manager's Challenge

The challenge for a marketing and sales manager is to maintain and build the market share of the brand through attracting new customers, and to ensure existing customer loyalty.

The brand will need promotion in a way that is sensitive to cultural differences. The manager will find opportunities to test products and use marketing information in order to provide ideas for new product developments. Protection of brand reputation can be secured by ensuring that its integrity is covered by auditing its social and environmental impact during the business process.

THE BENEFITS OF GETTING IT RIGHT

Cause-related marketing is an effective way of increasing the status of a brand as well as obtaining favorable publicity.

● Due to lack of funds, only half of the 1.5 million telephone calls made each year by children in Australia to the Kids Helpline could be answered. A partnership between Kellogg's Australia and the Kids Line charity collected over Aus $500,000, enabling more than 150,000 additional phone calls to be answered the following year.

The marketing and sales manager's response

ACTIONS IN RESPONSE TO CHALLENGE	WHO GAINS
● Use brands to communicate social or environmental issues.	**Your brand**
● Promote major brands by linking sales to a financial contribution for a social or environmental cause.	● Increased sales.
	● Differentiation in a crowded market place, with new routes to market.
● Form a partnership with a leading NGO to build brand integrity.	
● Carry out regular dialogue with other corporate departments within the company to ensure that the role of brand guardian is shared.	**Your customers**
	● Supporting a cause that they care about by purchasing a product.
● Commission independent social and environmental auditing of a brand at appropriate stages of its life-cycle.	**Social and environmental causes**
● Consider eco-labeling and other programs, but bear in mind that misleading claims can damage brand equity.	● Publicity and association with a well-known brand.
	● Access to corporate networks and resources.
	● Financial proceeds from cause-related marketing schemes.

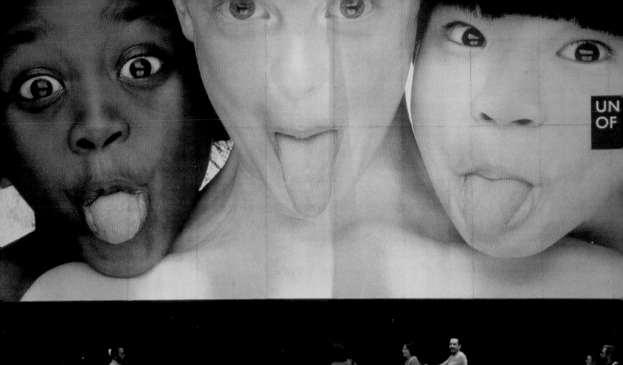

The campaign included media advertising and public relations activity, as well as exposure on seven million cereal boxes. Kellogg's benefited from extensive favorable media exposure. Sue Adkins, *Cause Related Marketing, Who Cares Wins*, 1999.

THE COST WHEN IT GOES WRONG

Marketing to populations of different ethnicities and beliefs calls for heightened sensitivity to cultural values.

● General Mills made a public apology after 12 million boxes of cereal containing the Bible in CD-ROM format were sent to grocery shops, prompting complaints by religious groups. One commentator stated:

"When Muslims, Buddhists, Hindus, Taoists, and millions of other Americans pick up this box of cereal and look at this Bible they are excluded."

The company later issued a statement that said, "It is the company's policy not to advance any particular set of religious beliefs. Inclusion of this material does not conform to our policy and we apologize." *Miami Herald*, July 23, 2000.

Conveying the right image
The bold and contentious method in which Benetton has chosen to advertise its brand of clothing has drawn both praise and criticism. While some of its chosen images have succeeded in appealing to a cross-cultural audience, others have been criticized as being in poor taste.

The Plant or Unit Manager's Challenge

The challenge of a plant manager is to ensure that the plant operates effectively in line with established corporate policies, taking local conditions into account.

A plant manager's responsibilities also extend to the company functions of human resources, purchasing and supply, security, and community relations.

THE BENEFITS OF GETTING IT RIGHT

Being seen to make a conscious effort to improve the environmental performance of the plant can bring benefits in terms of community relations and reputation.

- The managers of the Dow Chemical plant at Altona, in Victoria, Australia, made a public commitment to create and act on a voluntary Environmental Improvement Plan to improve health and safety and reduce the environmental impact of the plant.

Good neighbors
The Dow Chemical plant's environmental pledge improved its local and national relationships.

The plant or unit manager's response

ACTIONS IN RESPONSE TO CHALLENGE	WHO GAINS
• Ensure that the implementation of corporate policies are locally appropriate (in keeping with local tradition and culture, and of an appropriate scale and style). • Ensure safety of personnel and security of plant and equipment. • Ensure effective means of dialogue with stakeholder groups in the local community. • Work with local government on improving the physical and social infrastructure of an area. • Invest in the local community in school and business links and health education projects. • Offer support for the development of local businesses through mentoring and skills transfer. • Support the environmental performance of suppliers through training. • Support staff-volunteering efforts. • Recruit and purchase locally.	**Your company** • An improved reputation. • Winning and retaining a license to operate. • Developing a loyal and skilled workforce and supply base. **Your employees** • Satisfaction and motivation from contributing to the well-being of the local area. **Your community** • Business is generated for the purchase of supplies locally. • Transfer of skills into local supply base. • Improved local infrastructure.

The project has fostered a positive relationship between Dow, the Environment Protection Agency (EPA), the city council, and the community. Victorian EPA Chairman Dr. Brian Robinson said:

"This is the most significant change in environmental management seen in Australia in the past 10 years."

THE COSTS WHEN IT GOES WRONG

Companies may make investments in all the right areas, but this can be undermined if the plant manager does not have the correct operating procedures in place.

• Minera Yanacocha is a gold mine near Cajamarca in northwestern Peru, controlled by Denver-based Newmont Mining Corporation. Yanacocha invests in community programs and has built schools, roads, and sewage systems. However, after an incident in which mercury leaked during transportation, causing the hospitalization of 130 people, Yanacocha had to pay $12–14 million in clean-up costs and compensation, and was criticized by the International Finance Corporation of the World Bank for not having guidelines for the transportation of mercury.

Denver Post, October 29, 2000.

The Corporate Communications Manager's Challenge

The challenge of the corporate communications manager is to control the messages and communication channels between the company and its external audiences, and to build effective relationships with the relevant stakeholder groups.

The manager also directs communications within the company between management and employees, and leads the engagement of the business in public policy dialogue.

THE BENEFITS OF GETTING IT RIGHT

Opening channels of communication between the company, the media, and community groups can provide opportunities to raise the company's profile.

- Three packaging companies, Tetra Pak, Elopak and SIG-Comibloc, created the Alliance for Beverage Cartons and the Environment as part of a communications strategy to promote the eco-friendly nature of beverage cartons. In France, the alliance, operating as Alliance Carton Nature, formed a strategic partnership with UNICEF and created the "Brikkado" project. Schoolchildren bring in empty cartons which are then sent for recycling and converted into wrapping paper, which is designed by the schoolchildren. The wrapping paper is sold through French retailers at Christmas with profits going to UNICEF projects.

  UNICEF's public relations department promotes the program, which receives considerable press coverage and radio and television airtime, thus raising awareness of both UNICEF and the environmental nature of beverage cartons. CSR Europe.

THE COSTS WHEN IT GOES WRONG

Companies are often faced with a dilemma about how to react to accusations that they regard as false and damaging: resort to the courts and face extensive news coverage, or take no action.

- In 1997, McDonald's brought a court case against two people who circulated a pamphlet alleging that the firm's food was unhealthy, that its employees were exploited, and that its actions damaged the environment. The case lasted 300 days and generated extensive media coverage of the allegations. McDonald's won the court case, but opinion was divided on whether it was a wise strategy for them to sue the defendants and as a consequence be on the receiving end of considerable negative publicity, which portrayed a David and Goliath struggle between the two individuals and a large corporation. After the verdict, Reuters noted that the case was regarded,

"*by some experts as a public relations disaster, costing an estimated £10 million.*" "McDonald's Case Highlights Risks of Libel", *Reuters*, June 19, 1997.

However, a spokesperson for McDonald's responded by saying:

"*What if we had not challenged the allegations, what if people believed the allegations to be true and stopped coming to our restaurants?*" "McDonald's Case Highlights Risks of Libel", *Reuters*, June 19, 1997.

Corporate communications manager's response

ACTIONS IN RESPONSE TO CHALLENGE	WHO GAINS
● Ensure that systems and processes are in place to understand the perception of the corporate brand among different stakeholders. ● Inform management of changing expectations. ● Keep investors informed of company performance against their expectations. ● Support the human resource function by informing employees of business policies, practices, and decisions. ● Manage a two-way communication process between employees and management. ● Support community relations activity and build cross-sector partnerships. ● Ensure corporate communications supports brand positioning. ● Ensure open communications channels with suppliers. ● Ensure professional relationships with appropriate media and media commentators. ● Keep public agencies informed of the company's views on relevant matters and engage in dialogue on social, environmental, and economic development issues.	**Your company** ● Regular feedback on company via stakeholder relationships. ● Capitalizing on sound management practices to build goodwill among key audiences. ● Regarded as a serious player and consulted on relevant regulatory issues. **Your employees** ● More motivated and trusting of management. ● Good ambassadors in the community. **Your community** ● Realizing that their concerns are considered by your company.

Interconnected Management

The global forces for change and increased global competition have led to leaner, flatter organizational structures as senior managers attempt to create the conditions for speedy and decisive decision-making. The challenge under these conditions is to ensure interconnected management.

This is essential when companies are responding to emerging management issues that have cross-departmental implications. Interconnected management is characterized by managers carefully considering the impact of their decisions on the rest of the business. Signs of interconnected management in action will include regular interdepartmental communication and coordinating mechanisms. Interdepartmental turf wars and internal hoarding of data, practice, and knowledge are not conducive to this management style. The need for managers to adopt a collective and consultative approach to problem-solving and decision-making is particularly acute as the number of companies experiencing the emerging management issues first-hand continues to rise.

Open lines of communication and sound working relationships between functional managers are set to become increasingly important, as is cross-functional understanding of the cause and effect of decisions related to changing stakeholder expectations.

Systems to encourage information flows to and from front-line colleagues, whether in overseas markets or in customer relations, are crucial. The risks inherent in not achieving cross-functional understanding and good internal communication flows are damage to reputation, the cost of remedial action, and the cost of wasted management time.

The breadth of understanding that managers need to have of operations outside their areas of expertise is increasing rapidly. This is changing managers' job descriptions, professional training needs, rewards, and incentive programs. An interconnected management response to the emerging management issues is critical, and is the responsibility of the person missing from the meeting table – the chief executive officer.

Considering the implications of departmental decisions

The functional managers attending this operational meeting are engaged in interconnected management. Each manager asks pertinent questions of others, so that careful consideration can be given to the implications of what may appear at first to be unrelated actions by different departments.

Purchasing and supply manager
"I would like to invest in a fleet of fuel-efficient delivery vehicles. How should we structure the financing for this?"

Franchise manager
"How can we make our franchise contracts binding on levels of environmental performance?"

Human resource manager
"We are opening up a new plant in two years' time. Research shows we have the option to relocate some existing staff or to invest in up-skilling locally. What factors should we consider?"

Corporate finance manager
"We need to cut costs. One possible course of action is the closure of a plant. How will we assess the impact of closure and what criteria should we use for making the decision?"

Marketing and sales manager
"We want to link our next season's marketing campaign to "diversity and choice." How is this theme reflected in the company's workplace practices and purchasing policies? Will we be open to criticism if we follow this theme?"

Corporate communications manager
"We have heard that a TV company is running an exposé on the workplace practices of one of our longest standing suppliers. It is likely that we will be named as a principal customer. What do we know of the supplier's workplace practices? What measures were taken and recorded to ensure that we are not exposed?"

THE IMPACT ON INDUSTRY SECTORS

The emerging management issues will affect different industry sectors in different ways. Managers need to think not only about the issues affecting their sector but also about the issues that suppliers and their business customers are facing.

This is essential given the interconnections between today's global businesses, where effects on one company snowball through to various others. Understanding the pressures on customers and the needs they have is also important, and may provide stimulus for new business opportunities. Harnessing the creativity and entrepreneurial skills of business in order to find market-based solutions to the emerging management issues will produce faster and larger positive impacts.

The matrix relating the emerging management issues to industry sectors (see pp. 178–79) summarizes the main effects on nine key industries. Three sectors, the auto industry, financial services, and fast-moving consumer goods (FMCGs), are further examined, with examples of company responses.

How the emerging management issues relate to industry sectors

SECTOR	ECOLOGY AND ENVIRONMENT	HEALTH AND WELL-BEING
Auto	• Fuel economy in conventional vehicles. • Emissions contributing to global warming. • Development of hybrid vehicles. • Fuel cell technology and alternative fuels. • Recycling.	• Health and safety: vehicles and road safety. • Supplier relations. • Flammability fears over hydrogen-fueled cars. • Oversupply and mergers leading to plant closures and layoffs.
Financial services	• Exposure to contingent liabilities. • Lending terms take environmental performance of borrower into account. • Rise of ethical funds and investment screening. • Global warming's impact on insurance premiums.	• Effect of new gene technology on future insurance coverage. • Impact of HIV on insurance policies. • Pressure from governments to develop affordable health insurance for those without private cover.
Fast-moving consumer goods	• Life-cycle analysis on environmental impact of products. • Minimizing packaging. • Environmentally friendly refrigeration & storage. • Standards and certification.	• Development of genetically manipulated crops. • Foods and product safety. • Product labeling.
Information and communications technology	• Life-cycle analysis impact of hardware, extended product responsibility, and "take-back" legislation. • Positioning of satellite dishes. • Siting of transmitter masts.	• Health fears about mobile telephones and threat of class action lawsuits. • "Couch potato" syndrome, with risk of technology leading to less social contact. • Impact of repetitive strain injuries.
Extractive and utilities	• Depleting natural resources and research into renewable energy. • Pollution, global warming, and land damage. • Decommissioning. • Site issues for wind farms.	• Health and safety of operations and communities. • Impact of migrant workers on local health. • Effect of power lines on health of local communities.
Pharmaceutical and bio-technology	• Gene technology's effects on foods, crops, and medicines. • Animal cloning.	• Rising costs of prescription drugs. • "Frankenstein foods". • Biosafety. • Availability of affordable medicines in developing countries and the impact on patents.
Tourism and leisure	• Use of energy and materials – production of waste and pollution. • Impact on natural habitats, biodiversity, and natural landscapes. • Growth in sustainable tourism and ecotourism.	• Workplace conditions and benefits. • Sexually transmitted diseases among young employees. • Provision of healthcare services for tourists.
Retail	• Life-cycle analysis of products, including sourcing, packaging, and animal testing issues.	• Product labelling. • Growth in demand of organic foods. • Questions raised about links between health scares and intensive farming and food stores. • Impact of lifestyle changes on shopping habits.
Transportation	• Location of new roads, bypasses, rail tracks, ports, and airports. • Emissions (especially air transportation and road transportation).	• Road, rail, sea, and air safety. • Emissions. • Noise (especially airports).

	DIVERSITY AND HUMAN RIGHTS	COMMUNITIES
Auto	• Workplace conditions in plant and at suppliers. • Freedom of association and organized labor.	• Community relations around plants. • Integrated transportation systems. • Congestion taxes. • Restricted car use in urban areas.
Financial services	• Ethical lending. • Money laundering. • Third World debt cancellation. • Banking products for minorities. • Genetic testing and privacy.	• Serving the unbanked. • Pressure for reinvestment in communities. • Rise in microcredit programs. • Branch closures and access in rural areas. • Insurance discrimination.
Fast-moving consumer goods	• Conditions under which products are sourced and manufactured. • Diversity policies applied through supply chain.	• Community relations around plants. • Responsible marketing issues, especially to children.
Information and communications technology	• Internet hate sites. • Protection of copyright over the internet. • Privacy issues. • Decency. • Security for children on-line.	• Access by disabled or disadvantaged. • Abuse of services and impact on vulnerable consumers. • Geographical access and public service. • The digital divide.
Extractive and utilities	• Workplace conditions. • Use of private contractors and government personnel as security guards. • Joint ventures with oppressive regimes. • Ability to influence human rights issues.	• Impact on indigenous peoples and remote communities. • Community gain, for example, health and education provision. • Rapid development and site rehabilitation.
Pharmaceutical and biotechnology	• Genetic discrimination. • Animal testing.	• Local plant–community relations. • Integrity of product donations. • Critical press coverage over reluctance to supply cheaper medicines in developing countries.
Tourism and leisure	• Workplace practices, such as fair wages and freedom of association issues. • Sex tourism. • Kidnapping of tourists.	• Erosion of local culture and traditions versus needed investment and economic development. • Use of scarce water supplies.
Retail	• Conditions under which products are sourced and manufactured. • Development of fair trade and ethical trade relationships.	• Impact of out-of-town store developments and rural access. • Potentially more delivery vehicles as a result of on-line ordering. • Responsible advertising.
Transportation	• Workplace conditions. • Transportation of dangerous cargoes.	• Congestion. • New roads. • Removal of train lines. • Development of airports.

The Auto Industry

The mobility provided by cars, trucks, and motorcycles has been a major factor in economic development, and has resulted in an increased standard of living for many. With these advances have come congestion, pollution, extensive road building, and road accidents.

In 1950, there were some 2.5 billion people on the planet. Today there are over six billion. By 2050, there may be up to 9.4 billion. In 1950, there were around 69 million cars and trucks worldwide. Today, there are more than 10 times that number, and each year 55 million new vehicles are produced. If today's ratio of persons per vehicle is multiplied by the expected population growth, then the worldwide vehicle population will climb to nearly 1.1 billion by the year 2050.

Unless dramatically different forms of transportation are invented, the implications of this rate of growth are ever more congested roads and cities, more road accidents, and levels of pollution that increase the effects of global warming.

Technological advances have been harnessed by auto manufacturers to develop sophisticated safety features in cars, new advances in fuel-cell technology, and the production of hybrid vehicles that run on a mixture of gasoline and new fuels.

The use of e-commerce is reshaping the way that car manufacturers coordinate the purchase of parts. This has allowed a significant rationalization of the supplier base and, combined with oversupply in the industry, has led to a period of consolidation into a few giant firms, who have significant stakes in smaller firms.

- "From a peak of over 200 companies in the US in the early twentieth century, by the 1980s there were just 30 independent carmakers worldwide. In 2001, there were only 10 independent major players around the world, counting buyouts, alliances, and controlling interests." James Olson, VP External & Regulatory Affairs, Toyota Motors North America Inc. speech to US Conference Board, February 28, 2001.

The growing number of vehicles on the roads is creating problems with congestion. Many major cities around the world are now introducing controlling measures, such as congestion taxes and inner city tolls. Despite these measures, the demand for personal mobility, even with higher costs, shows no sign of being reduced.

However, as well as the usual information about vehicle performance, functionality, and design, customers are now also seeking information about the environmental impact and the health and safety features of vehicles before they buy.

THE EMERGING MANAGEMENT ISSUES
Ecology and environment

As a reduction in the number of cars on the road seems unlikely, consumers, environmentalists, and public authorities are putting great pressure on vehicle manufacturers to reduce the levels of pollution created by vehicles.

With a limited amount of research finance available, there is an ongoing debate in the auto industry as to whether resources should be applied to enhancing the efficiency of conventional vehicles, or to developing fuel-cell technology and hybrid vehicles.

- Several car manufacturers have announced development partnerships with companies in the oil and gas sector, such as Ford with BP and Royal Dutch/Shell with Daimler-Chrysler.
- Companies such as General Motors and Toyota are testing the use of technology to lessen environmental impact through a partnership for green technology research and development.

The manufacturer's return on investment for hybrid vehicles is uncertain as consumer acceptance is not definite. To succeed in this field, companies will need to market the cars as a must-have for trendsetters.

Car manufacturers have already made considerable progress in making vehicles more fuel-efficient.

- The EU has agreed with European car manufacturers that by 2008 average fuel consumption in new cars sold in the EU will be reduced by 25 percent from 1995 levels. The European Automobile Manufacturers Association.

- In July 2000, Ford US pledged to increase the fuel economy of sports utility vehicles by 25 percent by 2001. *Connecting with Society – Corporate Citizenship Report,* Ford, 1999.

Manufacturers have also developed Super Ultra Low Emission Vehicles (SULEVs), which produce far less pollution than other vehicles. Some campaigners and legislators are demanding the introduction of worldwide standards to provide the economies of scale that will drive down the product development costs of SULEVs.

Health and well-being

The car industry has concerns for the health and well-being of employees at its plants and at partner and supplier operations, and the health and safety of drivers, passengers, and other road-users. Research into new fuel technologies and types of vehicle are creating different safety concerns, such as the potential flammability of hydrogen-fueled cars.

Investing in safety
The publication by consumer groups of independent vehicle safety test results has helped to spur manufacturers to invest in improved design and sophisticated safety systems. Some brands have made safety part of their brand image.

Safety issues also extend from the auto manufacturers to suppliers of auto parts. In 2000, Bridgestone/Firestone became embroiled in controversy over the the safety of one of its tire specifications, which resulted in recalls.

Manufacturers are using new technologies to develop better safety systems for vehicles. For example, Ford is working on:

- Radar and lidar (laser radar) as tools for sensing an imminent accident and pre-arming the airbag system.
- Sophisticated restraint systems that can adapt to occupant characteristics and crash conditions.
- The application of Telematics (the connection of vehicles to information systems), combined with advanced sensors, to cut response time to crashes by alerting emergency services, and providing precise information about the location and severity of the crash and the number of occupants involved.

Connecting with Society – Corporate Citizenship Report, Ford, 1999.

The well-being of employees in the auto industry is threatened, as oversupply in industrialized countries is leading to industry rationalization, mergers, and acquisitions. These, in turn, are leading to restructuring, plant closures, and layoffs as capacity is switched to emerging markets. In the remaining workers, the result can be job insecurity and low morale.

Diversity and human rights

When car manufacturers invest in plants and operations in the emerging economies, they often find that there are less stringent local regulations relating to workplace conditions. By introducing world-class processes and health and safety systems, the companies can help to raise the local standards.

Manufacturers face difficulties in policing standards among overseas suppliers when direct contact is limited. However, if companies do not impose their world-class standards on their suppliers, or monitor them to ensure that these standards are adhered to, they may find themselves subject to pressure from domestic unions and international NGOs.

Toyota and Daimler-Chrysler have pledged to place five percent of their business with minority suppliers by 2002. By the same year, Nissan plans to have 25 per cent of its dealerships owned by minority groups.

Communities

Because of the nature and scale of vehicle manufacturing, car companies face significant community relations issues around their plants. The plant is often the sole or major employer in the area, leading to expectations from the community that the owners will invest in community projects, such as improving schools and medical facilities and providing affordable housing for local people. This can lead to communities becoming dependent on the plant.

As a major consumer of services, car plants create demand for a range of local suppliers. Many vehicle manufacturers invest in the development of a quality local supply base, which brings more money into the local environment.

Besides local communities, car manufacturers are also confronted by "communities of interest." These may include people affected by the noise, congestion, accidents, or pollution due to increased traffic flow who are demanding that there is less use of cars.

Traffic congestion is a major problem for most urban communities in the developed countries. Some cities are already approaching gridlock in rush hour traffic. Even in many large urban areas of developing countries, where car use is still relatively new, traffic congestion is intense.

- In Europe, road transportation of both passengers and goods nearly doubled between 1970 and 1996.
- Cars in Manila operate at an average speed of 7mph.
- On average, every car in Bangkok is immobilized in traffic for a total period of time equivalent to 44 days each year.

In response to this growing problem and that of lack of car parking spaces, manufacturers are experimenting with new programs to alleviate congestion.

- In Madrid, where 400,000 commuters vie for 200,000 parking spaces, Ford has teamed up with a consortium of public transportation agencies to make park-and-ride more attractive, contributing marketing expertise as well as funding for focus groups and other market research. Ideas include adding services such as shopping, car-washing, and dry-cleaning to locations where cars are dropped off.

Connecting with Society — Corporate Citizenship Report, Ford, 1999.

The Financial Services Sector

The financial services sector includes retail banking, investment banking, insurance, mortgages, and pensions. Innovations in technology, working practices, and financial products have combined to produce an industry sector that is experiencing profound change.

Automation and the growth of the internet are reducing the need for middle management and branch offices. Back office operations and call centers can now be stationed overseas where labor costs are lower, and on-line banking is becoming increasingly popular.

However, the increasing reliance on computerized transactions has lead to the specter of organized cybercrime, and an increase in money laundering.

Financial service companies face tough competition in core activities, such as credit card and savings operations, from new entrants, including supermarkets and other strong consumer brands like auto firms. These companies have the advantage of having access to extensive customer databases that allow them to cherry-pick customers from the traditional financial institutions.

The blurring of the boundaries between public and private sectors, and the growth of private partnerships for public infrastructure projects, is leading to the creation of new financing tools.

Corporate finance houses are responding to the increase in global markets by consolidating through mergers and acquisitions. This consolidation is leading to job losses.

● The ILO, in a press statement in February 2001, suggested that at least 130,000 finance jobs disappeared in Western Europe as a result of mergers and acquisitions during the 1990s, and predicted, "the disappearance of approximately 300,000 banking jobs between 1999 and 2002 through merger-led consolidation."

As the reach of the financial institutions grow, so they become the focus of government pressure to provide services for large numbers of disadvantaged, often unprofitable, customers who do not have bank accounts or any form of insurance.

As financial brands gain greater recognition, they face challenges from vigilante consumers and campaigning NGOs on a range of social, environmental, and ethical issues.

THE EMERGING MANAGEMENT ISSUES
Ecology and environment

Global warming is likely to generate substantial costs for the financial services sector, and the predicted increase in the number and impact of natural disasters will have a dramatic effect on the global insurance market.

- Some institutions are already offering better lending terms to companies with environmental systems in place, and are screening investments against environmental criteria. International financial services group ING has produced an environmental risk inventory for loan officers.
- There is greater interest and growth in environmental and ethical funds: the Co-operative Bank in the UK has made ethical lending the cornerstone of its marketing effort and internal vision and values. Institutions such as Morgan Stanley, Merrill Lynch, and Citigroup, involved in arranging finance for environmentally controversial projects such as the Three Gorges dam in China, face pressure and boycotts from campaigning NGOs.
- The UK insurance company CGNU seeks to measure environmental impacts, both directly (through property management, energy and water use, waste management, paper use, purchasing, transportation and travel), and indirectly, (through the way in which it conceives, designs, and delivers core business products and services).

Health and well-being

The insurance sector stands to be affected greatly by issues of health and well-being. There is increasing pressure from governments to develop affordable health insurance policies for those without private coverage. The long-term effects of HIV and AIDS also remain a significant issue.

Developments in gene technology raise the prospect of the ability to screen for genetic predisposition to diseases. This will affect the availability of life insurance, and questions will be raised about the ethics of denying coverage.

A difficult dilemma
The protests of animal rights activists have led to financial institutions facing a dilemma — whether to ignore the threats and risk retaliation on staff and property, or to bow to pressure and risk accusations of giving in to the rule of the mob.

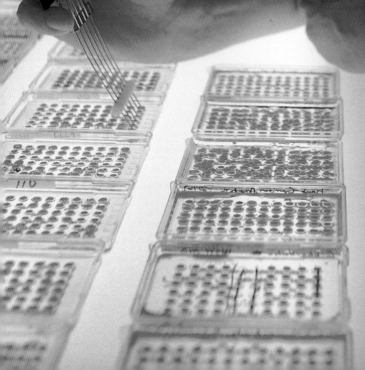

Diversity and human rights

Financial services organizations are having to respond to increased interest in ethical lending, including offering ethically screened funds and products. Extreme animal rights activists have adopted violent and illegal tactics, for instance with the objective of driving UK research laboratory Huntingdon Life Sciences (which tests drugs on animals on behalf of global pharmaceutical companies) out of business. Employees of its bankers and shareholders have been targeted. The Royal Bank of Scotland, Barclays, Credit Suisse First Boston, HSBC, and Philips and Drew have withdrawn their funding and services from the firm.

Advances in genetics threaten the rights of the individual. Genetic testing may lead to the emergence of "uninsurables," those people excluded from obtaining insurance policies because of a genetic predisposition to illness or disability. There are implications for privacy as well. Will individuals be forced to undergo screening to obtain insurance coverage?

Communities

Bank branch closures have led to debates in the media and campaigns highlighting the danger of loss of access to services for old, disabled, and rural residents. Banks are facing legislation to make them invest in local communities.

- The US Community Reinvestment Act stipulates that companies must reinvest in areas from which their funds are earned.
- The government of the Spanish region of Extremadura has proposed a tax on savings held by banks in the region. The banks will only be able to reduce the level of the tax if they reinvest the savings deposits in regional social programs. Banks have responded angrily to the proposal, arguing that their loans to small- and medium-sized enterprises should be considered as an investment in local social programs, and that the proposal goes against EU law.

Financial institutions are under increasing pressure to serve those without bank accounts or insurance. One specialized development is the growth of microcredit schemes and community enterprise finance, often funded by a mix of private and public capital.

Some institutions have developed community-based financial products or scholarships.

- The National Westminster Bank in the UK has developed new community financing products and is supporting the growth of credit unions.
- In South Africa, Nedbank and other banks tailored business loan products to meet the needs of street merchants, harnessing their ATM network for the purpose.
- The Spanish bank Caja Madrid has launched a scholarship program for research into biodiversity and environmental preservation in Spain.

Investing in communities
Many financial institutions have created foundations through which to channel community development work. As part of its activities, the Spanish bank Caja Madrid has launched a scholarship program for research into biodiversity and environmental preservation.

Fast-moving Consumer Goods

The fast-moving consumer goods (FMCG) sector (regularly purchased products such as food, beverages, beauty items, and household goods) is characterized by increasingly fierce competition, tight margins, and price-conscious consumers.

The globalization of markets and advances in IT distribution systems means that production of these goods can be rationalized in a few strategic regional centers. New product launches have also been speeded up so that it is now common for companies to launch products in many countries at the same time. At present, companies are trying to focus on their strongest international brands. Unilever, for example, is scaling down from 1,600 brands worldwide to concentrate on the 400 it feels have the greatest potential.

   Production and marketing of goods is influenced by demographic changes, such as the growing number of older customers in the industrialized world and a growing number of educated and affluent consumers in the developing countries who aspire to buy what is available to Western consumers. Simultaneously, many low-income consumers in developing countries need goods to meet basic needs.

Shopping overseas
Retailers selling fast-moving consumer goods have taken advantage of globalization and the increasing number of overseas travelers to become international brands.

Companies therefore tailor their products to different markets. More than half of Unilever's sales in India, for example, are in rural areas, so the firm has developed specific affordable products for these districts. *Unilever Social Report*, Unilever, 2001.

THE EMERGING MANAGEMENT ISSUES
Ecology and environment
The impact of products on the environment is now assessed through life-cycle analysis. In response to the findings, packaging is being minimized and advanced biodegradable forms are being developed. Environmentallyfriendly refrigeration and cold storage systems are also becoming more common. Eco-labeling is now a standard way of communicating environmental credentials.

Ethical produce
Many consumers do not mind paying a little extra for produce if they know that the people producing it, such as this young boy laying out coffee beans to dry, are treated fairly. Some manufacturers have ethically-sourced product lines as a way of differentiating their brands.

Health and well-being
Responding to consumer concerns, producers are also initiating labeling and education campaigns to inform purchasers about the conditions in which ingredients are grown and products manufactured. Some companies are being proactive and opening operations to public viewing.

- The Spanish food sector, represented by the Federation of Food and Beverage Industries (FIAB), and including companies such as Domecq, Koipe, Heineken Spain, Coca-Cola and Nestlé, run an "open doors" exercise in their processing plants, to show consumers that these companies apply the strictest health, hygiene, and safety controls. Forty percent of corporate members of FIAB are participating. FIAB has indicated that the sector needs to guarantee consumers quality foodstuffs and transparency, in order to prove that the sector has nothing to hide.

Diversity and human rights

FMCG firms that are sourcing from industrializing markets face demands to be more active in screening and improving the conditions under which their products are manufactured. In response, Mars has developed a Sustainable Cocoa Initiative in a partnership with industry, farmers, governments, and NGOs. Other companies have developed similar programs, such as the FairTrade coffee, tea, and chocolate brand.

Within industrialized markets, firms are also having to address issues to do with the diversity of their suppliers. At least one major FMCG firm has had to make significant changes in its labor force in Western Europe, after realizing that its loss of market share was due to its predominantly white male salesforce trying to sell its products to a largely Asian retail sector.

Communities

Providing jobs and generating associated economic activity are the most significant contributions to local communities made by FMCG firms. But it is now recognized that the most beneficial and sustainable community development work will come from the transfer of business skills and access to infrastructure. Established firms with highly honed marketing skills are coming under pressure to share their expertise to aid social and economic development in poorer markets.

- As Africa's largest private sector employer, The Coca-Cola Company has agreed to harness its marketing network in support of a UN-led campaign against the spread of malaria, tuberculosis, and AIDS. UNAIDS.

THE IMPACT ON SMALL AND MEDIUM ENTERPRISES

The emerging management issues are not just having an effect on large transnational corporations. Alongside the reach and scale of these companies, and fueled by many of the same forces for change, there is an explosion of small businesses.

Many of these businesses are operating in the informal economy and on a very local basis. However, developments in information and communication technology are enabling even the smallest firms to operate internationally, or to service and partner large companies. Many more employees are now working for small and medium-sized enterprises (smes), and the numbers of workers in these companies will grow in the future. Small enterprises need to respond to the emerging management issues and expectations from shareholders in the same way as larger companies, but they have different financial and managerial pressures.

The Relevance to Small and Medium-sized Enterprises

Smaller companies are under some of the same pressures and are experiencing the same issues of transparency and accountability as their larger cousins.

Many of the risks and opportunities associated with the emerging management issues are as applicable to small and medium-sized enterprises (smes) as they are to transnationals. The differences, such as they are, are largely of scale.

- Large companies are demanding evidence of good environmental practice from their suppliers, whatever their size. If a small firm wants to keep or win business, it will need to meet the stipulated standards.
- Most of the business regulations concerning health and safety, environmental performance, or discrimination apply to all firms, regardless of their size.
- Financial benefits from initiatives such as better waste management or reducing recruitment and training costs through improved hiring methods will apply, whatever a company's size.
- A small firm needs to be respected in its local community and its trade sector and trusted by its customers.
- The majority of smes will be operating on tight margins, where levels of efficiency and effectiveness can mean the difference between surviving or not.

The three overriding objectives for smes should be:
- Saving money by cutting costs.
- Improving productivity.
- Achieving more sales.

Demands on small companies
Small companies, especially those owned and run by a single person, often have to adhere to the same regulations as larger companies but have less financial room for maneuver.

Achieving objectives by acting on emerging management issues

EMI	SAVING MONEY	IMPROVING PRODUCTIVITY	GETTING MORE SALES
Ecology and environment	● Energy conservation. ● Lower waste disposal costs.	● Better waste disposal.	● Eligibility for corporate bidding lists. ● Products are chosen by eco-consumers.
Health	● Less time lost through employee sickness.	● Healthier and happier employees. ● Less absenteeism.	● More continuity in customer service.
Diversity	● Lower recruitment costs because staff are retained. ● Wider sources for new staff.	● Less downtime as new staff learn.	● Better understanding of diverse markets. ● Representative of markets served.
Communities	● Insurance and security costs reduced because there is less crime and vandalism.	● More motivated staff.	● Raised profile. ● Activity in networks, which helps to identify new business opportunities.

Managing the emerging management issues thoughtfully will help achieve these three objectives.

ECOLOGY AND ENVIRONMENT

There are many documented examples of how smes can save money and, at the same time, minimize their impact on the environment through energy conservation, recycling, and minimizing waste and excess packaging. Green Business Clubs and sharing good practice through local chambers of commerce or other organizations are common. Advice is also available on the internet.

Small and medium-sized companies that are seen to have good environmental management systems are viewed as being generally well-run businesses. This does not relate solely to environmental issues, because the process of obtaining certification itself can help improve a business's general systems and processes.

● Hopkins Catering Equipment of Leeds, in Yorkshire, England, supplies equipment to the catering industry. It is a family business, founded in 1957, and has a staff of 38 with an annual turnover of £2 million ($2.8 million).

In the mid-1990s, the second generation of the family took over the company and were advised by a business support service on ways of improving business efficiency. One recommendation was to seek accreditation to ISO 14001, the international environmental management standard, to show the company's commitment to best environmental practice and compliance with standards.

ISO 14001 certification placed emphasis on staff awareness and gave the company a structured approach to managing its significant environmental aspects, replacing a traditional ad-hoc and fragmented approach. The result has been improved efficiency in operations and fewer negative environmental impacts. *Helping smes on Environment*, Business in the Community – Yorkshire and Humberside, 2000.

As well as there being a solid business case for sound environmental practices, some firms are responding to the personal desire of employees to make a positive contribution to conservation and ecological issues.

● Communicopia.net is a small internet design firm in Vancouver, Canada. Its offices have been built using sustainable business materials. In addition, employees give 10 percent of their time to environmental and social projects, and the firm offers discount rates to NGOs. *Fast Company,* May 2000

HEALTH AND WELL-BEING

Sickness and absenteeism affect smes disproportionately more than transnational corporations, as one key worker's sustained absence may have a critical impact on the business. Health and well-being of staff in smes is therefore a crucial issue.

In order to be attractive
to employees or potential
employees, smes have to offer some
or all of the flexible workplace
practices and benefits instituted
by the larger companies.
However, the costs for an
individual sme to develop a range of
flexible workplace practices may be prohibitive.

There is therefore a trend for smes to group together to
achieve economies of scale, for example to keep
recruitment costs down, or to ride piggyback on the
facilities organized by a major employer, such as a
childcare service or a workplace gym.

To retain talented employees and to institute best
practices into the workplace, a manager of a sme may
have to make several commitments:

- A commitment to support work/life balance with
  flexitime, and provide support for care for the
  elderly and children.

- Long-term investment in measures to promote the health and well-being of employees, such as providing subsidized gym membership.
- A commitment to continuous improvement and learning for life.
- Submitting the firm to outside scrutiny from bodies such as the Investor in People organization, which certifies in 15 countries including Germany, Sweden, South Africa, and Bermuda.

Small firms can also provide creative perks to help attract and retain workers, as the examples of several California firms below illustrate:

- Cal Insurance & Associates Inc. gives employees every other Friday off.
- Respect Inc. gives each employee one paid day off a month to do volunteer work.
- Creative Wood Products offers all employees, regardless of their position in the company, profit-sharing, life insurance, and medical and dental insurance.
- E-greetings Network buys dinner for employees working overtime and gives all employees the opportunity to interview new recruits. *San Francisco Examiner*, October 6, 1998.

A successful method of reducing absenteeism and turnover is demonstrated by Grupo M, a clothing manufacturer in the Dominican Republic:

- Grupo M sells to companies such as Levi Strauss, Tommy Hilfiger, and The Gap. Over the past 12 years, the firm has adopted innovative policies that are aimed at removing social and economic barriers for its employees and the surrounding community. Grupo M is reported to have found significant bottom line benefits from their policies, including very low absenteeism rates, low staff turnaround after vacations, and no strikes.

   The programs adopted include a literacy effort (which has resulted in a 100 percent literacy rate among its employees), sponsorship of a local elementary school, scholarships that provide funding for international education, subsidized lunches for workers' children, full medical care for all employees and their families, and a recreational center for the community. *Human Rights – Is It Any of your Business?,* Amnesty International UK and Prince of Wales International Business Leaders Forum, 1999.

A job network in San Francisco illustrates how smes are coming together and pooling resources:

> Job Network is sponsored and directed by small business owners for small businesses. The program is designed as a portable human resources department that helps small companies to hire and train welfare recipients. The program provides training on customer service and communication skills, as well as information on how to deal with issues such as childcare and domestic violence. In addition, the program helps employees set short- and long-term career goals with a workplace specialist and assists them with job placement. *Los Angeles Times,* February 24, 999.

DIVERSITY AND HUMAN RIGHTS

Smes are responding to diversity and human rights issues on a "need to" basis (because they are subject to legislation ensuring no discrimination on various grounds) or on a proactive basis (because they see potential benefits for the company and for members of the community).

For many smes, compliance with legislation has not been a priority up until now. This is not because smes are deliberately flouting diversity and human rights regulations, but because laws in this area may seem like a distraction compared to the core activities of the business, such as meeting orders.

However, as a result of the global forces for change, smes are now exposed to risks if they do not consider diversity and human rights issues more seriously. Aggrieved minorities are more informed and better connected, more assertive, and ready to fight for their rights, in court if necessary. Compliance, therefore, is a rising issue. Acting beyond compliance, that is taking a proactive approach to diversity and human rights issues, can result in tangible benefits and competitive advantage.

Managers in smes have to work hard to attract and retain well-qualified, reliable, and honest employees. No manager will deliberately try to make this task harder. However, they may be unintentionally cutting themselves off from sources of staff. For example, the firm may only advertise vacancies in a journal read by a narrow cross-section of readers.

Managers of smes may also be unfamiliar with how adaptive technology and job reconfiguration can enable a disabled worker to join the business, or ensure that a valued coworker with a deteriorating physical disability can carry on working.

Managers should be sensitive to the pay and conditions packages that are most attractive to particular employee groups.

● Many migrant workers in the US are from Mexico and cross the border during the harvest season. Economic difficulties in Mexico led to an increase in the number of migrant workers and depressed wage levels at a time when the cost of living was increasing. Abuse of workers by unscrupulous employers was widely reported. One company, McKay Nursery, with 60 full-time employees, relies on these seasonal workers. The company provides stock options for the temporary workers and reports a 90 percent return rate each year of workers, aiding stability in the company. One-sixth of the company's full-time workers and managers were once migrant workers. Malcolm McIntosh et al., *Corporate Citizenship*: *Successful Strategies of Responsible Companies*, 1998.

Diversity and human rights issues apply in the marketplace as well as the workplace, and this holds true for small businesses.

Attracting talented staff
Managers of smes should not cut themselves off from potential sources of talented employees. If prejudices and language issues can be overcome, migrant workers, such as these from Mexico, are often an untapped pool of available labor.

● Travelsphere was the first British mainstream travel company to offer a specialized service for blind and partially-sighted people, creating a new market that generates more than £100,000 ($140,000) in sales.

The company has adapted some of its popular tours especially for blind and partially-sighted people. They provide tour information in large print and audio formats and, for deaf clients, use a "talk-type" system for letters. The company made only slight changes to their existing procedures, but opened up new horizons, both for themselves and their customers. As a result, Travelsphere differentiated its business and captured a new market ahead of their competitors. *British Government Report on Corporate Social Responsibility: Society and Business,* March 2001.

One of the hardest diversity and human rights issues in the marketplace for organizations of any size to grasp is that of meeting the needs of customers with disabilities, and not discriminating against them by, for example, offering an inferior service or an inaccessible one.

COMMUNITIES

Managers of smes will have contact with the whole range of communities that were identified in the Emerging Management Issues Defined section: geographical, communities of identity, and communities of interest.

The prosperity and condition of the local community in which an sme is based may directly affect the success of the business, especially if it is a company that mainly deals locally. Smes located in rural communities that are in decline will struggle to attract or retain employees as local services such as transportation and schools are reduced. Those based in urban communities that have high levels of crime and vandalism, high housing costs for employees, and heavy traffic congestion, will also find that recruitment and employee retention are difficult.

These scenarios are often the reason why managers in smes play an active role in community development, regeneration, and social development programs – their businesses depend on it. As spending by public authorities becomes tighter,

A community business

The success of the Seaview Hotel and Restaurant on the Isle of Wight (UK) is due to its owners taking the local community into account when making business transactions.

public–private partnerships between business and local authorities are gaining acceptance as vehicles through which business managers can make a contribution by providing know-how, leadership, and resources.

Small local firms can choose to support other local businesses through their purchasing decisions, and the local community through their human resource policies.

- Buying locally, employing local people, and saving resources turns a business into a community business. For the Seaview Hotel and Restaurant on the Isle of Wight in the UK, it is a philosophy that has also helped raise turnover from just £60,000 to £1.2m ($84,000–$1.7m) since the current owners bought the rundown hotel in 1980.

  The hotel buys food, wine, and beer from island farmers and fishermen, recruits staff from the island, and employs local people to make their furnishings and fabrics. It also buys bread and vegetables from the village store and capitalizes on the marketing network that the island's suppliers provide for it.

  The hotel identified the business benefits of staff development at an early stage. Training programs, apprenticeship courses, work placements, and visits for local schools have all contributed to low staff turnover.

  The owners recycle as much waste as possible, including passing on old beds to those in need and computers to the local school. The restaurant's bottles, paper and waste food are all separated and recycled. The hotel also uses low-voltage lighting and monitors water use. *British Government Report on Corporate Social Responsibility: "Society and Business,"* March 2001.

Investing in community involvement activities for smes may include raising awareness of the company and allowing time off to encourage employees to be involved in charities and community organizations, or to take on a useful role such as becoming a school volunteer. Alternatively, the company may support community involvement by allowing use of its premises and equipment.

● Hanna Andersson has been making and marketing children's clothes since 1983 from a base in Portland, Oregon. Giving back to the community is part of the culture at Hanna, and one that has special meaning for employees and customers alike. As Hanna's website says:

"Giving back makes sense both socially and financially, because businesses, like people, don't live in a vacuum — companies are greatly dependent on the community! Just for starters, our workforce is educated here and our employees use the transportation system. We believe that the long-term health of our company is vitally connected to the health of our community — you can't have a healthy company in an unhealthy community. We give back to our community by donating five percent of our pre-tax profits to charities."

Communities of identity

The interaction between a sme and communities of identity may be linked to the identity of the firm itself. For example, a business owned by a minority group living in a community may focus on building business relationships and customers within that same community. This is demonstrated by clusters of smes owned and managed by different ethnic groups that form in urban areas where migrants have settled down. Self-help and networking clubs and associations often form in these areas, such as ethnic business support groups. Coming together in these business communities of identity enables the smes to lobby public authorities and large companies to institute affirmative minority business plans. These plans stipulate a proportion of contracts that should be awarded to minority-owned business (which are known as minority set-asides in the US).

● Voice of the Red Sea is a small radio station in Eilat, Israel, which has an evening program called "To Give". The show was devised and is presented by Zilpa Grossman, who researches and presents the show voluntarily. The radio station provides air-time and backup. Listeners are encouraged to identify cases of hardship and the program helps to raise resources and solve social problems. The program attracts large numbers of listeners and provides an opportunity to use the power of the media to put something back into the local community. It has also raised the profile of the radio station with local politicians and other opinion formers. *The Globe*, June 6, 2000.

Communities of interest

The global forces for change, and particularly the revolution of values, have created a market segment defined by shared interest in an issue. In the same way as large and multinational corporations have seized on cause-related marketing, smes can use specialized marketing efforts to tap into these communities of interest.

- Guido's Pizza in Boise, Idaho, has the slogan, "Eat a Slice of Pizza, Help Save the Environment." A slice of pizza at Guido's may only cost $1.85, but patrons can take additional pleasure from the fact that a small portion of that price goes to help preserve a nearby park. *Christian Science Monitor*, January 2001.

- Nambarrie, based in Belfast, Northern Ireland, is the maker of Number-one tea. In 1998, it produced 100,000 special tea packages with a breast cancer awareness message provided by Nambarrie's nonprofit partner Action Cancer. Five pence from the sale of each promotional package was donated to Action Cancer. Nambarrie executives saw the initiative as, "a way to communicate a very positive message through our packaging."

The promotion was also seen as a way of strengthening the company's local brand image, and of giving something back to the community. Executives also reported that the campaign had benefited the morale of staff. In July 1999, the company was rewarded for the campaign by winning a Business in the Community Award for Community Excellence presented by the British prime minister, Tony Blair.

SIGNPOSTS

THE EMERGING MANAGEMENT ISSUES DEFINED

ECOLOGY AND ENVIRONMENT

A seminal work on business and the environment is *Changing Course* by Stephan Schmidheiny (Massachusetts Institute of Technology, 1992). Schmidheiny was the founder of the business organization The World Business Council for Sustainable Development (www.wbcsd.ch).

Other useful resources include: Conservation International (www.conservation.org); World Energy Council (www.worldenergycouncil.org); Worldwatch Institute (www.worldwatch.org); World Resources Institute and "Earthtrends" database (www.wri.org); the World Water Council (www.worldwatercouncil.org); and Business in the Environment (www.business-in-environment.org.uk).

HEALTH AND WELL-BEING

The International Labour Organization (ILO) has many reports and publications on international labor standards, covering topics such as health and safety, child and forced labor, and social protection. They also have a database on business and social initiatives (www.ilo.org). The Health and Well-being section of the European Foundation for the Improvement of Living and Working Conditions carries information on a range of European Commission titles and research (www.eurofound.ie/themes/health). Visit the Employers' Campaign on Work-Life and Balance for research and training information at: www.EmployersforWork-LifeBalance.org.uk; and the Boston College Center for Work and Family in the US (www.bc.edu).

For case study material on the effect of HIV and Aids on business, read *The Business Response to HIV/Aids: Impact and Lessons Learned* by Kieran Daly and Julian Parr (UNAIDS, PWIBLF, The Global Business Council on HIV/Aids, 2000).

DIVERSITY AND HUMAN RIGHTS

The resource website: www.diversityinc.com is produced by Allegiant Media and has a wealth of material, including a regular email newsletter on business and diversity issues. The business organization, The Conference Board (www.conferenceboard.org) publishes regular reports and hold seminars and conferences on diversity, as well as on other themes relevant for specific corporate functions.

Race for Opportunity and Opportunity Now at Business in the Community (www.bitc.org.uk) are, respectively, employer-led campaigns on achieving greater ethnic and gender balance in the workforce. The Employers Forum on Disability is a sister organization for disability issues (www.employers-forum.co.uk). Also, Ability Net (www.abilitynet.co.uk) offers advice on adaptive technologies for those with disabilities.

A number of NGOs campaign, monitor, and publish information about the interaction between business and diversity and human rights issues. Try Amnesty International, which has business advisory groups in 20 countries (www.amnesty.org); Human Rights Watch (www.hrw.org); and the resource website (www.business-humanrights.org). *Human Rights. Is It Any of Your Business?* by Peter Frankental and Frances House (Amnesty International UK and PWIBLF, 2000) and *Big Business: Small Hands. Responsible Approaches to Child Labour* (Save the Children, 2000) make useful reading.

COMMUNITIES

For a look at business and community relations, read Edmund M. Burke and Raymond V. Kilmartin *Corporate Community Relations: the Principles of the Neighbor of Choice* (ed. Burke, 1999) and *Companies and Communities: Promoting Business Involvement in the Community* by Michael Fogarty and Ian Christie (Policy Studies Institute, 1990). The Corporate Citizenship Company produces the bimonthly magazine, *Community Affairs Briefing*, which provides a comprehensive roundup of community issues for business (www.corporate-citizenship.co.uk).

THE IMPACT ON BUSINESS STRATEGY

For managers operating in an emerging economy or market in transition, look at Jane Nelson's *Business as Partners in Development* (PWIBLF with the World Bank and UNDP, 1986) and *The US Manufacturing Industry's Impact on Ethical, Labor, and Environmental Standards in Developing Practices: A Survey of Current Practices* (compilation and analysis by Ernest H. Preeg Manufacturers Alliance/MPAI and the National Association of National Manufacturers, 2001).

For the link between brands and the emerging management issues, a good case for associating brands with good causes is made in *Cause Related Marketing. Who Cares Wins* by Sue Adkins (Butterworth Heinemann, 1999) and *Making Money While Making a Difference: How to Profit with a NonProfit Partner* by Richard Steckel (High Tide Press, 1999).

US organizations The Conference Board (www.conference-board.org) and Business for Social Responsibility (www.bsr.org) have published reports on the social and economic impacts of business restructuring.

THE IMPACT ON COMPANY FUNCTIONS AND INDUSTRY SECTORS

For the impact on the emerging management issues on corporate functions, try the relevant industry associations or try national professional associations concerned with human resources or marketing.

THE IMPACT ON SMALL AND MEDIUM ENTERPRISES

A British government report and website www.societyandbusiness.gov.uk has examples of small firms responding positively to the emerging management issues. Shell LiveWIRE provides advice for young entrepreneurs about sustainable development (www.shell-livewire.org).

All websites active at the time of writing.

SEVEN STEPS TO
MINIMIZING RISKS

"Stakeholders want companies to make a profit,
but not at the expense of their staff and the
wider community."

INTRODUCTION

The emerging management issues are shifting away from the margins of commercial practice to become crucial aspects of mainstream management. How can you organize an effective response to these issues and turn the accompanying risks to your advantage?

First, the information in Global Forces for Change could be used to help develop a presentation to your colleagues on how stakeholder expectations are affecting your business. The examples in The Emerging Management Issues of how other companies have responded can be used as an aid to consider the likely risks and opportunities that your company may face. Then you need to integrate your company's response into management systems and practices, wherever possible using existing management procedures. This is the challenge that is explored in the following pages.

THE POWER OF ONE

Every manager has the power to initiate change within his or her sphere of influence. All managers can make decisions based on the suggested approach of minimizing risks and maximizing opportunities. The ability to exercise that power, given the demands on the time and energy of busy executives, will require a conscious and constant questioning of the way decisions are made and resources are allocated. You can meet these challenges by gaining the appropriate knowledge, applying the relevant skills, and breaking down the necessary actions into a series of manageable steps, outlined in the Seven-Step Process (*see* overleaf).

THE WIN-WIN SEVEN STEPS

The Seven-Step Process is a framework for action for managers and their teams based on good practice by companies experienced in responding to the emerging management issues and changing stakeholder expectations. Most companies manage their responses in an improvised fashion only, exposing them to risk. The Seven-Step Process can be used as a template to assess, plan, and monitor company activity. Each of the Seven Steps is founded on practical actions and the principle of continuous improvement. When the steps are followed, they will help you achieve wins for your business and wins for society.

Their importance is illustrated through the story of "Peter," a manager who enthusiastically embarks on a program of change in response to the emerging management issues (*see* pp. 212–13). However, the impact of his changes disappoints him and his colleagues because he does not know how to apply standards of professionalism and administrative rigor that he does to other areas of his business. Following the Seven Steps will help him do this in the future.

Using the Seven-Step Process

This process will help turn improvised responses to the emerging management issues into mainstream business practice. Study the Seven Steps and go through them with colleagues. Seek or create triggers for action. The steps are flexible enough to allow for business complexity, and the process is cyclical: results from the seventh step lead to fresh triggers.

1 Recognizing the Trigger

● **Spotting local triggers** ● **Getting ahead of the wave**
The process begins with an event that requires management attention and action: a trigger. It may come from a product or workplace crisis or from the introduction of new government regulations. It may also be started by a realization that costs are about to be incurred or potential benefits lost. Managers need to spot triggers or even initiate them in order to stay one step ahead.

2 Making a Business Case

● **Knowing the risks** ● **Spotting opportunities** ● **Building people**
● **Building the business** ● **Building reputation**
Sometimes, managers will be able to take the initiative and respond to a trigger in their own area of operation. More often, it will be necessary to undertake consultation and obtain buy-in from other colleagues and departments. A strong business case will need to be made for action.

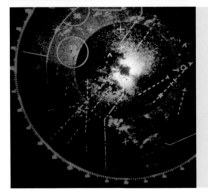

3 Scoping the Issues

● **Mapping issues on the corporate radar screen** ● **Engaging in dialogue with stakeholders** ● **Applying benchmarking**
● **Assessing business impact** ● **Using scenarios**
Working with the tools that help identify the range of issues likely to affect business, the next step is to make a risk and opportunity assessment on the likely impact of these issues on business operations. Priority areas and gaps in information and knowledge will emerge, suggesting necessary action and guiding broader strategy.

7 Measuring and Reporting

● **Understanding the reasons for measuring and reporting** ● **Building trust** ● **What to measure and how** ● **Looking ahead to the future**
It is vital to monitor and demonstrate whether the strategy is proving effective while making sure that targets are being met. This step involves measuring the impact of the company, reporting on its progress, and demonstrating transparency to ever more demanding stakeholders, while constantly looking ahead to the future.

6 Engaging Stakeholders

● **Communicating** ● **Offering incentives and motivation** ● **Talking about public policy** ● **Building partnerships** ● **Establishing community needs** ● **Training** ● **Overcoming obstacles**
It is necessary to effect change and implement the actions identified in previous steps by having regular ongoing dialogue with stakeholders. Key stakeholder groups need to be identified, channels of communication opened, community needs understood, partnership-building skills used, and obstacles overcome.

5 Integrating Strategies

● **Achieving quality and excellence** ● **Managing the supply chain** ● **Managing risks** ● **Creating new procedures and a win-win culture**
It is necessary to turn commitment into action: first, by integrating action into existing business processes, and second, by creating new policies and procedures. This step involves setting up a culture in which maximizing opportunities and minimizing risks, thus creating win-win situations, becomes instilled into the corporate DNA.

4 Committing to Action

● **Giving shareholder-added value** ● **Putting out signals** ● **Governance** ● **Demonstrating leadership**
With the key issues mapped out, it is necessary to commit to action and articulate that commitment, whether as an individual manager, a department head, or a senior executive. The commitment is to make decisions that minimize risks and maximize opportunities for both business and society, while recognizing their interdependence.

Working without the Seven Steps: Peter's Story

The Seven Steps are a process of organizing and aligning disparate elements within the business toward common goals. For those who would argue that such a process is unnecessary, here is a cautionary tale.

"Peter," an amalgam of several real-life managers, is a high-flying executive who has not used the Seven Steps. He runs the subsidiary of an international consumer goods company in an East European country. His personal values, as well as the lessons he learned from optional courses on his MBA program at a top US business school, make him receptive to the needs of the emerging management issues.

PETER'S INNOVATIONS

Peter joins the environmental task force of an international chamber of commerce. He makes it clear that he wants his senior management team to include women, and asks for female employees to be promoted throughout the firm. To engage with the local community, he instructs local managers to develop links with schools adjacent to their factories and to encourage their employees to get involved.

THE CONSEQUENCES

Peter thinks he has done enough to address the issues. It comes as a shock to discover that the reverse is true.

- Prominent local environmentalists accuse Peter of hypocrisy, claiming that although he joined the business environment taskforce, the plants for which he is responsible are not tackling excessive pollution levels. These allegations come despite the fact that the previous managers deliberately suppressed information about the pollution, and it was Peter who implemented a major clean-up.
- At the annual meeting of the parent company, activist shareholders accuse the corporation of encouraging a corporate culture that discriminates on the grounds of sex and race. The CEO asks Peter to provide data to demonstrate that equal opportunities policies are in place. Peter has no such data.

- Local managers report a backlash from staff who are angry at being told to volunteer. Employees see this as a throwback to the old Communist regime, when citizens were expected to "volunteer" for community action on Saturdays.
- Local newspapers report criticism about the company among local community leaders, who accuse the firm of abandoning groups that it traditionally has assisted. The paper fails to report that the company is now supporting a number of local schools in the same area.

GOOD PRACTICE

Peter's experience illustrates that simple awareness of the emerging management issues is not enough. A professional response is required, as in other areas of management practice. The implications of a change in policy and practice need to be thought through before the change is made, and procedures and systems should be in place to ensure that implementation is having the desired effect. Business media are contributing to a growing awareness among managers that something needs to be done. The Seven-Step Process is a vehicle to turn increased awareness into sustainable change.

Learning lessons from Peter

There are a number of lessons Peter can learn from his experiences:

- Publicizing the environmental improvements he instigated and discussing some of the remaining problems with environmental NGOs would have given him a solid foundation. When the media criticized the company, he would have had a credible, independent third-party voice to speak up for him and the company.
- Peter and his colleagues could have backed up their claims to be an equal opportunities employer with evidence of their policies. Change needs to be monitored so that continuous improvement can be demonstrated.
- Surveying employee attitudes toward community activities in advance of implementing his employee volunteer program would have enabled Peter to have avoided confrontation. Even a quick consultation could have helped to identify sensitivities about issues such as enforced volunteering.
- Peter could have given guidance and training to his managers as to why they should get more involved in their local communities, how to do so, and what to watch out for. Working as a team, they could have better managed the transfer of support to schools, rather than peremptorily withdrawing support from local organizations that had long relied on the company, creating a positive attitude to the company rather than ill will.

STEP 1 RECOGNIZING THE TRIGGER

There are many different types of events and incidents that may be the trigger for a manager to take action in line with the *Everybody's Business* management approach.

Trigger situations will range from those that are not of the company's own making, such as changes in government regulations, to a crisis due to a breakdown in business procedures, such as the need for a product recall or poorly executed business activity leading to critical media coverage. The news media regularly report on major businesses falling foul of a problem related to the emerging management issues. This in itself should be sufficient evidence of the importance of making regular reviews of areas where the company may be vulnerable.

Whatever its cause, the trigger represents an opportunity to focus the team or company's attention, not only on the reaction to an incident, but also on the wider subject of the emerging management issues and the firm's response to changing stakeholder expectations. It is better to be in control than to be forced to react under pressure. It is advisable to get ahead of the wave by creating your own trigger and using it as an opportunity to initiate the Seven-Step Process, rather than waiting for a crisis to emerge.

RECOGNIZING LOCAL TRIGGERS

In the immediate working environment of local managers, there are many triggers for action. Some of the most common ones to look out for are:

- Local residents objecting to a new facility or expansion of an existing facility.
- High sickness or absenteeism rates.
- A major customer demanding some form of change in company behavior.
- The local media campaigning against your business.
- Groups of campaigners holding demonstrations outside a store or facility.
- Difficulty in recruiting and retaining talented employees.

STAY AHEAD OF THE WAVE

A trigger can be created in many ways (*see* Identifying Triggers for Action, pp. 216–17). The trigger may emerge in the form of a specific request by a senior manager, or from results contained in research carried out into stakeholder perceptions of the company. It may develop from internal debate and discussion that has been encouraged by an external speaker, or by questions raised in employee work improvement programs, work councils, or briefings. Functional managers are likely to encounter triggers sparked by operational factors, and those working in different industry sectors will experience sector-specific triggers.

Identifying triggers for action

TRIGGER	HOW IT MAY AFFECT YOUR BUSINESS
Shareholder resolution	There has been a marked increase recently in the use of shareholder resolutions to pressure firms. Resolutions filed for annual meetings require a formal management response and can be embarrassing for executives if they expose questionable business practices or impacts. Friends of the Earth, which has published a guide for shareholder activism, is one of a number of campaigning organizations buying stocks in target companies in order to propose resolutions at annual meetings.
Pressure from international investors	Screening services such as the Dow Jones Sustainability Index in the US or the FTSE 4-Good Index in the UK provide data that is used by institutional investors and analysts in assessing companies. Members of the Association of British Insurers, who control a quarter of the British stock market, plan to publish disclosure guidelines on social and environmental information that large investors expect to see in annual reports. After monitoring compliance, they share information with investors.
Pressure from NGOs	NGOs can have a major influence on corporate practices, as was demonstrated in the "Fatal Transactions" campaign by NGO Global Witness. This was to encourage the diamond industry to change business practices that inadvertently supported regimes engaged in conflict in Africa. The regimes used the proceeds of a trade in illicit diamonds to buy arms and support their armies. The diamond company De Beers Consolidated Mines was concerned about the prospect of an NGO campaign aimed at boycotting so-called "blood diamonds." The company worked to head off a boycott by promoting systems that tracked diamonds from mine to finger (*Financial Times*, July 12, 2000; *International Herald Tribune*, August 23, 2000).
Legal requirement from a regulatory agency	There may be a legal requirement to take action and change business. For example, the European Commission brought forward the deadline for introducing regulatory agency bans on CFCs, agreed in the international Montreal Protocol of 1987.
Government call to action	Pressure on companies to act can be leveraged without resorting to the statute book. The South African government encouraged companies operating in the country to help finance job creation programs to help reduce the country's 30 percent unemployment rate.

The regulatory trigger
Under the Montreal Protocol of 1987, chlorofluorocarbons (CFCs) were outlawed. This triggered companies to look for alternatives, such as tetrafluoroethane gas.

TRIGGER	HOW IT MAY AFFECT YOUR BUSINESS
Economic downturn	Increasing numbers of bankruptcies, rising unemployment, and the social unrest resulting from economic downturn can trigger cooperation among companies to cushion the impact for the employees and communities affected. Such a period in the Philippines in the 1970s saw companies coming together to form the Philippines Business for Social Progress to coordinate relief and social investment.
Employee action	Staff within a company may instigate a chain of events. In February 2001, the US Department of Labor ordered a subsidiary of the largest US electric utility, Southern Utility, to pay a projected $5 million damages and reinstate whistleblower Marvin Hobby in his high-level executive position. This followed Hobby's 10-year battle against dismissal after going public over the disposal of the subsidiary's nuclear plants to another company.
Competitor action	More companies now provide attractive product differentiation by incorporating new characteristics that appeal to consumers with heightened social and environmental awareness. Market pressures mean that competitors may be required to follow suit.
Customer action	Boycotts, or threats of boycotts, have been aimed at companies in a range of sectors, notably those in the fur industry, investors in South Africa during the apartheid period, and more recently, companies producing foodstuffs containing genetically engineered ingredients.
Customer demand	Tougher environmental and social criteria by companies in the business to business sector are forcing operational changes by suppliers. They risk losing significant amounts of business if they are not in a position to comply.
Product crisis or personnel crisis	When goods are not up to standard or processes go wrong, the result can be an urgent need to rectify the situation. Examples include Coca-Cola's partial recall in Europe in 2000, following the identification of contaminated product in Belgium, and Texaco's introduction of new diversity measures as a result of litigation over claims of racism from employees. The crisis triggered by the outbreak of foot-and-mouth disease that swept the UK farming industry in 2001 may lead to consumer and political pressure for an overhaul of food production methods. It could also result in changes in relations between producers and supermarkets.
Pressure from a new CEO or nonexecutive director	A nonexecutive director brought in from outside as part of a preparation for a public stock offering may stimulate action. They can ensure that issues such as the environment and diversity are dealt with seriously. This is part of the process of reassuring investors and analysts that the company intends to remain in business and is not a transient operation. For companies seeking external financing, it may be part of the procedure to obtain permission for raising capital, especially where such capital is scarce.
Inspiration	Rather than reacting to, or planning for, specific events, the trigger may come from a fresh vision. One CEO attended the 2001 Davos World Economic Forum of business leaders and politicians and left convinced that his company needed to seriously address the subject of corporate citizenship. He subsequently ensured that policies and practices were introduced.

STEP 2 MAKING A BUSINESS CASE

When a trigger occurs, it may lead to immediate local and tactical action or to a more wide-ranging strategic review of business operations.

In both situations, if you are the manager responsible, you will have to weigh up the plus and minus points of action or inaction, consider likely outcomes, and recommend which course of action to take based on a considered business case.

The business case for action is made by analyzing the associated risks and opportunities, costs or savings. Arm yourself with the best arguments and examples in order to persuade colleagues and senior management that something needs to be done; the ability to marshal the arguments and to articulate the business case will be crucial to securing buy-in and subsequent internal collaboration.

There is no single all-encompassing business case. It will be different depending on the circumstances, although it will usually be structured with the same elements. A business case is usually articulated as a positive or negative argument for action or inaction, as a cost or loss, or as a saving or a gain, in relation to something of value to the business. Value will be measured in a variety of ways: market share, reputation or trust, employee morale and performance, relationships with business partners, and the cost of capital.

When collecting information and gathering data to build a business case, you can choose from one of two approaches, depending on your organizational and management culture:
● An emerging management issues perspective.
● A business needs perspective.

Making a Case from the Emerging Management Issues Perspective

Effective responses to the emerging management issues, from the viewpoint of business strategy, functional responsibility, industry sectors, and small and medium-sized businesses, were illustrated in The Emerging Management Issues.

Business case arguments from this perspective can be presented as opportunities or risks for each issue. It is possible to produce a summary of opportunities and risks that are likely to be encountered frequently for each of the issues (see pp. 220–23).

Siemens stock exchange listing
Additional reporting requirements for a stock exchange listing may provide a business case. The listing of Siemens on the New York Stock Exchange in March 2001 was the opportunity for an enhanced drive on the company's environmental and social practices.

The business case for the emerging management issue:
Ecology and environment

OPPORTUNITIES	RISKS
● Energy savings through cleaner technologies and conservation.	● Fines for breaches of regulations.
● Cost savings through new packaging, requiring less waste disposal.	● Expenditure in new plant or equipment required as a result of stringent regulations on emissions.
● Growing market for ecologically efficient technologies, products, and services.	● Increased insurance costs due to global warming.
● Market opportunities for market leaders through raised performance standards from regulators and customers.	● Limits to physical development or exploration because of threat to habitats and landscape.
● Becoming brand or company of choice for consumers interested in corporate environmental consciousness and conservation.	● Rising landfill and disposal costs.
	● Increasing take-back legislation, specifying that producers accept responsibility for disposal of material such as packaging.
	● Loss of consumers, or interest group action, due to spills and contamination or use of materials from non-sustainable sources.
	● Inheriting environmental liabilities as a result of merger or acquisition.
	● Disqualification from bidding for contracts that require adherence to specific standards.

PREVENTING POLLUTION: 3M

In its environmental policy, US conglomerate 3M says that it is: "more environmentally effective, technically sound, and less costly to prevent pollution at the source than to use conventional end-of-pipe procedures." The company has eliminated 771,000 tons of pollutants and saved $810 million with its Pollution Prevention Pays effort. *Visions: Socially Responsible Investing*, 3M, 1998.

"3M is moving beyond an era of compliance with environmental regulations toward one focused on sustainable development. We are convinced that, in the future, the most environmentally responsible companies also will be the most competitive companies." L. D. DeSimone, Chair and CEO of 3M, quoted in John Dalla Costa, *The Ethical Imperative*, 1998.

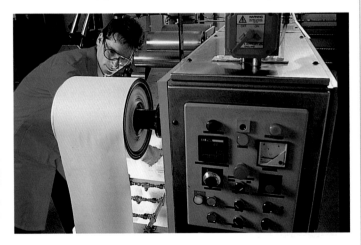

A cleaner process
The technical staff at 3M manufacture cleaning products without the use of solvents, a process that helps to cut down on harmful emissions being released into the air.

The business case for the emerging management issue:
Health and well-being

OPPORTUNITIES	RISKS
● Growth in market for products and services oriented to health and well-being.	● Costly recalls and damaged reputation due to consumer and interest group action on health and safety aspects of products.
● Productive employees and good company morale as a result of comprehensive employee healthcare or health insurance.	● Costs of absenteeism or low productivity due to overworked and stressed employees.
● High retention rates of staff because of controlled recruitment and training costs, and flexible working practices.	● High turnover of trained staff unable to achieve work/life balance who leave, possibly to go to competitors who are offering more flexibility.
● Savings on absenteeism when employees are motivated.	● Loss of trained staff and costs of secondary care for victims' families resulting from HIV/AIDS.
● Lower sickness rates because of health promotion via company communication channels.	● Time-consuming litigation from employees claiming for work-related illness or injury.
	● Expensive provision of basic healthcare if state system is ineffectual.

WORKING TO PREVENT DISEASE: ESKOM

Eskom is the state owned power utility of South Africa. It is one of the world's largest electrical utilities, and has a workforce that is 85 percent male, 68 percent of which are between the ages of 30 and 49.

Educating the workforce about AIDS

Eskom has supported the foundation of the South African Business Council on HIV/AIDS as a way of combining health resources with other companies.

"Eskom, South Africa's main electricity utility, has estimated that AIDS could cost 15 percent of its payroll by 2005. The firm has invested $750,000 in AIDS education and distributing condoms to its workers, and is working with the government and the mining companies to reduce HIV infection among prostitutes working around its power station."

"Corporate Hospitality," *The Economist,* November 27, 1999.

The business case for the emerging management issue:
Diversity and human rights

OPPORTUNITIES	RISKS
● Competitive edge gained by attracting and retaining the best employees from a diverse pool of talent, if effective policies and practices in place. ● Access to preferred supplier status if stipulated standards of performance are met. ● Higher market share won from concerned consumers because of independent verification of standards. ● Familiarity with the needs of diverse minorities spurs new product development and penetration in minority markets.	● Damage to reputation and loss of consumers or business-to-business orders if human rights violations are alleged to have been carried out by the company or its suppliers. ● Disqualification from bidding for contracts that require adherence to specific standards. ● Increased costs in replacing employees who leave because of a climate of discrimination or lack of belief in advancement possibilities. ● Lengthy litigation costs, and if cases are upheld, large fines, with risk of class action suits for discrimination. ● Added transaction costs if company actions perpetuate corrupt practice.

POLICING THE SUPPLIER: C&A

In 1999, UK retailer C&A placed an advertisement in the *Financial Times Responsible Business Magazine* saying that 100 suppliers and 400 individual production units that once supplied C&A were now barred following audits of their workplace conditions by C&A's Service Organization for Compliance Audit Management (SOCAM) team. SOCAM auditors made unannounced visits to over 1,400 production units throughout the world. C&A's aim was to improve conditions rather than shut companies down, and when 40 of the suppliers took corrective action, they were allowed to work for the retailer again.

Monitoring the supply chain
An auditor from SOCAM visits one of the organizations that supplies C&A to ensure that they conform to the workplace standards that are set by the retailer.

The business case for the emerging management issue:
Communities

OPPORTUNITIES	RISKS
● A bank of goodwill formed by good community relations providing early warning of potential problems before they become crises.	● Expensive and time-consuming clashes with antagonistic local communities.
● Share risks, gain access to information and expertise, and benefit reputation by forming partnerships with local communities that are of common identity or interest.	● High security costs if operating in physical conflict with local communities.
	● Adverse effect on expansion or relocation plans if local community not brought on board.
● Influence quality of the local supply base by sharing good practice and investing in local training.	● Costs of remedial education when state system produces undereducated workforce.
● Attracting potential client businesses as well as ensuring an attractive location for employees by investing in local economic development programs.	● Pressure from governments to provide low-cost services to unserved markets.
● Mitigate opposition to planning applications through dialogue.	● Danger of community relations issue becoming a high-profile cause for campaigning NGOs.
● Better employee skills from employee volunteering in the community.	● Backlash from raising but not fulfilling local expectations to provide jobs and social investment.

NURTURING A SUPPLIER:
KUAUI MARRIOT BEACH RESORT

Staff at the Kuaui Marriott Resort and Beach Club, part of the Marriott International Group, worked with a local food bank to create a program called Hui Mea'ai (this translates from Hawaiian as "an association providing things to eat"). Chefs at the hotel wanted to offer local dishes to guests. The challenge was to source the quality and quantity of food required. With the Kuaui Food Bank, a local NGO, the hotel helped establish a farm and created a new fresh produce brand. This is sold to many other restaurants and hotels. The result was quality fresh indigenous food and local economic development (*Green Hotelier*, July 1999).

Benefiting from partnership
George Liechty, director of food and beverage, displays some of the fruits of the mutually beneficial partnership between his hotel and a local NGO.

Making a Case from the Business Needs Perspective

An alternative way of building a business case is to approach it from the perspective of building people, the business, and the corporate reputation.

The examples of opportunities and risks presented by the emerging management issues can be used as prompts to help create a business case expressed in these three terms.

BUILDING PEOPLE

A company needs to use every opportunity to build its people by attracting, retaining, and developing the most talented employees at every level throughout the organization.

Recruiting new employees

McKinsey research concluded that only three percent of organizations have sufficient staff talent to reach five-year organizational objectives (*The War for Talent*, McKinsey, 1998). Therefore, it is imperative that you create the workplace conditions that will attract the best staff to your company: potential employees look for adequate remuneration, flexible and family-friendly workplace practices, the opportunity to progress, and a small but increasing number also want employers who share their personal values, for example, a belief in human rights or support for disadvantaged communities.

- Allied Dunbar (now part of Zurich Financial Services) ran recruitment advertisements that mentioned the firm's community involvement, prompting four times as many responses as other advertisements in the same series.

Retaining employees

The factors that influence retention are similar to those that attract employees, but are modified by exposure to real life in a firm. They include respect, fair treatment, interesting work, fair reward and recognition, good communication, and management that follows words with action. Research by Bain and Co., quoted in *Winning with Integrity*, *Business in the Community*

> The face the organization presents to the outside world matters to us, call this the dinner party effect. When we meet someone and tell them where we work, what does the label say about us?
>
> Stanton Marris, *Magnetic Attraction – The Potential of Talent and the Corporate Brand*, Shared Learning Project, 2001.

(2000), concluded that there is correlation between firms with high employee retention and those with greatest customer retention and greatest profitability.

- Oil company Chevron in San Francisco expanded its environmental community outreach program after learning that 75 percent of employees described themselves as environmental activists.
- Danube Knitwear in Baja, Hungary, introduced preventative healthcare services for employees, such as screening for breast and ovarian tumors, and testing for osteoporosis, which the Hungarian health service could not offer. Staff turnover, said the firm, fell sharply and "loyalty and mentality" have changed "tremendously." The company consequently joined with other local employers to share their experience through the "Caring Employer's Club."

Financial Times Responsible Business Magazine, Financial Times, 1999.

Developing employees

People are aware that security of employment is being replaced by security of employability. As a result, employers wishing to develop and retain staff offer opportunities for learning and personal development.

- General Motors offers access to distance learning to MBA level via the internet to 88,000 white-collar workers. This is through GM's university and partners: a private company, Columbia Business School, Stanford University, the University of Chicago Graduate School of Business, and the London School of Economics. "GM Spins Web for Staff," *Financial Times*, April 5, 2001.

BUILDING THE BUSINESS

A company can build the business through a number of means. These include reducing and avoiding costs, increasing sales, and boosting profits.

Reducing and avoiding costs

Lean corporations are constantly seeking ways to eliminate unnecessary costs. Savings may be direct and current, such as in improved environmental performance, or avoidance of potential future costs. For example, investing money in

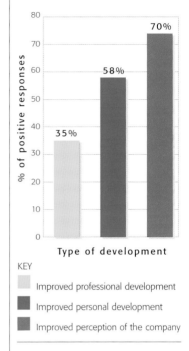

How employees respond when employers support volunteering

KEY

☐ Improved professional development

■ Improved personal development

■ Improved perception of the company

Positive responses to employer-supported volunteering

IT consultants FI Group (now Xansa UK) surveyed staff whose volunteering had been supported by their employers. Seventy percent reported that, as well as personal or professional development, they had an improved perception of their company.

response to the emerging management issues can reduce the costs of remedial education for new recruits who are below necessary educational standards, and avoid the potential costs of litigation for failings in diversity and human rights.

● The US computer business Unisys has reduced its manufacturing emissions, notably hazard waste, by 92 percent since 1988. More efficient production systems and avoiding disposal costs save the company $6 million every year. *Visions: Socially Responsive Investing,* Neuberger and Berman, 1998.

● US insurance giant American General settled claims that it charged African–Americans more for insurance than whites with a payment of $206 million. UPI, 2000.

● The cost to restaurant chain Shoney Inc. to settle a class-action suit brought by 20,000 employees for alleged discrimination was $132 million. John Weiser and Simon Zadek, *Conversations with Disbelievers*, 2000.

Boosting profits

Sound management of the emerging management issues can help increase sales and boost profits, support winning contracts, and help develop new routes into markets.

● Procter & Gamble Italy worked with ActionAid to raise more than $1.65 million (over 3 billion lire) for health centers and water projects in Africa. Some 170,000 consumers responded to leaflets in packs requesting donations. Sales of

Mutual benefits
Proctor & Gamble's support of ActionAid in Africa helped to alleviate the meager living conditions of the poor as well as increase the firm's sales.

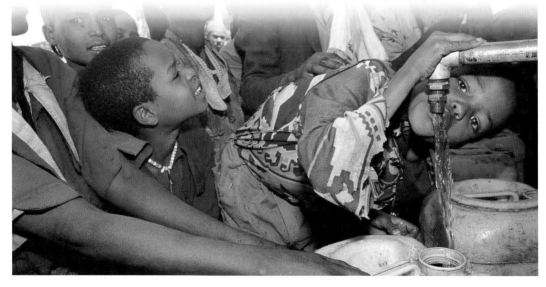

Dash laundry products rose by five percent during the promotion. Glen Peters, *Waltzing with the Raptors*, 1999.

- UK construction firm John Laing actively supports and contributes to UK community development projects. They believe this track record and their understanding of community needs aided their selection for a $128 million, seven-year regeneration project in Greater London. The leader of the local town council said the project was "much more than a housing program, and Laing met our wider goals of social and economic regeneration."

BUILDING REPUTATION

A company can help to build its reputation by gaining the trust of both the public and its own employees, and securing a license to operate.

Goodwill and a license to operate

Companies operating on a global scale require opportunities to establish themselves locally, access markets, earn a good reputation, and gain a license to operate. Managers must understand political and governmental systems in the countries in which they are operating, and be able to access officials and politicians. Engaging proactively with policy-makers to build trust is essential, and creatively managing the emerging management issues can help achieve these goals.

- The International Center for Alcohol Policies was established in the mid-1990s to help reduce alcohol abuse worldwide, promote understanding of alcohol's role in society, and encourage dialogue and partnerships between the alcohol industry and the public health community. Sponsors include Diageo, Allied Domecq, Heineken, South African Breweries, and Fosters Brewing Company. Jane Nelson, *Competitiveness and Communities*, Prince of Wales International Business Leaders Forum, 1999.

Changing expectations of corporate behavior provide both a threat to brand and corporate reputation and an opportunity for differentiation in a crowded marketplace.

- UK home improvement store B&Q encouraged partnerships between its stores and local disability groups to develop training in disability awareness and improve service

> "It takes 20 years to build a reputation and five minutes to ruin it."
>
> Warren Buffett.

provision for disabled people. Specific needs of people with disabilities are addressed by local staff and local groups. The long-term benefits are improved reputation, increased sales to disabled people, an increase in employee satisfaction, and for the disabled, access to stores that meet their needs.

Winning Over Stakeholders

It is important to know which arguments to use for different stakeholders if they are to be convinced of the need for action and provide the appropriate support or capital for necessary expenditure.

Each stakeholder group has its particular concerns and agendas and will therefore be swayed by different information. A good source of data will be the actions and activities of competitive companies in a similar industry sector, or in studies by industry or trade associations. Above all, you will be required to build and maintain trust with stakeholders who will often be geographically far-flung. The test for whether trust is granted is when you are given the benefit of the doubt during a crisis. In the table below, some of the most popular arguments are listed in the form of expression a manager may use to a range of key stakeholders.

Making a business case to different stakeholders

TO SHAREHOLDERS	TO FELLOW MANAGERS	TO CONSUMERS	TO BUSINESS PARTNERS
● We are alert to these issues as part of a culture of innovation. ● Action is an integral part of our quality management system. ● We take action now, saving costs later on in a global war for talent. ● These issues are important to attract recruits.	● Every part of the business should minimize risks and maximize opportunities. This applies to all staff on all types of contracts. ● We need to attract talented staff by creating a win-win culture appealing to those with similar values. ● The company will build trust with stakeholders.	● We know you have a choice. We want you to trust in us and to believe that we will correct any honest mistakes we make. ● We will minimize our negative impacts and maximize our positive contribution to society because it is in our and your best interests.	● Complex relationships with different types of business partners are necessary today. ● Stakeholder engagement provides learning, improves transparency, and increases accountability. This carries over to our relationship with you.

STEP 3 SCOPING THE ISSUES

The process of scoping will help you to identify and assess the significance of risks and opportunities that your business faces in the light of the emerging management issues and rising stakeholder expectations.

Scoping involves a number of procedures, and there are tools available to aid you in the process. These include mapping the issues, stakeholder consultation, benchmarking against other relevant companies, business impact assessment, and the use of scenarios.

Mapping the Issues on a Corporate Radar Screen

Start by brainstorming the social, ethical, and environmental issues facing the company, using a mock radar screen to map their relative or potential importance to your company.

You can use a variety of criteria. For example, are the issues live or dormant? Approaching or receding? You could map issues using a scale of probability, showing which ones are most likely to actually impact on the business.

Whichever criteria you choose, you will require market intelligence to map the issues accurately. Trade media, industry association reports and conferences, commissioned studies, competitors' web sites – all of these are potential souces of

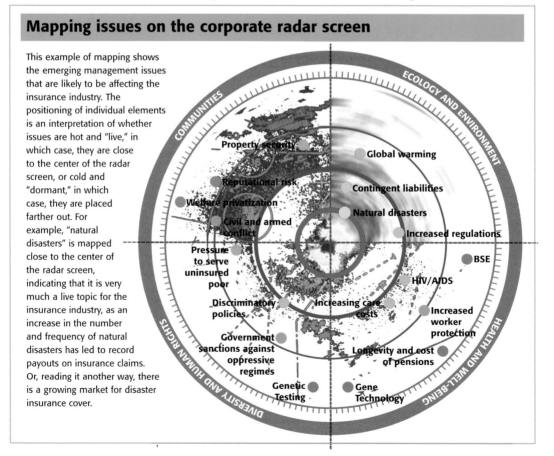

Mapping issues on the corporate radar screen

This example of mapping shows the emerging management issues that are likely to be affecting the insurance industry. The positioning of individual elements is an interpretation of whether issues are hot and "live," in which case, they are close to the center of the radar screen, or cold and "dormant," in which case, they are placed farther out. For example, "natural disasters" is mapped close to the center of the radar screen, indicating that it is very much a live topic for the insurance industry, as an increase in the number and frequency of natural disasters has led to record payouts on insurance claims. Or, reading it another way, there is a growing market for disaster insurance cover.

COMMUNITIES
ECOLOGY AND ENVIRONMENT
HEALTH AND WELL-BEING
DIVERSITY AND HUMAN RIGHTS

Property security
Global warming
Reputational risk
Contingent liabilities
Welfare privatization
Natural disasters
Civil and armed conflict
Increased regulations
Pressure to serve uninsured poor
BSE
HIV/AIDS
Discriminatory policies
Increasing care costs
Increased worker protection
Government sanctions against oppressive regimes
Longevity and cost of pensions
Genetic Testing
Gene Technology

opinion and data on how the emerging management issues may be affecting your business or industry sector. A number of these key specialized sources are listed in Signposts at the end of this section (see p. 302).

TRACKING THE DEVELOPMENT OF ISSUES

An issue which is important to a company today may not be tomorrow. On the other hand, events may result in a subject that was on the edge of the radar screen gaining relevance rapidly. Keeping track of the shifting development dynamic of issues is a constant process.

In *When Good Companies Do Bad Things*, Peter Schwartz and Blair Gibb provide a useful analysis of how issues can come to prominence by looking at how issues of concern to NGOs may emerge over time, highlighting five distinct phases of development:

Tracking the emergence of issues

EMERGING	CAMPAIGNING	CODIFYING	MONITORING	CONSULTING
				Environment
			Gender/race	
			Third World minimum wages	
			*Human rights	
			Learning organizations	
		*Family-friendly		
			*AIDS	
		*Community		
	Genetically modified food			
Human genetics				
	*Disability			
	*Sexual orientation			

Key
* = Issues more of concern in developed countries

● Emerging – an activist NGO floats an issue as being a dilemma or a concern.
● Campaigning – NGOs, usually in a coalition, initiate a campaign to which public opinion either responds strongly, as with the long-running baby food formula controversy, or weakly, as was the case with the Disney boycott campaigns, fought by Southern Baptists over Disney extending spouses' benefits to same-sex partners.
● Codifying – with enough public response, governments, sometimes with intergovernmental bodies and NGOs, participate in drafting new laws, regulations, and codes.
● Monitoring – NGOs become active monitors of legal, regulatory, and code compliance.
● Consulting – NGOs are resources for companies in future policy decisions.

Tracking issues
An assessment of where selected issues might be positioned in 2001 in the Five Stage Model developed in Peter Schwartz and Blair Gibb, When Good Companies Do Bad Things, *1999.*

Stakeholder Consultation

As part of the scoping exercise, take stock of the interests and concerns of each of your company's principal stakeholder groups. Assess what actions might be taken to alleviate risks and meet stakeholder needs and expectations.

Each business will have its own particular version of this assessment (see Responding to Stakeholder Interests, below), based on various sources: surveys of attitudes among employees and influential opinion-formers, market research,

Responding to stakeholder interests

Six key stakeholder groups are identified below. The second column lists their needs or reason for being; the third, the issues which are on their agenda today in light of the emerging management issues; and the fourth, how management might respond. Managers can create their own stakeholder interest matrix.

STAKEHOLDERS	NEEDS	TODAY'S AGENDA	POTENTIAL MANAGEMENT RESPONSES
Investors	Return on investment	Corporate governance and ethics.	• Ensure compliance with best practice in corporate governance.
		Rise of interest in ethical investments.	• Ensure measurement and reporting of ethical impacts to institutional investors.
		Concern with operational, social, and environmental risks, and exposure through merger and acquisition (M&A) activity.	• Ensure adequate risk assessment management processes are in place. • Ensure due diligence procedures incorporate social and environmental issues.
		Vulnerability of corporate reputation.	• Ensure reputational assurance processes in place.
Employees	Jobs, reward, and recognition	Prospect of downsizing and manufacture relocation.	• Consult with employee representatives regularly, keeping them informed of potential operational changes and personnel implications. • Work in partnership with local authorities to mitigate impact of closures or downsizing.
		Pressures on health and well-being.	• Work toward best practice in employee relations and benefits, including flexible working and life-long learning. • Ensure processes are in place to monitor employee attitudes, concerns, and learn from their ideas.

from investors and analysts, and intelligence gathered across the organization. A process of stakeholder dialogue not only provides an ongoing source of information, but also allows two-way communication between company and stakeholder groups. It thus identifies areas of mutual interest or of potential conflict.

This process of stakeholder consultation may sound arduous and negative for companies, with extra burdens, more pressures, and more conflicting interests to balance. However, there is a beneficial side. Managers and organizations who understand these developments will be better placed to

STAKEHOLDERS	NEEDS	TODAY'S AGENDA	POTENTIAL MANAGEMENT RESPONSES
Customers	Safe, reliable products	Consumers making purchasing decisions based on environmental, sourcing, and workplace practices; human rights and diversity, and animal welfare issues.	● Ensure that life-cycle and business process impacts of products and services are understood, and steps taken to minimize negative impacts. ● Promote positive programs that appeal to consumer concerns.
Suppliers	Regular orders, prompt payment	Compliance with customers' environmental and workplace standards.	● Form networks or clubs of suppliers and help them to build their capacity to meet changing standards.
Government	Thriving private sector, providing employment opportunities, serving citizens, and paying taxes	Attracting foreign direct investment (FDI).	● Negotiate appropriate terms during relocation and the opening of new operations.
		Establishing public–private funded projects.	● Enter public–private partnerships. ● Engage in public policy dialogue to help improve efficiency of public sector delivery and institutions.
		Looking to offload some areas of public service delivery.	● Business opportunities in previously government-run institutions.
Local communities	Employment opportunities and contribution to the local economy	Planning gains in return for awarding a license to operate.	● Initiate regular dialogue with local community representatives.
		Support for social and physical infrastructure, such as education and health.	● Undertake community needs assessment. Offer community cash and noncash contributions.
		Displacement and relocation of indigenous peoples.	● Handle with sensitivity and show respect for ancient rights and customs.

spot and exploit new market opportunities. They will also achieve sustainable business while simultaneously using their power to improve social conditions. They can build up a bank of trust as well, which will be useful if the company ever faces criticism.

By minimizing the negative and maximizing the positive impact of the emerging management issues, value-added results can be achieved for shareholders at the same time as value-added results for society.

Benchmarking Against Other Companies

By benchmarking itself against other firms, a company can gain a sense of its own relative performance and record its improvement and progress over time.

Benchmark policies, procedures, and practices, focusing on performance or resulting reputation, in tandem with one or all stakeholder groups. The process can be done entirely in-house, may involve in-house self-measurement with an external compilation of comparative data, or may be carried out completely externally.

Benchmarking is part of the spirit of creative swiping that successful sustainable organizations practice. Consider a number of samples to benchmark against:

- Other businesses in the same sector.
- Businesses within a particular function such as marketing.
- A recognized business grouping such as the Fortune 500 or the Financial Times 100 (FTSE 100)
- An externally generated listing of the Most Admired Companies (listings such as the Most Admired Companies to Work For are published by *Fortune* and the *Financial Times*, among others)
- Your company's own list of companies against which it benchmarks for other purposes.

Your company may also be a member of mutual learning networks with groups of organizations such as these.

> Benchmarking is a process of systematically comparing your own organizational structure, processes, and performance against those of best practice organizations, for the purpose of achieving sustainable business excellence.
>
> British Quality Foundation, 2001.

Assessing Business Impact

A useful process to follow during scoping is business impact assessment. This can be particularly beneficial when dealing with emerging issues of communities, for example, in the context of a market in transition, or in a newly industrialized country.

This tool, developed by Jane Nelson of The Prince of Wales International Business Leaders Forum, looks at what impact the business actually has – both positive and negative. One way of appreciating the impact of the business is to think of corporate activity in three broad segments. The first, and most important of these segments in terms of impact, comprises core business activities, everyday operations, and business links. This is detailed in the table overleaf (*see* Assessing the Business Impact of Core Business Operations, p. 236). Social investment, the second segment of corporate activity, is a process of managed involvement with the community and social issues. The third segment is business engagement in the formulation of public policy.

SOCIAL INVESTMENT

Sometimes labeled corporate citizenship, social investment is based on a recognition of enlightened self-interest, centered on creating sustainable partnerships based on mutual benefits for business and society. It incorporates traditional corporate giving and philanthropy and can be thought of as a continuum, with philanthropy at one end and enlightened self-interest at the other. Not exclusively cash-focused, it takes many forms, releasing a range of noncash corporate assets for community development, such as cause-related marketing tie-ins. Activity in social investment bridges the functions and operations of a company and can be used as a tool to address business issues.

- In 2001, Cisco offered 8,500 employees facing layoffs the option of being paid to help a local charity if they pledged to do so for one year. Cisco paid one-third of their salaries if they committed to help a nonprofit use of the internet, with a two-month period of grace at the end of the year to find a position at the company.

Assessing the business impact of core business operations

Of the three categories of business impact: core business, social investment, and engagement in public policy, core business operations have the greatest potential to have substantive and sustainable impact. Eight categories of core business activities are listed below, along with corresponding potential multipliers and corporate examples.

CORE BUSINESS ACTIVITIES	BUSINESS MULTIPLIERS	EXAMPLES
Generating investment and income	● How much investment and income is a company generating in host countries and communities? ● How is it allocated between taxes, wages, shareholders, business partners, and communities?	"As economic engines, Shell companies are now providing more than $51 billion in tax revenue each year" *People, Planet and Profits, The Shell Report,* Shell, 2001.
Creating jobs	● Looking at issues of quantity and quality in direct jobs as well as changes, through job creation or loss, over time. ● Assessing the wider job creation multipliers in indirect jobs. *Assessing impact* *Coca-Cola has assessed the positive impact it has had on job creation in different national markets as it has expanded globally.*	The Coca-Cola Company employs some 30,000 people. It also employs thousands more through bottling partners and its network of customers. The vast majority of these people are nationals of host countries, locally hired and trained. In the University of South Carolina's 1995 study of Poland, it was estimated that for every direct job, 10 jobs were created by Coca-Cola.
Building local business systems	● Finding local joint venture partners. ● Investigating backward linkages or upstream relationships. ● Looking at forward linkages or downstream relationships.	The San Miguel Food Group (SMFG) is a major chicken producer, and corn feed represents about 60 percent of its production costs. In the past, Filipino farmers couldn't compete with foreign imports of corn feed. San Miguel worked with the government and with NGOs, such as the Philippines Business for Social Progress, to train the farmers to improve their productivity and ability to negotiate and deal with traders. Access to credit, organic fertilizers, hybrids, and markets were targeted. Corn marketing contracts were signed by SMFG with some 30 groups of farmers. *Philippines Enterprise* *The Phillippines Business for Social Progress is an alliance of companies which, among many development projects, has been marshaling business resources to develop indigenous rural enterprise.*

CORE BUSINESS ACTIVITIES	BUSINESS MULTIPLIERS	EXAMPLES
Developing human resources	• Skills development and quality of life in the workplace. • Building human capital along the value chain and in local communities.	Gas company BOC has a longstanding commitment to the development of both technical and managerial skills in the 60 or so countries in which it operates. It has established welding schools, for example, in Poland, South Africa, and Russia, which are aimed at helping to develop local technical skills. The services at these centers are not only targeted at experienced welders, who may or may not be BOC staff, but also at small-scale entrepreneurs and unemployed youth.
Sharing international standards and world-class business practices	• Health, safety, and environmental standards. • Worker's rights and human rights standards. • Ethical business practices. • Quality standards and management practices.	Responsible Care is the chemical industry's voluntary initiative that encourages improvement in all aspects of health, safety, environmental performance, and openness in communication about its activities and its achievements. It is global, targeted at any company involved in the production, handling, use, transportation, or disposal of chemicals. This gives it an outreach to about 86 percent of the chemical industry.

"One of the most important competencies that business can bring to support the development of host countries and communities is business management skills; a customer focused, task-driven, results orientation which can be applied to tackle sustainable development challenges as well as commercial ones." Goran Lindahl, then-CEO ABB, presentation to UN Secretary General, New York, 1997.

Supporting technological development and transfer	• The nature and extent of research and development. • Linking hardware, such as equipment and materials, with software, including skills, managerial systems, and information. • Access to the benefits of technology.	In the early nineties, Norsk Hydro led the launch of a research program called MARICULT (Marine Cultivation), to clarify possibilities for increased sustainable production and the harvesting of food and raw materials from the oceans. The team includes experts from the Norwegian and international marine science community. Openness has been fundamental to the initiative, and government agencies, environmental organizations, and the media have been given free access to the research planning.

Sustainable production research

Experimental basins at Solbergstrand, near Drøbak in Norway, are being used for testing the possibilities of sustainable production of food and raw materials from the ocean.

Based on a model and examples from Jane Nelson, *Competitiveness and Communities*, The Prince of Wales International Business Leaders Forum, World Bank, and UNDP, 1999.

Assessing the business impact of core business operations

CORE BUSINESS ACTIVITIES	BUSINESS MULTIPLIERS	EXAMPLES
Establishing physical and institutional infrastructure	● Preparation for unintended consequences. ● Physical – plant and machinery, roads, dams, transportation systems, telecommunications, water and sanitation, domestic waste management, housing. ● Institutional – legal and financial systems and standards.	Prior to merger with MMC Marsh McLennan in 1999, Sedgwick was one of the world's leading international risk consulting, insurance and reinsurance brokering, employee benefits, and financial services groups, with operations in some 60 countries. It was the first international broker licensed to operate in China. In May 1996, Sedgwick played a lead role in establishing the China Employee Benefits Forum. It was a nonprofit organization owned by its members, which included over 25 foreign-owned companies, several Chinese enterprises, many universities, and government ministries. The forum was established in response to a number of drivers, such as the need for social security reform (a key element of general Chinese economic strategy) and the need for adequate resources, which could then be accessed through public/private partnerships. There was also the desire to ensure that employers, both domestic and foreign, became contributors to the social security system.
Providing appropriate products and services	● Product creation. ● Product marketing and distribution. ● Product use and impact. ● Product access.	Worldwide demand for fish is rising, but it is estimated that about 70 percent of the world's commercial fish stocks are overexploited or fully fished. Unilever is the owner of several major frozen fish companies and brand names. As a key customer of the fishing industry, it is well placed to help foster a more sustainable approach to fishing. In February 1996 it formed a conservation partnership with the World Wide Fund for Nature (WWF). The objective was to use market forces and the power of consumer choice to create incentives for sustainable fishing, by establishing a certification program. In 1997, the Marine Stewardship Council (MSC) was established as an independent, self-financing body to implement this objective. Unilever has committed to source all of its fish from fisheries certified to MSC standards by the year 2005.

"... most of our potential impact is outside our direct control – when our raw materials are produced and when consumers use and dispose of our products. We have to understand and work with others to minimize these impacts."

Niall FitzGerald and Morris Tabaksblat, joint chairmen, Unilever, Unilever Environmental Report, 1997.

PUBLIC POLICY

Scope the company's contribution to society through its involvement in the formulation and implementation of public policy. Business representatives can advise elected officials, and serve on government taskforces, or employees can be assigned to assist in a government department for a period. More typically, becoming involved in public policy means contributing to the development of business views and ideas inside trade associations, industry sector bodies, or general employers' representative organizations. These are promoted as a collective business contribution to public policy. How to handle public policy to optimize positive impacts for business and society is discussed further in Step Six, Engaging Stakeholders (*see* pp. 260–86).

Using Scenarios

There is still the "X Factor" – what might be coming over the horizon? Many organizations use the device of scenarios as a way of attempting to answer this question. Scenarios are not forecasts of the future, but a way of anticipating what may happen and a way of planning for different possible futures.

Some organizations develop their own scenarios. Typically this is done by a team of people who examine drivers and trends in the fields of politics, economics, technology, the environment, and social issues.

The team has to identify what Peter Schwartz calls the predetermined elements versus the critical uncertainties. From these, the objective is to derive two or three consistent visions of the future (Peter Schwartz, *The Art of the Long View*, 1992).

The process of building scenarios can help participants to envision the future of the business and the need for action in response to changes. Scenarios can be used as a practical tool in the scoping of risks and opportunities of the emerging management issues. They can also be helpful at other stages of the seven steps:

- Scenarios may be the trigger (Step One) that prompts a company to take the emerging management issues seriously.
- Scenarios can be a way of involving the board and senior management team in understanding a business case. This helps to secure their commitment to research the impact of the emerging management issues (Step Two).
- Scenarios may lead to action (Step Four).
- Scenarios may help to shape priorities and inform the business process (Step Five).
- Scenarios can be developed with, or presented to, employees in training, and to management and staff in briefing (Step Six).

Scoping in Action

In undertaking scoping, a business will miss things if it hands the task entirely to consultants or outsiders. Instead, assemble a team – a hit squad – from different functions and levels of seniority across the business.

You will almost certainly discover that there are people with passions and expertise that you can use. External advisers may help to facilitate the process, and help access specialized expertise as needed. Such as squad will reinforce the benefits of interconnected management, described on page 174.

The potential application of scoping can be illustrated with the case of an imaginary enterprise: "Everybody's Business Inc," based on real-life companies all over the world. This fictional company established a hitsquad to scope out risks and opportunities presented by the emerging management issues, and the impact of changing stakeholder expectations for their business.

The company had not faced any dramatic crisis or wakeup call. The trigger was a series of seemingly isolated developments in which some nonexecutive directors had belatedly seen a pattern: results of surveys on perceptions of the business, no ranking in company awards lists compared to peers, poor performance at university recruitment fairs, poor retention of those who did join, and rising inquiries from business customers about environmental performance.

THE HIT SQUAD IN ACTION

The board instructed executive managers to assemble a cross-company team with people from different nationalities, a range of business functions, and varying lengths of service and seniority in the company. This hit squad drew together a range of inputs for scoping:

- There was a fresh reading of recent employee satisfaction surveys, customer complaints, and focus group reports.
- Future scenarios were developed by managers and facilitated by an outside expert.
- The squad made an exhaustive keyword search for the company and its key competitors on the internet, particularly focusing on websites critical of business.

- A specially expanded version of the company's regular reputation profile survey was extended from its usual focus on analysts, investors, and politicians to include a wider range of opinion formers from civil society organizations.
- An announcement about the hit squad was made on the company's global intranet, generating a substantial number of unsolicited inputs from employees.
- The squad carried out a public policy development review showing that compliance costs could be reduced.

Suggestions from the employees lead to an extra strand in the scoping exercise: a challenge from the CEO to employees to identify environmental projects for the company that could demonstrate payback in three years or less.

A country manager had already completed a mini-version of a similar scoping exercise in a project with his local chamber of commerce. This demonstrated how the company was having a positive impact on the local economy through a range of business multipliers. The same manager was asked to lead an exercise with colleagues from across the firm to see if those impacts and multipliers were applicable on an international level.

External consultants working with the hit squad on the scoping exercise took individual members on a carefully programmed series of visits into the community and to events where issues of business and society were discussed. These included debates organized by an environmental group and by an alliance of businesses interested in their impact on society.

From this rich mix of inputs, a series of possible risks and potential opportunities for the company were identified. They were ranked according to the probability of them occurring and the extent of the negative or positive impact on the business and its stakeholders. The hit squad made sure to look for activities that might lead to early wins in order to gain confidence among colleagues in the business.

Several of the issues required further research and had long-term strategic implications. These formed the basis for a report especially prepared for the board, which included recommendations for stretching of existing company policies and practices or new additional elements.

STEP 4 COMMITTING TO ACTION

You have gathered evidence and mapped the challenges that lie ahead. Now it is time to act, demonstrating your personal commitment, engaging your team, and gaining support from your company.

You are being asked to commit to actions that minimize risks and maximize opportunities presented by the emerging management issues and by rising expectations, to the benefit of business and the wider community. A vocabulary has evolved to describe the subject of this commitment: corporate social responsibility, socially responsible business, enlightened self-interest, good corporate citizenship. Some companies aspire to the notion of sustainable development, which is development in this generation that does not prejudice possibilities for future generations.

The term "sustainable business excellence" is often used to emphasize that a company is striving to be a leading example of good practice and that it is built to last. Such businesses use the triple bottom line of economic prosperity, social equity, and environmental quality as a principle to aspire to, or as a way of measuring and defining their success, whereas other companies just use the financial bottom line.

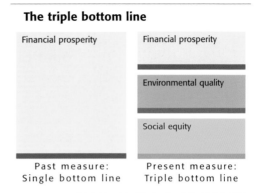

The triple bottom line

Financial prosperity	Financial prosperity
	Environmental quality
	Social equity
Past measure: Single bottom line	Present measure: Triple bottom line

Adapted from John Elkington, *Cannibals with Forks*, 1997.

"Society depends on the economy and the economy depends on the global ecosystem, whose health represents the ultimate bottom line."
John Elkington, *Cannibals with Forks*, 1997.

Aiming for sustainable development
Sustainable development involves the simultaneous pursuit of economic prosperity, environmental quality, and social equity. Companies aiming for sustainability need to perform not against a single financial bottom line, as they used to, but against a triple bottom line.

Behind all of these phrases is the concept of ensuring long-term shareholder added value by simultaneously adding value to society. Your commitment will act as a compass, directing you toward a win-win management approach in your decision-making and in your dealings with others. This is no soft option or flight of fancy, but is practical and achievable.

What are the implications if this approach is not adopted?

It would be a paradox indeed if, in their competition to provide the means of life ever more efficiently, business managed to destroy much of what sustains life... It is a sobering thought that half of the world's 500 largest economies are corporations who are answerable in law only to themselves and their stockholders. We have to rely on the internal values of those that control them to keep them honest and decent; and we must hope that those values are focused on what is good for all of us, not just themselves; that they think of themselves as communities fueled by purpose, rather than as the personal properties of their owners. This, it seems to me, is the ethical challenge for this century. Charles Handy, Foreword: *Sowing the Seeds of a Sustainable Future*, Environment Foundation, 2000.

Considering Commitment

What does it mean to commit yourself, to gain the commitment of your team, and that of the company? For you as an individual manager, it means considering a new set of criteria when you make decisions.

For example, if you are responsible for selecting suppliers, stipulating quality, and managing costs, you can negotiate conditions related to the emerging management issues such as environmental performance or workplace conditions.

Securing the engagement and commitment of your team will mean finding appropriate opportunities to emphasize to them the implications of the global forces for change, assessing the impact of the emerging management issues, and determining a team plan of action.

Gaining companywide support will depend on your authority in the business, your ability to influence others, and the strength of the case you build for change. It will mean helping the business through a reassessment of its values, mission, vision, and operations. It will require discussion and dialogue with stakeholders in order to understand their hopes and concerns, and the impact of the company's actions on them.

SIGNALING COMMITMENT

As a manager, you can signal commitment in a variety of ways, most directly by considering all the relevant factors when making business decisions and taking appropriate action as a result.

It is also important to give the correct signals to both internal and external audiences. As a team or unit manager you can do this in several ways:

- Discuss your business decisions with colleagues and explain why certain choices have been made.
- Invite external speakers to visit in order to share their experiences and encourage discussion among members of your team.
- Undertake practical action in the community to demonstrate that the firm is committed to the well-being of its neighbors.

GlaxoSmithKline set up a Corporate Social Reponsibility Committee to oversee business and society issues, headed by its chairman, Sir Richard Sykes.

Facing the Challenge, GSK, 2001.

The Dow Chemical Company's involvement in local communities is based on a simple rationale: we live here, too. In addition to investing time, money, and other resources in these local communities, Dow has established Community Action Panels in each of 26 local communities where they have a significant business presence, in order to develop two-way dialogues with local residents and community leaders. Each panel addresses issues of importance to the community as a whole (not just fence-line issues relating to the Dow facility). In Terneuzen, Netherlands, for example, this has led to a traffic safety campaign around the Dow site.

Dow Public Report, Dow Chemical Company, 1999.

At a corporate level, companies express top-level commitment in a number of ways.

- Ford Motor Company aims for "leadership in corporate citizenship and sustainable business practices."

We see no conflict between business goals and social and environmental needs. I believe the distinction between a good company and a great one is this: a good company delivers excellent products and services; a great one delivers excellent products and services and strives to make the world a better place. Bill Ford, chairman of Ford Motor Company, *Connecting with Society*, Ford Corporate Citizenship Report, 1999.

- Following the merger of BP and Amoco and the acquisition of Burmah Castrol, the new combined BP committed to a long-term strategy of "beyond petroleum," communicated widely through advertisements and public relations.
- The vision of TXU, an American electric utility, is "to be the most admired energy company in Europe." Not the biggest, the best, or the most profitable, but "the most admired."

To signal the company's commitment internally and externally and access expertise at the same time, it may be advisable for the business to join an organization that promotes responsible business pactices. A variety of institutions welcome business members and share experience and techniques in finding win-win solutions to business issues (see Signposts, p. 302).

Companies can also sign up for a code promoting sustainable business principles, such as the Global Compact, which was launched by

"We see no conflict between business goals and social and environmental needs."

Kofi Annan, secretary general of the United Nations (*see* Expectations of Intergovernmental Institutions, p. 84). Groups of businesses in India and in the Nordic countries have banded together in associations to promote the compact.

Ensuring Oversight

How can you ensure the appropriate level of engagement from managerial colleagues? One way is to establish cross-functional teams and task forces with responsibility for guiding and monitoring progress.

At the senior corporate level, oversight requires integration with existing governance structures. Integration can be achieved by introducing mechanisms that are sensitive to the culture and existing practices of the firm. Several of these mechanisms were detailed by Jane Nelson, Alok Singh, and Peter Zollinger in their report *The Power to Change*, Sustainability and PWIBLF (2001), and some are listed below.

- A dedicated board committee, such as Rio Tinto's Social and Environmental Accountability Committee; Ford's Environmental and Public Policy Committee; and Coca-Cola's and 3M's Public Issues Committees.
- Integration into existing board committees; for example, an expanded role for the audit committee.
- Independent advisory panels to advise the board, such as BT's European Stakeholder Advisory Panel and Dow Chemical's external advisory panel.
- An internal management group reporting to the main board, such as Shell's Sustainable Development Council, and Ford's Corporate Governance Group. Diageo has created a subcommittee of the main board charged with corporate citizenship, chaired by CEO Paul Walsh, with other members drawn from different business functions and key markets.
- Appointment of an executive board director responsible for these issues, as BP has done.
- Stakeholder representation on boards. This is a mechanism that is integral to the supervisory board structure of Germany and the Netherlands.

DEMONSTRATING LEADERSHIP

If you are a member of the board or senior management team of an operating unit, you need to demonstrate leadership when making the commitment to sustainable business practice. As stated in *The Power to Change*, Sustainability and PWIBLF (2001), this may involve:

● Personally serving on external NGO boards, emphasizing that you expect those who are reporting to you directly to pay attention to these issues, and talking to financial analysts about the issues.

● Addressing the issues at annual meetings and in communications to shareholders.

● Using the influence you have with suppliers, trade associations, and other businesses in localities where you have significant presence.

● Taking up the question when serving as a nonexecutive director on other company boards.

"Once a company has made a public commitment to achieving broader social, economic, and environmental objectives, it becomes more exposed and more likely to attract criticism when commitments don't match action. Such criticism is not always fair or accurate, but a reality."

The Power to Change, Sustainability and PWIBLF, 2001.

College boycotts
Having publicly committed to better supplier workplace practices, some clothing manufacturers were unable to satisfy student activists that conditions had improved. As a result, the students urged a campus boycott of those manufacturers that supplied college apparel.

STEP 5 INTEGRATING STRATEGY

The strategy for integrating the culture of responding to the emerging management issues into the company's corporate DNA has two main stages.

The first stage is to review existing business processes to see how sophisticated they are. This will identify policy areas that can be stretched to take the emerging management issues into account. The second stage is to consider whether additional elements of policy are needed to supplement those that already exist.

Where possible, it is preferable to stretch existing processes and policies. This requires minimal extra bureaucracy and training as established systems are already in place. Process revisions are more likely to be successful in operational areas linked directly with the firm's ongoing commercial objectives. The path of least resistance is usually found by working with the status quo rather than trying to subvert it.

Aspects of the emerging management issues that are already integrated into existing business systems are health and safety and environmental management. These have become accepted as mainstream business issues. Innovation in the fields of diversity management, community relations, and social impact is also occurring. New policies may be required in these areas.

Reviewing and Stretching Business Processes

Business processes are multilayered and are not mutually exclusive. Over the years, companies will have adopted and adapted a range of processes to suit their particular circumstances and evolving needs.

To decide on the best way of integrating a new strategy, a manager should ask:

- Which processes are my company most comfortable with?
- If stretched, which processes will address the issues raised by the scoping exercise?
- Which processes do not lend themselves to adaptation?
- Which processes do I have influence over?
- How sophisticated is my company's approach?

It is possible to map the level of your firm's adoption of business processes on a scale of basic to progressive. Such mapping is shown in the tables on pages 250–55 for five key business processes, with examples given of activities found at advanced levels of integration. If your company's approach is at a basic level, there are opportunities to stretch the policies to a progressive level, as illustrated in the examples. The need for your company to introduce new procedures and practices can then be considered by means of a policy audit.

QUALITY AND EXCELLENCE

A company with an advanced approach to quality and excellence is highly results-oriented and customer-focused. The business will be applying benchmark techniques to the emerging management issues, employing quality systems, and seeking assessment from quality institutions.

Examples of the advanced approach

- British Telecom publishes social and environmental reports that are assessed by the British Quality Foundation and the European Foundation for Quality Management (EFQM).
- Tools to measure the quality of community engagement are available from the Center for Corporate Citizenship at Boston College and at the American Productivity and Quality Center.

Examples of the progressive approach

- Telefonica de Espana require all subcontractors to have ISO 9000 certification, and provide support in the form of resources and training through in-house programs and quality teams. CSR Europe.
- Lloyds TSB Bank worked in partnership with local education authorities and other educational bodies to apply the EFQM Business Excellence Model in UK schools as part of its corporate citizenship program.

What is your company's approach to quality and excellence?

BASIC	INTERMEDIATE	ADVANCED	PROGRESSIVE
• Little or no adherence to quality, excellence, or best practice systems and approaches.	• Commitment to established systems, such as total quality management. • Achievement of ISO 9000 quality management standard or equivalent. • Application to production, manufacturing, and service sector in traditional operational areas.	• Quality management and excellence processes are applied to production and manufacturing. • Awareness of risks from poor management of emerging management issues. • Extension of awareness to nontraditional areas, such as community relations.	• Need for value and transferability of quality and excellence processes to help improve efficiency and effectiveness is recognized. • Proactively engaged in and sharing good practice.

SUPPLY CHAIN MANAGEMENT

Companies with an advanced approach to this business process will specify that suppliers meet minimum standards, adhere to codes, and adopt certification related to the emerging management issues.

Examples of the advanced approach

- Banana producer Chiquita Brands International encourages suppliers to adopt operating standards stipulated under the "Better Banana Project" certification program.
- Some firms offer capacity-building of suppliers by providing mentoring, advice, and training for environment and workplace practice issues. Benefits of these programs include lower costs from greater efficiency, less exposure to risk, higher quality, and innovation in development.

Examples of the progressive approach

Supply chain relationships are seen as opportunities to contribute to local economic and community development.

- ABB (South African Breweries) support small business start-ups to help build a local supply base.
- UK retailer Littlewoods supports minority-owned business with affirmative purchasing programs.

What is your company's approach to supply chain management?

BASIC	INTERMEDIATE	ADVANCED	PROGRESSIVE
• Price and specified minimum quality levels are all that is important. • Relationships are confrontational or adversarial with little loyalty or trust on either side. • Contracts are on a one-time basis, even if repeated.	• Long-term shared destiny relationships are based on mutual benefit. • Buyer and supplier have regular dialogue, feedback, and performance reviews. • Suggestions for improvements of process and quality flow both ways. • A more cordial buyer-supplier relationship, with trust built over time (sometimes referred to as partnership sourcing).	• Globalization, revolutions in technology and communications, customizing products or services, and pressures on costs lead to more complex and integrated systems. • Extended producer responsibility and take-back legislation is responded to. • Suppliers are screened for inappropriate conduct in labor, diversity, or human rights issues.	• Recognizes the inter-dependency of community and business prosperity. • Extra effort put into supply-chain relationships to find synergies and ways of leveraging positive impact.

COMPLIANCE

Companies with an advanced attitude toward compliance are adopting global company standards or codes that go beyond local legal requirements. Some of these businesses define compliance in terms of the expected standards of ethical behavior, and include ethics in their training procedures.

Examples of the progressive approach

Companies with this approach are going beyond compliance, both in terms of areas for which standards are set and the level of standard aspired to.

- BP is setting higher than necessary targets to reduce those emissions that contribute to depletion of the ozone layer and global warming.
- In Europe, some companies and regulatory authorities are developing co-regulation (regulation that is formed on a consensual basis).
- Corporations can make compliance an internal obligation. Shell country managers sign a letter each year saying that they have complied with the contents of a statement of general business principles, and that they have introduced policies and practices as directed.

> "It is not good enough simply to do what the law says. We need to be in the forefront of these [social responsibility] issues."
>
> Anders Dahlvig, chief executive, IKEA, quoted in *Financial Times*, February 8, 2001.

What is your company's approach to compliance?

BASIC	INTERMEDIATE	ADVANCED	PROGRESSIVE
• Typified by minimum baseline compliance with legal requirements, and basic internal self-regulation. • Reactive rather than proactive.	• Compliance through a dedicated internal audit structure, with mandatory regulations. • Limited, internal compliance culture. • Conservative approach to developing issues. • May engage in debate over forthcoming public policy changes, but only through trade or business associations.	• Recognizes the cost savings and benefits of going beyond compliance. • Signs up to comply with voluntary as well as mandatory standards in areas represented by the emerging management issues. • Looks ahead to prepare for regulatory pressures as a result of changing expectations. • Internal and external audit processes in place. • Has direct dialogue with policymakers.	• Sees competitive advantage in setting higher compliance standards. • Transparently engages with policymakers to establish good practice standards. • Independent verification of their own compliance. • Hope to enjoy a lower level of regulatory overseeing as a reward for progressive and proactive approach.

RISK MANAGEMENT

Companies with an advanced approach to risk management will recognize and plan for nonfinancial risks at all stages of the product or business service life-cycle and through the supply chain. Social and environmental impact studies are carried out. Both business and societal costs and benefits are incorporated in risk analysis and business case calculations.

Examples of the advanced approach

- New corporate governance codes from major stock exchanges have been introduced, which stipulate broad definitions of risk. Some stock exchanges are making the regular reporting of risk assessment obligatory.
- Reputation risk can be managed through frameworks such as that developed by the management consultants PricewaterhouseCoopers. The system they have developed is based on integrating quality management techniques, addressing reputation strategy, reputation management systems, assurance, and reporting.

What is your company's approach to risk management?

BASIC	INTERMEDIATE	ADVANCED	PROGRESSIVE
• Few if any formal risk management systems in place. • Risk features little in decision-making. • Sticks to what is tried and tested.	• Risk management is associated with health and safety and product liability, including that through the supply chain. • Informed by insurance availability and cost. • Regarded as a specialized function within internal audit and legal departments.	• Recognizes that risk is both financial and non-financial. • The management of reputational risk, based on the brand and corporate reputation down the supply chain and through the business process life-cycle, is seen as vital. • Understands that the risk assessment process includes communication and dialogue.	• Reduces risk potential by engaging in forums on enabling environment and public policy. • Forms partnerships with nontraditional partners to collaborate on areas of mutual interest. • Has the capacity to turn risks or potential risks into opportunities. • Is aware of the need to carry out comprehensive due diligence studies across social, ethical, and environmental criteria for alliances, joint ventures, partnerships, and mergers and acquisitions.

Examples of the progressive approach

- McDonald's faced negative press and pressure over levels of waste from food containers and packaging material. Along with a number of other companies, such as the Bank of America and United Parcel Services, it joined forces with the Alliance for Environmental Innovation, a nonprofit advocacy group that is a joint project of the Environmental Defense Fund and Pew Charitable Trusts. The Alliance reported that McDonald's eliminated more than 26,000 tons of packaging between 1991 and 1998, saving the company an estimated $12.2 million in 1997 and 1998 alone.
- Conflict in many parts of the world impairs business performance. Mining firms Rio Tinto and De Beers are now recognizing that they have a role to play in conflict resolution and prevention by virtue of their economic influence, networks, and physical presence in conflict zones. Risk assessment and risk mitigation processes can be applied in such situations. Jane Nelson, *The Business of Peace, International Alert,* Council on Economic Priorities, Prince of Wales International Business Leaders Forum, 2000.

INNOVATION

A business with an advanced approach to innovation will encourage staff to make calculated risks in order to speed up the pace of service and product innovation.

Examples of the progressive approach

- In the UK, Business in the Community and several other organizations are collaborating on the Innovation Through Partnership project. This encourages businesses and nonprofit organizations to feed their experience from working together back into the business and the community.

"Companies that are breaking the mold are moving beyond corporate social responsibility to corporate social innovation. These companies are the vanguard of the new paradigm. They view community needs as opportunities to develop ideas and demonstrate business technologies, to find and serve new markets, and to solve longstanding business problems." Rosabeth Moss Kanter, "From Spare Change to Real Change," *Harvard Business Review,* May/June 1999.

What is your company's approach to innovation?

BASIC	INTERMEDIATE	ADVANCED	PROGRESSIVE
• An organization built to wither. Slow to adapt, it is bureaucratic, and follows a not-invented-here culture.	• Innovation is boxed off as a separate research and development function or responsibility; the company is product-driven, technology-focused, and poor at picking up signals from the marketplace.	• Innovation is encouraged throughout the business. • All employees understand that they should take calculated risks and go the extra mile in customer service. • Employees contribute their experience to speed up the pace of service and product innovation.	• Forms partnerships with civil society sector institutions as an integral part of its policy of responding to the emerging management issues. • Far more creative and eclectic about where it finds new insights and skills.

Adding New Operational Policies and Practices

The second stage of integrating strategy involves adding to the company's policies and practices if stretching of existing policies will not be sufficient to take the emerging management issues into account.

As a manager, you may come across many different situations in which policies and practices need to be revised or new policies created.

- To adapt existing policies, for example, a company might have an employee diversity policy that needs to establish diversity policies for purchasing, marketing, and community relations in addition to employment practices.
- Where a new policy has to be established, for example, a policy for responsible marketing of the company's products to children.
- After a merger or acquisition, where the original firms have disparate policies that need to be consolidated and developed.
- When a new business starts up, where there is a blank sheet of paper regarding policies.
- When a company is establishing commercial operations in a market with a very different culture.

CONDUCTING A POLICY AUDIT

Where there are gaps in the content of existing policies, an audit can be carried out. This can be done in the first instance for each of the emerging management issues, asking questions that reveal how the issues relate to each other.

Policy areas to audit include crisis management, due diligence processes for takeover or merger targets and alliances, advertising and promotional policies, and procurement procedures. If a scoping exercise suggests that a particular issue is likely to present significant risks or opportunities, a new policy area may be warranted. The exercise can also help to communicate within the company the serious nature of any potential impact. An example of a policy audit for the human resources area is given below.

POLICY CHECKLISTS

Specific policy areas may require the formation of a task force, council, or department in order to oversee policy formation, implementation, and review (see pp. 258–59).

- Voss Fabrik S/A of Denmark established a health and well-being committee that included managers and employees.
- The CEO and president of J. P. MorganChase heads a diversity council that oversees employment practices.
- Pitney Bowes established a department that is responsible for

Audit your human resources policies

This is an example audit illustrating how you could frame an audit of your company's human resource policies. Pose questions to cover a range of topics, starting with those raised during the scoping exercise, and use the answers to consider whether your existing corporate policies and practices need revising.

ECOLOGY AND ENVIRONMENT	HEALTH AND WELL-BEING	DIVERSITY AND HUMAN RIGHTS	COMMUNITIES
• Are newly inducted employees aware of the company's stance on environmental management?	• Are incentives given to encourage life-long learning? • Is mentoring in the workplace encouraged? • Are health-screening and health education services available? • Are provisions adequate to allow for dependant care?	• Is equal pay given for equal work regardless of gender? • Is recruitment practice free from age, gender, or racial discrimination? • Are standards of workplace conditions for suppliers clearly communicated and audited?	• If layoffs are necessary, are outplacement and other support services provided in the local community? • Do managers of plants or geographical divisions have to account for the state of community relations? Are these part of performance-related pay?

both diversity employment issues and multicultural markets. They are geared to encouraging integration and inter-disciplinary learning.

● GlaxoSmithKline has community partnership teams to support its corporate citizenship activities.

Policies related to the emerging management issues are detailed in the checklist overleaf. Practical examples of policies can be obtained from professional and specialized institutions, or industry trade organizations. For example, policies on managing disability issues are covered by the Employers Forum, which works in the UK to share best practice, producing guides and briefings on disability policy. Transparency International is a Berlin-based coalition against corruption, which has more than 75 national chapters and is promoting codes against bribery.

If it is not clear which institution to go to for advice, business associations promoting responsible business practices can point you in the right direction (*see* Signposts p. 302).

INTEGRATING IN STAGES

Most companies have some policies that address the emerging management issues, but these will have been developed on an *ad hoc* basis and not as a coherent response. Integrating strategy may seem daunting, but it need not be if it is tackled in stages. Some of these stages will take more effort and receive less support than others.

First, consolidate all existing policies into a coherent strategy. This can then be stretched to accomodate emerging management issues. Policy gaps then need to be filled. Start with the easiest targets: policies where people can see the benefits quickly. This gives fellow managers the confidence that the company can change. Finally, tackle the hard-to-dos. These will take a lot of effort, but getting support will then be easier.

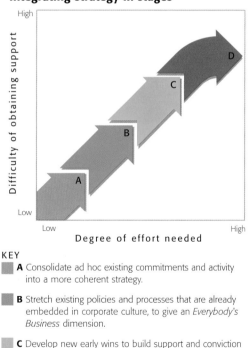

Integrating strategy in stages

Difficulty of obtaining support (High / Low)

Degree of effort needed (Low / High)

KEY

A Consolidate ad hoc existing commitments and activity into a more coherent strategy.

B Stretch existing policies and processes that are already embedded in corporate culture, to give an *Everybody's Business* dimension.

C Develop new early wins to build support and conviction that can make a difference.

D New policies and processes to tackle the hard-to-dos where the company may be breaking new ground or having to make major changes in operations.

The emerging management issues policy checklist

ECOLOGY AND ENVIRONMENT

- Is your company formally committed to sustainable development? This is development that meets the needs of the present without compromising the ability of future generations to meet their own needs.

- Is there an environmental management system with objectives and procedures for evaluating progress? This minimizes negative impacts, as well as allowing transfer of good practice and a product life-cycle analysis for major products, and provides the means to monitor key suppliers.

- Is there continuous striving for improvement in the efficiency with which your company uses all forms of energy and materials? This includes reducing the consumption of water and other natural resources, and a decrease in emissions of hazardous substances. Programs should be in place for monitoring the use of energy, water, and materials, and for measuring emissions.

- Is there a commitment to use and produce recycled and recyclable materials? Efficiently designing and minimizing packaging can increase product durability in a process of reducing, reusing, and recycling.

- Has your company considered the impact on global warming from its activities? Appropriate programs, for example, company tree-plantings, can offset carbon emissions.

HEALTH AND WELL-BEING

- Does your company have policies for the health and safety of all employees? Are these communicated to and understood by employees?

- Does your company maximize the participation of employees in corporate governance structures? They can be engaged in improving the work environment. Employees further benefit by being offered flexible working practices and job referral services.

- Is commensurate treatment provided for part-time workers, regarding pay, promotion, and training?

- Are open-book policies maintained? Do your employees understand financial statements, and are efforts made to reduce job insecurity?

- Does your company offer training opportunities and encourage mentoring to maximize promotion from within the organization? Training and support can extend to work–life management, retirement planning, and the care of dependants.

- Is health screening provided by your company? It can also encourage healthy workplace practices, with bans on smoking, the encouragement of physical exercise, and support for those with drug and alcohol issues.

- Does your company offer outplacement services, retraining, and severance benefits in case of layoffs or closures?

DIVERSITY AND HUMAN RIGHTS

- Does your company have written policies containing measurable objectives to promote diversity and empowerment in the workforce? These should be regularly reviewed against performance.

- Are there explicit policies against discrimination in hiring, salary, promotion, training, or termination of any employee? These would apply to gender, race, age, ethnicity, disability, sexual orientation, or religion and include policies against harassment and bullying.

- Does your company pay comparable wages for comparable work?

- Does your company meet or exceed internationally recognized labor standards and conventions in all the places it operates? These standards include freedom of association, absence of age discrimination, the right to engage in collective bargaining, and a minimum wage.

- Does the company have a supplier code of conduct? In tandem with this, a monitoring system can be used to oversee the employment practices of key partners, suppliers, and distributors to encourage alignment with its own policies.

- Does the company support organizations that practice and promote the concept of fair trade and human rights compliance?

- Does the company know where its products are manufactured and the human rights issues involved?

COMMUNITIES

- Has the company established formal mechanisms to promote two-way communication and partnerships with the local communities in which it operates?

- Is the community seen as an important stakeholder, included in decision-making? Does the company inform it about operations and plans, and of the impacts of the company's activities?

- Does the company use its procurement and investment practices to improve local economic and social development?

- Has the company established programs that encourage contributions, employee volunteering, and help in kind to the community?

- Does the company focus on at least one critical community issue? Company power and financial and political weight can be employed to create positive social change.

- Do employees serve as volunteers and board members in local organizations?

- Does the company run joint marketing campaigns with social causes and organizations?

Adapted from *Winning with Integrity*, Business in the Community, 2000 (UK); *Starter Pack on Social Responsibility*, Business for Social Responsibility, 1998 (US); and *Standards of Corporate Social Responsibility*, The Social Venture Network, 1999 (US).

STEP 6 ENGAGING STAKEHOLDERS

A key component in the implementation of any corporate strategy will be the engagement of stakeholders affecting or affected by business operations.

Effective stakeholder engagement involves open, two-way communication, the commitment of fellow managers and employees, active involvement in public policy, maintenance of stakeholder partnerships, an appreciation of the needs of the community, and an understanding of how business may address those needs.

Communication and Dialogue

Building sustainable relationships with stakeholders requires investment of time and resources, as well as a genuine willingness to listen and learn from their perceptions of the company or business unit, however far from your understanding of reality they may be.

If, as a manager, your responsibilities include overseeing stakeholder communication activities, there are a number of guiding principles to keep in mind when engaging with stakeholders.

PRINCIPLE ONE: OPEN TWO-WAY COMMUNICATION CHANNELS

Stakeholders increasingly expect to be able to enter into dialogue with the companies that make an impact on their lives. This communication should be two-way. The internet is a useful tool, since it allows intensive and low-cost interactive communication. Incorporating feedback mechanisms will help you to understand how your messages are being received and interpreted by your target audience. This can help you to sharpen your communications in the future.

● The Royal Dutch/Shell Group of Companies has run a coordinated global corporate communications program to encourage dialogue and engagement with stakeholders after research showed the company's policies, practices, and principles were not well understood. The program focused on opinion-forming stakeholders, including fund managers, journalists, other businesses, academics, politicians, and leaders of NGOs. The campaign includes press and television advertising, a website, media relations, publications, stakeholder forums, and conference platforms. Measurable targets were set, including the proportion of global opinion-formers who saw the advertising.

"Dialogue is not something which can be turned on and off like a tap. We will never again retreat behind our barricades — we are committed to continuing the process of discussion." Sir Mark Moody-Stuart, then Shell Chairman, quoted in *Listening and Responding, The Dialogue Continues,* Royal Dutch/Shell Group of Companies, 2000.

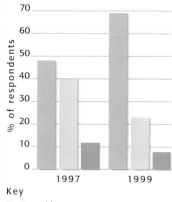

Shifting attitudes toward Royal Dutch/Shell among opinion-leaders

Mori research for Royal Dutch/Shell, 2000.

Key
- Favorable response
- Neutral response
- Unfavorable response

Positive campaign outcome
Opinion-forming stakeholders expressed greater favorability toward Royal Dutch/Shell following its communications campaign in 1998. The results of this poll helped to shape the company's policy on issues such as human rights and the environment.

PRINCIPLE TWO: ENSURE THE INTEGRITY OF YOUR MESSAGE

What grounds does your company have to communicate on a particular theme? Integrity comes from long-term engagement with an issue, following an investment of effort and resources that allows knowledge to be institutionalized over time. If you focus on themes and issues with which your company has a proven track record of engagement, you can advance your corporate message.

- IBM has a history of leadership in education initiatives dating back more than two decades. Successive CEOs have championed systemic education reform in partnership with other businesses, public officials, and educators. The IBM Reinventing Education program involves substantial cash and in-kind assistance to a number of demonstration projects. This started in the US, and is now in other countries including Brazil, Singapore, and Vietnam. When IBM communicates with governments and policymakers on education issues, it can draw on the integrity of a sustained, long-term, and substantial commitment to the subject.

PRINCIPLE THREE: GAIN CREDIBILITY THROUGH PARTNERSHIPS

Many people doubt the credibility of information originating from companies. Forming partnerships with non-governmental organizations or academic institutions can help address the repercussions of the emerging management issues. Partnerships provide a vehicle for jointly-branded commercial activities, influencing perceptions of all parties, such as in the alliance between Starbucks and Conservation International promoting shade-grown coffee.

PRINCIPLE FOUR: ENSURE COHERENCE AND CONTINUITY

Your company is open to criticism if it is inconsistent – for example, if it claims to care for the environment but is responsible for avoidable pollution through poor systems and negligence. Different messages communicated for short-term expediency to flatter and appeal to different audiences will be found out, discrediting you in the eyes of stakeholders.

- Monsanto ran a major press advertising campaign in 1998, setting out its views on genetically modified organisms (GMOs). The company stressed that it wanted to be part of an informed public debate on the issue. A few months later, following some critical attention, Monsanto was seen to be refusing invitations from reputable media to be interviewed on the question. One leading commentator became so frustrated that he wrote a major press article highlighting the Monsanto silence. The company's leaders later admitted the major mistakes they made in the way they handled both the GMO issue and their communications about it.

"We've learned that there is often a very fine line between scientific confidence on the one hand and corporate arrogance on the other... It was natural for us to see this as a scientific issue. We didn't listen very well to people who insisted that there were relevant ethical, religious, cultural, social, and economic issues as well." **Robert Shapiro, former CEO, Monsanto, quoted in** *Business Week***, September 11, 2000.**

Avoiding open communication
Monsanto's response to growing negative commentary on GMOs was to retreat from the debate. This had the effect of reinforcing suspicions about the subject and fueled further critical coverage and protests by activists.

PRINCIPLE FIVE: SPEAK THE LANGUAGE OF YOUR TARGET AUDIENCE

Stakeholder communication requires the same professionalism as any other form of the business communication process. In fact, because you may be dealing with very different sets of audiences, extra sensitivity is needed. The style of language used in business communications may not be suitable when talking or negotiating with community groups or campaigning pressure groups. One technique to overcome this obstacle, until you are well practiced in this area, is the use of an independent facilitator or partnership broker to act as a go-between. A broker may be an individual working alone or representing an institution which specializes in this role. They are likely to have experience in both public and private sectors, will command respect and authority, and be perceived by all parties as neutral.

How to communicate with stakeholders

HAVE TWO-WAY COMMUNICATION	REMEMBER TO:	PRACTISE THE 5Rs:	BE AWARE THAT:
● Engage in dialogue with a broad range of stakeholders and on a wider range of issues. ● Consider using interactive communications. ● Learn to listen, not just to talk. ● Always check that you have heard accurately. ● Prepare to change your policies and practices as a result of dialogue.	● Convince sceptical colleagues that stakeholder engagement is worthwhile and necessary. ● Be brave. ● Make sure that the corporate communications team understands and has the necessary information on hand. ● Keep all staff informed. ● Create a goodwill bank among external stakeholders. ● Provide feedback to stakeholders. Make sure they know you have listened and acted on what you have learned.	● Research. Find the best communications channels for each stakeholder. ● Realism. Do not make too big a claim about what the company is achieving. ● Relevance. Ensure the substance of the communication is relevant to the concerns of target stakeholders. ● Reliability. External verification of key performance indicators will enhance the reliability and the credibility of data that you present. ● Repetition. Facts do not speak for themselves, so key messages need constant repetition.	● Some, if not all, of the emerging management issues (and perhaps your business) may be new to some stakeholders. ● Measurement metrics for assessing how well the company is doing may not exist. If they do, they may be hard to understand or not widely known. ● Fellow managers may have reasonable fears about being in the firing line if the company raises its head. ● Stakeholder engagement today may be seen as a distraction and an abdication of leadership. Look for the early wins that will build confidence and support.

Gaining Commitment from Colleagues

If changes in strategy, policies, and practices are to be effective, then one of the most important stakeholder groups to get on board is fellow managers and employees in the business.

This can be achieved by ensuring that job descriptions and performance targets reflect the company's aspirations to follow an Everybody's Business management approach. These can be reinforced through employee review and recognition systems.

- J. P. Morgan Chase's efforts to promote diversity include scorecards measuring women and minority representation and employee survey results that influence bonuses.
- Texaco withheld part of a bonus due when goals in diversity were not reached.
- The performance of Adidas country managers is measured against human rights policies and influences their annual bonuses. Bad scores result in cut or lost bonuses. Robert Crawford, "Adidas's Human Rights Policy Back on Track," *Financial Times*, December 20, 2000.
- Some 75 percent of companies responding to a survey of Standard and Poor's 500 said they incorporated environmental performance criteria in executive compensation. They included Alcoa, Black and Decker, Cinergy, Dow Chemical, FPL, Hasbro, Millipore, Philips Petroleum, Raytheon, and Conoco.

Employee commitment and enthusiasm can be encouraged through volunteering programs supported by employers. Research suggests that these can raise employee morale and productivity, improving skills levels for the benefit of business and employees.

Popular volunteering programs include company challenge days, mentoring programs, matched company giving to employee fund-raising events, organized time banks, and development assignments in the community.

- In 2000, companies from bankers Citigroup in Hong Kong ran "A Heart to Share," which recognizes employees who complete eight or more hours of volunteer service in a year.

> "I was not sure whether I had the skills and experience to complete [the project] successfully, but found that by using my own initiative and developing my own ideas, I could succeed in an environment which was quite unfamiliar to me."
>
> Development Assignment Employee, The Cecile Network, 1999.

Engaging in Public Policy Dialogue

A key stakeholder relationship to manage is that between business and government, whether directly with regulators, politicians, and intergovernmental organizations, or indirectly through trade associations and organizations representing industry.

Your company may only communicate with government and its agents when there is a clear threat to commercial freedom or competitive advantage from issues such as business taxes, environmental regulations, labor legislation, and planning permits. Yet public policy is a key determinant of the business environment and needs consistent, continuous management.

Strong, long-term relationships with politicians and civil servants can help your company spot issues as they appear on the radar screen. The European Union and the US Federal Government have guidelines for lobbying. Good practice in relationships with government is characterized by transparent processes, accountability, and consistency in the positions that a business publicly espouses. With increased scrutiny of corporate behavior, consistency is the key to credibility. Ensure that the stance you take as a business is consistent with the position taken by the industry associations to which your company belongs.

MAKING PUBLIC POLICY WORK

Businesses are increasingly called upon to contribute to the effective implementation of existing public policies. Examples include business people serving on boards of public institutions, acting as mentors to public officials, and providing staff and expertise to improve the running of public institutions such as schools and hospitals.

Executives contribute by serving on government taskforces, reviewing policy areas, and identifying new policy options. When poorly thought through and executed, such involvement can be tokenistic, and it may give business undue and inappropriate influence. Conversely, well-conceived and professionally implemented involvement, engaging successful business people and businesses in examining policy options, can produce creative solutions, cost savings, more efficient delivery, and greater scale of impact of public services.

Some of the most effective engagement in new public policy formulation comes when a business is encouraged to translate its own skills and experience. A business can benefit from the experience staff gain when they serve on the boards of public institutions, and from the institutional knowledge gleaned over time through long-term engagement with public policy issues.

Companies can join forces with government to help promote an enabling environment for private enterprise. They can support standards in governance, contribute to economic, social, and environmental policies, and promote ethical business practices. Examples of this include:

- The National Business Initiative in South Africa, through which employers are supporting the government's reconstruction program.
- In Brazil, the Institute for Quality Education engages businesses in a program that helps to improve achievement levels in mathematics and Portuguese in schools, working in close partnership with education authorities, school principals, and teachers. The institute was initiated by the São Paulo American Chamber of Commerce.

Engaging Stakeholders Through Partnerships

Partnerships and alliances between business and government, business and NGOs, or between all three sectors, will increasingly become common practice.

Before your company embarks on a partnership, it is helpful to consider the roles of the public sector and of civil society. Recognizing the different roles and characteristics within these sectors is the first stage in understanding the potential of partnerships and the dynamics of the partnership-building process. Each sector has a different contribution to make to social and economic development. The schematic overleaf, The respective contributions of different sectors, interprets the

The respective contributions of different sectors

Business operates in a complex environment interacting with government and civil society institutions. This schematic illustrates the many roles that each sector plays in the development process. The foundation for successful interaction between the sectors is represented by core roles, as follows:

the rule of law; the creation of wealth through investment and trade; and the social cohesion of communities, which is determined by civil society through institutions or individual citizens.

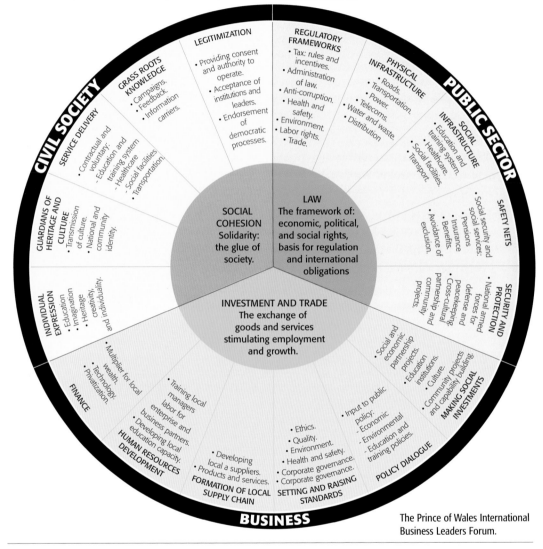

The Prince of Wales International Business Leaders Forum.

distinctive contributions that can be made by civil society, government and the public sector, and by business.

Forming partnerships with different stakeholder groups can be advantageous for a business. As a functional manager, these links may satisfy your specific needs.

- As a brand manager you might wish to take advantage of the growing number of ethical consumers, and form a partnership with a charity or NGO to run a cause-related marketing or social advertising campaign.
- As a purchasing manager, you may have been asked to take active steps to purchase from ethnic minority small businesses. Forming a partnership with a business advisory service will help you to find appropriate companies and build their capacity to join your tender list.
- As a local plant manager, you may have been invited to join a partnership with local government and other local businesses to develop a long-term vision for the future of the area and a strategy to achieve this vision.
- As a human resource manager, you may want to implement a retiree volunteer program and will need to form partnerships with local community groups and local government departments or their contractors.

SUCCESSFUL PARTNERSHIPS

Many companies have formed partnerships with NGOs and other entities to address specific emerging management issues. These have benefited society, the environment, and the business by creating win-win situations.

- Consumer goods firm Diageo adopted a partnership approach in order to help build the profile of its gin brand Tanqueray. Fundraising for AIDS/HIV charities was supported by sponsoring the Tanqueray AIDS rides in the US. The approach increased awareness of the brand among key target audiences and achieved higher sales.
- Telecommunications firm Telenor, as part of its strategy to enter the telecommunications market in Bangladesh, supports the development of small mobile phone businesses run by unemployed rural women. The project has been undertaken in partnership with local institutions and the international microcredit organization, the Grameen Bank. After a pilot project involving 250 women in rural villages, predictions are of 50,000 users within five years.

Fundraising rides
Tanqueray, a leading gin brand owned by beverage company Diageo, has supported cycle rides to benefit HIV and AIDS charities since 1994. Over $160 million has been raised for these charities. The Tanqueray brand has earned over 280,000 media mentions and increased sales as a result of the association with the rides.
Diageo Corporate Citizenship 2001 Guide.

- The Forest Stewardship Council (FSC) is supported by donations from foundations, governments, and individuals and membership fees. Member companies include the UK firms B&Q, Boots the Chemist, Do It All, Homebase, and Habitat, and the US firms Home Depot Inc., Wickes Inc., and Lowe Inc. American retailers who sell over a fifth of all wood used in US building are signatories.
- Global healthcare company SmithKline Beecham (now GlaxoSmithKline), the World Health Organization (WHO), local and national government bodies, local, national, and international NGOs, and community-based organizations formed a partnership to attempt to eliminate the tropical disease lymphatic filiariasis. Each partner has slightly different motivations for engaging in the partnership, but each is working toward one common goal.

  From 1998, GlaxoSmithKline donated the amount of the drug Albendazole needed to treat all people vulnerable to the disease, estimated to be 1.1 billion people worldwide. The target date for elimination of the disease is 2020.
- The Global Partnership for Youth Development (GPYD) is a World Bank Business Partners for Development Program, which convenes business and civil society to work with government to explore the benefits of partnership. GPYD is co-convened by the International Youth Foundation and Kellogg. It has also worked with American Express to promote careers in tourism. *World Bank Partners in Development,* World Bank, 2000.

Certified forests
Forests covering two million hectares have now been certified by FSC-accredited bodies in several countries including Bolivia, Brazil, Costa Rica, Honduras, Mexico, Papua New Guinea, Poland, UK, US, and Zimbabwe.

Examples of partnerships

From Johannesburg to St. Petersburg, from Shanghai to Santiago, businesses are forming partnerships with each other, with NGOs, and with government to tackle the emerging management issues. These partnerships may tackle the issues on a local, national, or international basis, or approach them from an industry-specific perspective.

BASIS OF PARTNERSHIP	ECOLOGY AND ENVIRONMENT	HEALTH AND WELL-BEING	DIVERSITY AND HUMAN RIGHTS	COMMUNITIES
Industry-specific	● Responsible Care: the chemical industry's response to concerns about the manufacture and use of chemicals.	● Pharmaceutical companies, the World Health Organization, and national governments: fighting malaria.	● The US Apparel Industry Partnership: working to raise workplace standards among suppliers.	● Youth Careers Initiative and the International Hotel and Restaurant Association: raising skills levels for the hospitality industry.
International	● World Business Council for Sustainable Development with International Chamber of Commerce: inputs at Rio+10 conference.	● Pharmaceutical company Eli Lilly and World Health Organization: working to combat mental health problems.	● Amnesty International: Amnesty Business Support Groups in over 20 countries.	● The International Youth Foundation: improving the quality of youth programmes.
National	● McDonald's, UPS, and other US companies: the Alliance for Environmental Innovation.	● Thailand Business Coalition on HIV and AIDS: leveraging resources and campaigning to fight ignorance and disease.	● Northern Ireland Employer's Initiative: teaching skills to prisoners participating in work release programs.	● Canada's IMAGINE campaign: persuading more businesses to become involved in the community.
Local	● Groundwork Trust: a UK network of public/private partnerships for environmental improvements and job creation.	● IBM, CARE International, and local institutions: improving water access and quality in Byumba, Rwanda.	● Sportswear company Pentland Group, Siakot Chamber of Commerce in Pakistan, and the ILO: helping to improve workplace conditions at a local level.	● Hydro Aluminium Aardal, a subsidiary of Norsk Hydro in a small Norwegian coastal community: helping reduce accident rates in the workplace and to homes.

CRITICAL SUCCESS FACTORS

When businesses, NGOs, and governments are starting or seeking to sustain cross-sector partnerships, there are a number of key requirements.

● A shared, clear vision of the purpose, bold goals, and strong leadership to make the vision a reality.

● The ability to communicate the vision to stakeholders.

- A strategy to give effect to the vision.
- A genuine engagement and clear accountability between the partners.
- An organizational capacity to implement the ideas and plans of the partnership.
- Time to develop mutual trust between the partners so that each feels able to articulate what they bring to the party, what they need to take away, and, importantly, what they cannot do or conceive of. If there is sufficient trust, it will be possible for underachievers to be taken to task by their peers.
- Entrepreneurial skills with the knowledge of how to mobilize resources from many different places.
- A passion for excellence and continuous improvement.

Choosing an NGO partner

Managers may need to develop a partnership with an NGO, whether to help deliver a particular program or to provide a means for testing and shaping corporate policy.

NGOs are not all the same. They may be ad hoc, local activists, or coherent committees, and may have international brand status. As a manager, you need to allow for these different types of NGOs and to engage with them in the appropriate manner.

- Be clear about the purpose of developing the partnership, whether it is for dialogue, assistance, or project management.
- Set the duration of the partnership: decide whether it is to be a onetime or an ongoing project. There may be potential to expand the reach of the partnership geographically or in terms of those helped by the partnership.
- What is your business looking for? It may require NGOs with technical expertise, project management abilities, entrepreneurial talent, peer group credibility, or media relation skills.
- Is the NGO you are considering representative, or does it claim to be?
- What scale do you need the NGO to operate on? NGOs can operate on a local, national, or international basis.
- If the purpose is to find an NGO partner able to manage a project for the company, then the selection criteria for the NGO will be very similar to that for choosing a commercial partner or supplier. Your decision will then be based on the NGO's track record and its reliability, peer group review, whether or not the NGO meets appropriate standards for your company, and their competitive pitch.

Finding Win-win Scenarios

Business and society are interdependent. It therefore makes good business sense to maximize the benefits that accrue as a result of your business operations to both business and society wherever possible.

In order to do this and create win-win scenarios, there are three key considerations:

- What do the communities need? To discover this, you should undertake a community needs assessment.
- How can my company address social issues in the local community? This could be by providing product, premises, purchasing, power, promotions, people, or profit (*see* the Seven Ps, p. 276).
- How can my company's help and participation in the community help address business needs? Engagement with communities can help build the business, develop employees, and improve corporate reputation.

Three phases of business–community partnerships

WIN–WIN

Phase 3 — Mutual benefit and respect. / Confident. Providing and receiving help to/from business.

Phase 2 — Arrogant. Aiming for gain from charitable associations. / Struggling to see what to offer/ask for from business. Amateurish cash requests.

Phase 1 — Limited or no involvement with charity. / Cynicism and disbelief. Ignorance of working with business.

Business   Voluntary organizations

Stages to mutual benefit
Partnerships between NGOs and business can produce mutual benefit, as long as they evolve through a number of development stages and mature into win-win relationships. Adapted from *The Two-Way Street*, Taskforce 2002, BITC, and NCVO, 1998.

UNDERTAKING COMMUNITY NEEDS ASSESSMENT

In order to understand the requirements of a community, you will need to carry out a community needs assessment. Only by doing this can you accurately identify a community's priorities and match them with your business contribution. Whether the community needs assessment is defined by a geographical community or by one defined in a different way, the principles are very similar.

For example, a business that has significant local presence, such as a mine, a manufacturing plant, or a major distribution depot, will carry out a process consisting of a number of concurrent steps:

- Identifying local community needs using formal surveys, focus group discussions, and informal conversations with different stakeholder groups such as employees, local community leaders, and public officials. This may extend to local opinion-formers such as newspaper editors and journalists, business associations, and campaigning NGOs. Back-up data can be sourced from local government agencies about community characteristics such as crime levels and numbers of single parent families.

- Examining how any overall community program themes of the parent company might be translated into a local context.

- Exploring ways of contributing to established agendas for business action from a local Chamber of Commerce or equivalent organization.

- Assessing which of the key community needs most strongly correlate to issues of business concern. For example, concerns about high truancy rates in local schools may coincide with the business's concerns about vandalism to company property that turns out to be caused by absconding school pupils.

- Considering what corporate contribution might be available to help address community needs. If employees are to be encouraged to get involved in community initiatives, establish their concerns and interests in the community.

This process is likely to produce a long list of possible community needs for the business to address. In order to decide where to focus business effort, it is helpful to plot likely community impact of business support along with likely positive impact on the business (*see* Maximizing impacts for business and the community, opposite).

Several factors are essential in forming a successful local partnership that benefits both business and society.

- Availability of competent local partners, whether public, NGO, or both, or a willingness to build the capacity of such partners. A strong partner may mean more chance of a significant positive impact and all-around benefits.

"Discuss with colleagues what are the needs of the community in which your business operates, and think how you can collectively address them, for example by establishing a citizenship committee."

Diageo's Corporate Citizenship 2001 Guide,
Diageo, 2001.

Maximizing impacts for business and the community

The managing director of a public relations firm is a volunteer school board member at an urban school.

The impact of her involvement is heightened for the school when:
- The firm offers work experience placements to the school's design and English students.
- The firm helps the school to develop and implement a marketing strategy including a website.

The impact for the business is heightened when it plays a more active role with the school:
- Young staff at the firm work on the school account. They learn new skills and become more enthusiastic about their employer.
- The quality of the firm's work for the school is seen by other business people who are school board members. This leads to new commercial commissions.
- The firm is able to offer a permanent job to a student from the school on work experience, who demonstrates design flair.

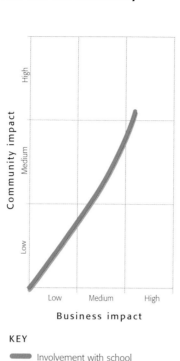

KEY

━━━━ Involvement with school

- A commitment to a win-win partnership. This is more likely to produce sustainable impacts and commitment.
- The ability to leverage resources from other sources.
- Cultural sensitivity. This is needed particularly when working across public, NGO, and business sectors.

Who might undertake a community needs assessment?
- One or more local staff or enthusiastic younger employees teamed up with older colleagues who are already involved in the local community in their personal life.
- A Community Affairs Department that can help your company directly or provide introductions to experienced external consultants.
- Local intermediary organizations that promote socially responsible business practice may have listings of consultants who could undertake an assessment (*see* Signposts, p. 302).

Addressing Community Need

There are a variety of ways in which a company can contribute to community need through social investment. Cash contributions can be important, but a company has access to many more resources.

A useful device to help you remember the range of contributions a company can make is the Seven Ps. These are: product, premises, purchasing, power, promotion, people, and profit.

You should consider these seven categories as a template when your company is planning any social investment. The examples on the following pages illustrate how the Seven Ps can be used to support education and local communities, help bridge the digital divide, and support people with disabilities.

The Seven Ps of corporate contribution

RESOURCE	HOW IT WORKS
Product	● Your company can contribute products and services. This may be a product that is in stock, or a product that is still perfectly usable but no longer saleable, perhaps because the packaging is out of date or features an out-of-date promotion. It may also be a product and/or equipment that the company has bought for itself, but which is now redundant for the business.
Premises	● Your company can provide free accommodation to NGOs and access to business premises out of office hours. Surplus premises may be provided for conversion into small business incubators or hostels for the homeless.
Purchasing	● Your company can use purchasing power to advance social goals. This may include commitments to buy a certain percentage of goods and services locally or from small or minority-owned businesses, charities, and NGOs supported by the business.
Power	● Companies frequently underestimate the power they have to open doors for NGOs and community groups, the influence they have with other businesses, and the communications channels they have available to support the work of community organizations.
Promotion	● Your company can undertake cause-related marketing campaigns which will also promote a social cause or organization.
People	● Perhaps the most significant corporate resource is the ability to mobilize the expertise, passion, and time of the people within the organization for some community cause. Many firms now encourage employee volunteering and support the volunteer efforts of staff with time off, back-up information and training, and cash contributions to NGOs and staff causes.
Profit	● Your company can support social causes and NGOs with financial support. Increasingly, however, this is linked to where there are opportunities for the company to support in other ways.

How business is supporting education

Businesses recognize that helping to improve education is one of the most valuable contributions that can be made to support social and economic development. There are also positive knock-on effects for society, such as a reduction in the crime rate, reduced poverty, and less social alienation. Business benefits because there is less burden on employers for the costs of remedial education for employees.

Community discovery
With support from the Discovery Channel Global Education Fund, boys at St. Jude Primary School in Luwero, Uganda, learn about African wildlife.

RESOURCE	EXAMPLES
Product	● The Discovery Channel, via the Discovery Channel Global Education Fund, supports rural and disadvantaged communities in Africa and Latin America with technological resources, training, and culturally appropriate educational programming for teachers and students.
Premises	● As part of the Toyota Teach program in South Africa, Toyota makes premises available for seminars and workshops to help advance science and mathematics development. By 2001, the program reached nearly 40 primary schools, over 1,000 teachers, and some 45,000 students. Evaluations indicate marked improvements in teachers and students who have been exposed to the program.
Purchasing	● WH Smith, the UK bookseller and stationery chain, has made £1.5 million ($2.25 million) worth of books available to schools in its Ready Steady Read promotion.
Power	● Vandenburgh Foods, a Unilever subsidiary, established the Rama Nutrition Education Project in Natal, South Africa, in the mid-1980s. The initiative is an integrated community nutrition project that teaches schoolchildren the basic requirements of a healthy diet and shows them how to plant tiny, highly-productive vegetable gardens, using recycled household waste as compost. The company has developed relationships with school authorities, teachers, research institutes, and universities throughout the project to maximize the project's educational and research benefits.
Promotion	● Cadbury Schweppes joined forces with Save the Children to support special needs education around the world. The promotion raised about £1.5 million ($.2.25 million) over a six-year period through on-pack promotions and special events.
People	● DHL Worldwide Express in Panama supports the local Junior Achievement organization, encouraging entrepreneurs among local fifth and sixth grades. A DHL senior manager sits on the organization's Board of Directors, and two other staff members act as program advisers.
Profit	● Aracruz, a paper-pulp company in Brazil, worked with Rede Interdisciplinar de Educação (RIED) to provide teacher training in elementary level classroom theory and practice in public school systems. They worked in the municipalities of Aracruz, Ibiraçu, João Neiva, São Mateus, Conceição da Barra, and Pedro Canário. A total of 607 teachers were trained, to the benefit of some 28,000 students. ● Since 1988, the ICWI Group Foundation has invested over £38 million ($68 million) in educational programs in Jamaica, including scholarships for employees' children, community grants for NGOs and schools, and the development of a Science and Learning Center.

How business is supporting local communities

Local community regeneration and development can benefit from a variety of inputs from business, such as assistance for job creation through aiding start-ups and small business growth; business development through local purchasing and subcontracting programs; raising education and skills levels by investing in training; support for the viability of sports, leisure, and arts activities; community crime prevention movements; and environmental conservation.

RESOURCE	EXAMPLES
Product	● In Brazil, the private foundation of the Globo TV network and the Federation of Industries of São Paulo, in conjunction with the National Industrial Training Service, have developed a television program called Telecurso 2000, which is broadcast every morning on the main channel and during the day on educational channels. Education and training concepts are applied to everyday situations that Brazilians face. The TV program is supported by materials made widely available through newsstands and by an accreditation process through government-supported examinations.
Premises	● Miami-based law firm Steel Hector and Davis LLP provides office facilities to a number of charitable projects, including the Volunteer Lawyer's Project of Southern Florida.
Purchasing	● German-based car company BMW has an environmental management system called Zeus, which is an on-line information system used for the registration of environmentally friendly material from suppliers, and which gives advice on safe disposal of materials.
Power	● Hewlett Packard has joined forces with i2 Technologies to create Aidmatrix: a new online, nonprofit e-marketplace to link businesses with surplus goods to charities managing aid and disaster relief.
Promotion	● Boots, international provider of wellbeing products and services, helps to raise awareness of health issues such as breast cancer by providing information for customers through its extensive network of stores.
People	● The Youth Business Initiative is an international program to encourage and support young people starting out in business, offering access to financing and volunteer mentors from companies. YBI has helped over 45,000 people in a dozen countries.
Profit	● In the UK, Shell created Livewire, which provides advice, information, and mentors to help young people start their own business. Shell's worldwide operating companies are replicating the program.

Community healthcare
BOC has supported the provision of healthcare for local Indian communities by providing a mobile clinic.

How business is tackling the digital divide

Not all countries are in a position to benefit from the opportunities and economic prosperity that information and communications technologies offer. Few in Africa have access to the telephone, much less the internet. In some countries, access to independent news sources remains restricted. There are also growing divisions within countries. Different standards of education accentuate the ICT skills gap and with it the digital divide within and between countries.

RESOURCE	EXAMPLES
Product	● Cellular Corporation, a telecommunications company, is working with 120 homeless shelters across the US to give homeless people access to voicemail boxes free of charge. The aim is to aid contact between the homeless and prospective landlords and employees. ● AOL Peace Packs is an initiative to bring the benefits of the internet revolution to developing countries. Internet service provider AOL equips Peace Corps volunteers with the packs, which consist of two PCs, a printer, a digital camera, and internet connectivity. Hewlett Packard provides hardware for most packs.
Premises	● New technology firm CISCO provides equipment to internet cafés in poor areas, developing countries, and to schools and training centers. It is committed to establishing IT training academies in 24 of the poorest nations.
Purchasing	● Rather than purchase commercial IT support, for example to develop a website, companies can sponsor young trainees to do the work. This approach was used by corporate members of the UK Government's Policy Action Team on IT and Social Exclusion.
Power	●Consultants Accenture are working with the United Nations Development Programme Digital Opportunity Initiative, with the aim of building a global strategy to bridge the digital divide within 10 years.
Promotion	● Tesco, the UK supermarket business, has run a Computers for Schools program since 1992. Customers collect vouchers that are valued according to their level of purchase and these can then be redeemed by local schools. The program has provided over 30,000 computers for schools plus IT training for teachers.
People	● Czech Republic IT and internet company ALMS has used the technical knowledge of its staff in IT, public relations, and project management to help develop a web site offering information and advice on HIV/AIDS to Czech youth. The company formed a partnership with a local NGO and medical school to provide, via the web, facts, information, and an on-line virtual consulting room. ● The McGraw Hill group of companies has expertise in educational and professional publishing, information, and media services. As part of a signature corporate citizenship program supporting education, the company has embarked on a project to encourage volunteers who help as mentors over the internet.
Profit	● The ClubTech program is a joint program run by Microsoft and the Boys and Girls Clubs of America (B&GCA) to "technology-enable" virtually every club over five years by establishing technology centers, developing and delivering relevant curriculum and content, and providing program management and computer training for staff. Microsoft is donating $100 million in cash and software to bring technology access and programs to more than 3.3 million under-served children and teens in 2600 Clubs nationwide.

Access to technology
Microsoft's donations of money and software are helping to bridge the digital divide that exists between well-off and disadvantaged children.

How business is supporting those with disabilities

It is estimated that one in every four customers is either disabled or is close to someone who is. People with disabilities are an important slice of the market and a significant part of the labor market as well. Yet, organizations that are committed to diversity often fail to address disability issues. Many of the adaptations made for disabled people, such as improved access, can result in benefits for all staff and customers.

RESOURCE	EXAMPLES
Product	● UK utility company Thames Water gave 900 computers, and Microsoft have given free software, to The Leonard Cheshire Workability Scheme, which gives computers and IT training to 10,000 under 34-year-olds, with the goal of getting them back to work. The project also involves a buddy program. ● US Bank Wells Fargo & Co. is installing talking ATMs at all of its Californian locations.
Premises	● IBM, BT, Hewlett Packard, and Microsoft all host AbilityNet centers in their UK corporate premises. AbilityNet is a charity offering advice to individuals and organizations about adaptive technologies available to help people to stay at or get work, or enjoy greater personal freedom via the computer.
Purchasing	● United Utilities, which has had a long charitable association with the Royal National Institute for the Blind (RNIB) in the UK, needed expert advice on how to become more responsive to the needs of disabled employees and customers. The company bought in RNIB professional expertise on a consultancy basis. RNIB's sister organization, the American Foundation for the Blind (AFB), works to provide technical expertise with individual companies and industry bodies, such as those in construction and transportation.
Power	● Diversity Services is a New York-based employment agency that works with firms such as AOL Time Warner, UPS, and Federated Department Stores. It recruits workers who are disabled, HIV positive, or recovering from cancer. One-quarter of the company's temporary workers go on to permanent positions, a rate three times that of the average employment agency. Diversity Services helps employers tap the estimated 70 percent of America's disabled people who are capable of work but unemployed. ● Tricon Restaurants in Australia runs a Jobsplus program that specifically recruits people with disabilities into the company. Tricon reports that retention levels are 4.5 times higher than with other employees, there were no workplace accidents over a two-year period, and there is a high level of job satisfaction among the Jobsplus recruits.
Promotion	● Target Stores in the US and BT and McDonalds in the UK responded to prompts from disability rights campaigners by including disabled people in their general advertising. They aim to show a cross-section of their customers. Flora sponsors the London Marathon, and in 1999 the event's designated charity was WhizKids, an organization that seeks to enhance the mobility of disabled children.
People	● High-tech companies in Silicon Valley have encouraged employees to volunteer for an on-line service that helps dyslexic school children and students with their homework and study assignments. A student emails his or her projects to the volunteer, who corrects spelling and layout.
Profit	● BT sponsored Typetalk. This is an innovative program enabling deaf people to use the telephone system. By calling the Typetalk exchange on a specially adapted telephone with typing facilities and screen, they can converse over the phone. Trained operators act as the interpreter to and from the printed word. ● The Marriott Foundation, of the Marriott Hotel Group, developed and supports the Bridges program, which helps young adults with disabilities move from high school to work, with training and awareness-raising for employers and prospective employees.

KEY POINTERS

Whether your company chooses to support education or another issue, it is worth keeping in mind some pointers that will save time and ensure that your company's contribution is well received on the ground.

Supporting education

When supporting schools, it is worth considering how wider economic and social regeneration projects in the school's area will make the school more effective. Companies need to keep a balance between providing much-needed equipment or materials and ensuring that corporate branding of any donations is appropriate for the educational setting and the age of the children concerned.

Supporting local communities

For many companies, philanthropic and charitable giving develops over time into more partnership-based activities, in which employees are engaged in sharing skills as well as company resources, and in which there is both business and community benefit. It is advisable not to allow a community group or project to become too reliant on support from one company in case business circumstances change.

Tackling the digital divide

Helping communities overcome the digital divide requires more than just donated computers. Four areas need to be addressed simultaneously: telecommunications links for internet connections; access to appropriate computer models and software; relevant content; and access to training, capacity building, and ongoing technical support. The need for this combination lends itself to a partnership approach between hardware and software donors and trainers.

Supporting those with disabilities

Working with disability projects can help businesses understand how to make their own workplaces, products, and services accessible to disabled employees and customers. This should include regular disability awareness and equality training and ensuring disabled access to buildings.

USING THE COMMUNITY AS A TOOL KIT

Many communities and companies have benefited from alliances and partnerships. The conclusion to be drawn from these positive relationships is that there is a wealth of potential beyond the factory gate or office window for managers who are willing to think creatively. The challenge for you is not necessarily to do different things, but to do things differently. You should try to think of the community as a tool kit. It is simply a matter of learning which tools are available, and which of them is best for which job. The tasks outlined below show how to use them.

Health warning

As with any tool kit, misuse of the equipment can result in injury or damage to pride and reputation. Transparency in purpose is paramount when entering into relationships with the community. Doing the right deed for the wrong or hidden reason can backfire.

TASK: Build the people

COMMUNITY TOOL	HOW TO USE THE TOOL EFFECTIVELY
Send young managers on community development assignment	● Monitored programs based in community organizations involve not only the application of technical and professional skills but also encourage the development of interpersonal skills such as communication and negotiation skills. In a corporate setting, managers can often buy their way out of a problem because they have access to funds and resources. In a community organization, they will have to rely on a natural wealth of tact, diplomacy, and lateral thinking.
Seek imaginative routes to build diversity through the recruitment process	● Access to jobs for ethnic minority groups can be difficult, as they may not have links with traditional avenues of information for vacancies, such as employment agencies or local newspapers. An alliance with a local community group drawn from the minority can provide a cost-effective way of ensuring that opportunities reach a broader mix of potential applicants.
Support employee volunteering efforts	● Challenge days, time off for volunteering, and matching funding for charitable fund-raising helps to boost employee morale, aid intercompany communication, and develop employee skills. All these are devices that, time and time again, have been shown to contribute positively to employee loyalty and motivation, to breaking down hierarchical communication structures that block effective flow of information and, if carefully selected, aid employee training.

TASK: Build the business

COMMUNITY TOOL	HOW TO USE THE TOOL EFFECTIVELY
Invite customers and suppliers to join corporate community initiatives	● The informal atmosphere and the feel-good factor of working together for a common cause can help build lasting personal relationships and improve communication on commercial issues.
Create supplier clubs or networks and share good practice in environmental management	● This helps to identify cost savings in the supplier's operations, improving their efficiency and reducing their environmental impact. Better suppliers are better for your business.
Develop partnerships with further education colleges' research and development departments	● As well as providing access to up-to-date thinking and research capabilities, these relationships can help spot potential recruits at an early stage.
Link sales of products with good causes	● Through a cause-related marketing campaign, you can help to raise awareness and increase resources for the cause. It appeals to the growing number of consumers looking for ways to buy for a better world.

TASK: Build the licence to operate

COMMUNITY TOOL	HOW TO USE THE TOOL EFFECTIVELY
Make non-commercially sensitive research and information available	● The company can provide information that they have used, for example on transportation patterns, or geological reports to authorities, community groups, libraries, and schools.
Allocate managers to government task forces or committees	● Managers can lend their specialized expertise and knowledge to address social and community-related issues.
Invest in mutually beneficial infrastructure	● Helping to build efficient transportation systems, and investing in sports and artistic venues will help the company's reputation.

SKILLS AND TRAINING

New management skills are required to deal with emerging management issues, changing expectations, and increased scrutiny. Continuous learning and people development are key ways of enhancing these skills. Some organizations are already investing in these areas. Many large firms have their own corporate universities, others buy in executive management programs, and sponsor staff to enroll in MBA programs and other courses at business schools and management centers.

The cycle of learning

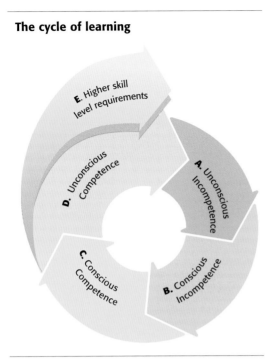

E. Higher skill level requirements

D. Unconscious Competence

A. Unconscious Incompetence

C. Conscious Competence

B. Conscious Incompetence

Learning process
Individuals have to go through a circular process of learning, from a point where they are not aware that they have a knowledge or skill gap, through to being able to apply new skills unconsciously. If there is no reinforcement to this skill level, then that skill may deteriorate. However, the platform of a new level of skill can be used to start a new cycle (E). **Adapted from Harvey Dodgson,** *Journal of Business Research,* **December 1987.**

It is crucial for those responsible for commissioning this training and liaising with business schools to incorporate the emerging management issues into their specifications.

Organizations such as the Corporate Citizenship Unit and the New Academy of Business run courses. CSR intermediary organizations listed in Signposts (*see* p.302) can provide details of local training providers.

Given the speed of change and the complexity of business today, it is perhaps not surprising that managers face a paradox. Top managers do not know what people on the front line know and are experiencing. Conversely, those on the front line may not understand what top management has to understand to do their jobs properly. Therefore, top management may not have the framework for getting crucial intelligence.

As well as the need to develop technical skills in areas such as diversity and human rights, and supplier conduct codes and verification, there are some broad generic skills that need to be developed. These include:

● Moving from a product-led basis to a customer focus to stakeholder focus. In recent times, managers have been exhorted to adopt a customer-led rather than product-led approach. Now, managers have to be able to identify and optimize the needs of different stakeholders, including, but not exclusively, customers. This means being able to engage actively in two-way communications with stakeholders and finding opportunities to build trust.

● Creative-swiping: "stealing with pride." The ability of a company to stay future-alert and to learn not just from other businesses but also from what is happening in other sectors. Management guru Peter Drucker, for example, has long argued that some of the best learning for businesses about how to motivate their people is to be found by studying how the best of voluntary organizations enthuse their volunteers.

● Connectivity: looking for the unusual but practical

synergies. Again, these may be across sectors. One community-based NGO – Community Links, in the East End of London, England – has developed such a successful approach to the identification of community needs that major firms such as Thames Water and Shell have hired them to run training courses for groups of their managers.

- Leveraging own business resources through participating in win-win partnerships with other businesses and/or with other sectors.
- Networking like crazy: proactive stakeholder management, creative swiping, connectivity, and leveraging all require that managers with the ability to network intensively and with a much broader range of people and organizations.
- Being alert to the future: scanning regularly for future developments on a broader canvas with greater sensitivity.

IMPLEMENTATION:
WHAT GETS IN THE WAY?

Managers and companies already working on policies in response to the emerging management issues report that the hardest part of all is implementation: making it happen, and helping the whole organization to understand what is involved. What gets in the way of implementation?

Many of the obstacles in the way of effective implementation of policies to achieve sustainable business excellence are the same as those that hinder attempts to improve business performance and enhance long-term prospects. Ultimately, it is an issue relating to the quality of management. Barriers to implementation include:

- Policies are insufficiently thought through.
- Over-identification with one or only a few champions in the company means there has not been buy-in to the policies from senior management overall.
- The rationale and eventual benefits of the new policies have not been articulated or actively sold.
- Sceptics and opponents of business change have not been handled effectively.
- Poor business performance undermines support.
- Staff have not been trained sufficiently to implement the new policies.

- Reward and recognition systems have not been brought into alignment with the new policies and priorities.
- External audiences have been allowed to interpret the new policies as meaning far faster or more dramatic changes or results than the company has actually signed up for or has intended.
- Organizational inertia may manifest itself in continuing membership in outside organizations promoting policies that are inconsistent with the company's new policies.
- Local management misunderstands policies.

These obstacles are the result of one or more essential preconditions for mastering change being absent.

Requirements for mastering change

As with all other aspects of management, there are several preconditions needed for the successful mastering of policy change. As shown here, if even one of these preconditions is missing, the result will be suboptimal performance or failure to achieve sustainable business excellence. For example, without buy-in from staff, there will be organizational resistance to change. (Adapted from a chart produced by EPPA.)

COMMUNICATION	UNDERSTANDING	BUY-IN	ABILITY	CAPABILITY	RESULT
Continuous feedback and sharing	Why, what, and where to change	Motivation, ownership, and accountabilty	Competence and power	Tools and resources	
✗	✓	✓	✓	✓	Incoherent implementation
✓	✗	✓	✓	✓	No motivation or purpose
✓	✓	✗	✓	✓	Resistance to change
✓	✓	✓	✗	✓	Don't know how approach
✓	✓	✓	✓	✗	Frustration

Even companies that avoid these pitfalls might find themselves criticized for some activities that are ultimately a finely balanced decision. There may equally be no settled consensus on what is the correct sustainable business practice to follow. These are areas that measuring and reporting can help to clarify.

STEP 7 MEASURING AND REPORTING

There is growing interest in how to measure different aspects of business operations as managers increasingly have to report their company's results to different audiences.

It is not enough simply to minimize the negative and maximize the positive impacts of a business for its stakeholders and for wider society. As was made clear in Global Forces for Change, stakeholders are no longer prepared to trust what companies say. There has to be proof.

Reasons to Measure

Whether adopting or adapting an existing code or standard, or developing a code from scratch, it is important to be clear about why measuring is required.

Your company's motivation for measuring might include one or more needs:

- To benchmark performance and set targets for continuous improvement. This enables a manager to assess the impact of a business operation and to make comparisons with other firms.
- To answer specific allegations that have been made against the company. When confronted with media criticisms that it was exaggerating aspects of its operations, cosmetics retailer The Body Shop International developed rigorous and publicly transparent methods of measuring.
- To understand concerns of a particular group of stakeholders. When planning to build a fifth terminal at London's Heathrow Airport, the British Airports Authority embarked on consultations with the local communities.
- To help you spot where there may be a need for new policies. A number of companies based in the US did not have processes in place to measure general employee satisfaction levels, nor to monitor the mix of employees recruited from different ethnic groups. If they had done so, they may have been able to head off rising dissatisfaction among their African-American employees, which escalated to legal action and led to critical press coverage.
- To demonstrate your company's difference from your competitors. Increasingly, companies are under pressure to measure the conditions under which goods are made and produce is grown. Some promote a commitment to fair conditions via the Fairtrade movement, which offers a seal of approval in several countries. Similarly, the Forest Stewart Council certifies companies that produce paper and pulp products to environmentally-friendly standards.
- To satisfy regulatory requirements from governments or international conventions.

A fair deal for suppliers
The effectiveness of businesses operating practices related to the emerging management issues can be measured at the source of the product, for example the conditions for artisan craft workers. Oxfam awards a Fairtrade mark to companies that can demonstrate that their suppliers have decent working conditions and pay.

- To communicate within the business and to ensure all line managers understand the seriousness of commitments.
- To earn third-party endorsement through external awards and certificates of approval.
- To provide the data that a commercial customer may require in order to put a firm on its tender list. Car manufacturer GM insists suppliers must be ISO–14000 compliant by 2002.
- To build trust with internal and or external stakeholders.

Building trust

It is important that managers are sensitive to the level of trust that stakeholder groups have in the company. This will help in determining strategies for building relationships with stakeholders. As production becomes more generic, the added value to a business comes from intangibles: knowledge, brand, and reputation. In a global information economy, trust is increasingly valuable for businesses.

- Consumers ask: "Do I trust this brand? Do I trust this company?" This is especially true as e-commerce becomes more widespread.
- Local communities ask: "Do we trust this potential inward investor as a neighbor of choice, or do we fight it as a dangerous intruder?"
- Employees and freelancers ask: "Is this an organization I trust and with whom I want to be associated?"
- Joint venture or business partners ask: "Will our reputation and financial standing be affected if we associate with this business?"

These questions are most relevant for the large mutinational companies and brands, whose behavior may be reported around the world, impacting on their corporate reputation. Yet soon, even small businesses, especially if they are in a supply chain to multinational companies, will have to confront similar questions. In the past, a business did not need to explain itself, or could simply make assertions about its performance. Increasingly, it has to provide hard evidence to justify its claims, and stakeholders want to be involved in probing those claims. Arguably, organizations, businesses, NGOs, and governments move from left to right along a spectrum:

Ignore ▸ Listen ▸ Listen ✚ Act ▸ Involve ▸ Include

John Drummond, Director, Corporate Culture plc, 2000.

Suppliers with a monopoly and companies with no real business competition can afford to be on the left of the spectrum. Increasingly, however, organizations have to listen to their voters, customers, clients, and patients and act upon what they hear. The leading companies are those that include users in the process of identifying problems and potential solutions.

WHAT TO MEASURE AND HOW?

But, what should you be measuring? There are a bewildering array of codes of conduct, principles, auditing techniques, and assessment criteria in the marketplace. The 1990s saw the introduction of a plethora of measurement devices designed to help companies assess impact and performance, especially in the field of ecology and environment.

These devices have been followed more recently by developments to assess social and community impact and performance. A range of measurement codes have been developed, each of which deals with a specific problem.

- The CERES Principles (1989), which were formerly known as the Valdez Principles after the *Exxon Valdez* affair, were drafted by CERES (the Coalition for Environmentally Responsible Economies) to demonstrate business practices that are environmentally sound.

- Following the spate of high-profile cases around the world about sourcing and manufacturing conditions, several codes were introduced to address these issues. These include the US Apparel Industry Partnership (1997), the World Federation of Sporting Goods Industry Code of Business Practice Concerning Child Labor (1995), the Code of Labor Practices for the Production of Goods licensed by FIFA (the International Federation of Football Associations), and the Ethical Trading Initiative in the UK.

Sea change
Apart from causing widespread ecological damage and harming local livelihoods, the Exxon Valdez disaster was a trigger that led to greater efforts by business to measure their environmental impact.

EXXON VALDEZ

- National and international bodies from different trade sectors produce guides that are specific to the key concerns of their members. Examples include the German Publishing Industry Code on Paper Recycling, and the Pacific Asian Travel Association Code for Environmentally Responsible Tourism. In addition, the International Chamber of Commerce has produced a Code on Bribery and Corruption, a Code on Advertising Practices, and a Charter for Sustainable Development.
- A growing number of national business associations are producing their own guidelines on responsible business practices for their members. Examples include the Federation of Greek Industries, the Federation of Korean Industries' Charter of Business Ethics, and Kedainren (a grouping of Japanese Employers).

In November 2000, the Ethos Institute for Business and Social Responsibility in Brazil launched social responsibility indicators for:
- Values and transparency
- Workplace
- Environment
- Suppliers
- Consumers
- Community
- Government and society

Some international agencies have worked with corporations specializing in metrics to produce standards such as the SA 8000, which is issued by the Council of Economic Priorities Accreditation Agency (now called Social Accountability International). The SA 8000 standard is a voluntary code for companies interested in auditing and certifying labor practices in their facilities and those of their suppliers and vendors. It is designed for third-party verification, which is increasingly being undertaken by a growing number of independent verification bodies.

An established measurement tool is the Business Excellence Model of the European Quality Foundation, which includes a section titled "Impact on Society" alongside its people, customer, and key performance results categories.

One of the most comprehensive measurement devices is the Global Reporting Initiative (GRI). This aims to:

"promote international harmonization in the reporting of credible and relevant corporate environmental, social, and economic performance information to enhance responsible decision-making."

GRI began in 1997 as an initiative of CERES and the United Nations Environment Program. It involves a growing number of multinational companies, including Procter & Gamble, GM,

Ford, and TXU, which are piloting the GRI measurement metrics. The aim is to elevate sustainability reporting practices worldwide to a level equivalent to financial reporting. Revised GRI Guidelines were published in June 2000. These guidelines encompass:

- Economic factors, such as wages and benefits, labor productivity, job creation and investments in training and other forms of personal development.
- Environmental criteria, including the impacts of processes, products, and services on air, water, land, and human health.
- Social factors, including employee retention, labor rights, and wages and working conditions at supplier operations.

Summary of measurement indicators

The Business Impact Taskforce in the UK reported a series of measurement indicators suitable for companies at different levels to measure against. Small companies, or those just starting to measure, should only tackle level one indicators. Larger companies, with greater measuring skills, can add level two and three indicators as well.

LEVEL OF MEASURING	WORKFORCE INDICATORS	MARKETPLACE INDICATORS
LEVEL 1 Measurement indicators for small companies and those just starting to measure and report.	● Workforce profile. ● Staff absenteeism. ● Number of legal non-compliances on health and safety, equal opportunities, and other legislation. ● Number of staff grievances. ● Upheld cases of corrupt or unprofessional behavior.	● Customer complaints about products and services. ● Advertising complaints upheld. ● Complaints about late payment of bills. ● Upheld cases of anticompetitive behavior.
LEVEL 2 Measurement indicators that can be added when measuring becomes more sophisticated.	● Staff turnover. ● Value of training and development provided to staff. ● Pay and conditions compared with local equivalent averages.	● Customer satisfaction levels. ● Customer retention. ● Provision for customers with special needs. ● Average time to pay bills to suppliers.
LEVEL 3 Additional measurement indicators for large corporations and multinationals.	● Impact evaluations of the effects of downsizing, retraining, and other measures. ● Perception of the company regarding issues such as equal opportunities and work–life balance.	● Extra sales gained attributable to social policy/cause-related marketing. ● Customer loyalty measures. ● Recognizing and catering to diversity in advertising and product labeling. ● Perception of company as a desirable commercial partner. ● Social impact, cost of benefits of products/services.

The GRI suggests 103 different measurement indicators. GRI itself recognizes that there may be intermediate stages toward comprehensive measurement and reporting, especially for smaller firms. In the UK, a two-year Business Impact taskforce, involving business leaders from a variety of business sectors, published a report in November 2000. They recommended a series of measurement indicators, with levels of sophistication depending on the size and situation of the firm. The intention is to "demonstrate the essence of what should be reported – to identify the main areas which it will profit a business to measure and manage business performance" (*Final Report*, Business Impact Taskforce, November 2000).

ENVIRONMENT INDICATORS	COMMUNITY INDICATORS	HUMAN RIGHTS INDICATORS
• Overall energy consumption. • Water usage. • Quantity of solid waste produced (weight/volume). • Upheld cases of prosecution for environmental offenses.	• Cash value of community support as percent of pretax profit. • Estimated combined value of staff company time, gifts in kind, and management costs.	• Compliance with international human rights standards with regard to employees and other stakeholders and absence of upheld cases against the company. • Confidential grievance procedures. • Wage and employment agreements
• Greenhouse gas emissions. • Other emissions, such as ozone and radiation. • Use of recycled materials. • Positive and negative media comment about environmental activities.	• Individual value of staff time, gifts in kind, and management costs. • Positive and negative media comment on community activities. • Project progress and achievement. • Leverage of other resources.	• Progress measures against adherence to stated business principles on human rights as stated by UK Law and international human rights standards. • Proportion of suppliers and partners screened for human rights compliance.
• Level of recyclable waste? • Net carbon dioxide/greenhouse gas measures and offsetting effect. • Environmental impact over the supply chain. • Environmental impact, benefits, or costs of products/services against best in class.	• Impact evaluations carried out on community programs including: improved educational attainment, number of jobs created, professional support for community organizations, and environmental enhancement or conservation. • Perception measures: of the company as a good neighbor.	• Proportions of suppliers and partners meeting company's standards on human rights. • Proportion of company's managers meeting the company's standards on human rights within its area of operation. • Perception of the company's performance on human rights by employees, the local community, and other stakeholders.

Reporting codes of practice for the emerging management issues

This is a sample of codes, standards, and principles, covering business behavior against one or more of the emerging management issues. They are sponsored by intergovernmental organizations, individuals, religious groups, and business associations. Some are self-assessment tools, others need external monitoring.

SPONSOR	ECOLOGY AND ENVIRONMENT	DIVERSITY AND HUMAN RIGHTS	HEALTH AND WELL-BEING	COMMUNITY
BUSINESS ASSOCIATIONS				
America Apparel	✔	✔	✔	
Caux Round Table	✔	✔	✔	✔
Confindustrial (Italy)	✔	✔	✔	
Federation Greek Industries	✔	✔	✔	✔
International Chambers of Commerce	✔	✔	✔	✔
Toy-Makers		✔	✔	
STAKEHOLDER GROUPS				
CERES	✔	✔		
Consumers International	✔	✔	✔	
SA 8000		✔	✔	
Interfaith	✔	✔	✔	✔
Global Reporting Initiative	✔	✔	✔	
INTER-GOVERNMENTAL				
ILO		✔	✔	
OECD	✔	✔	✔	
UN Global Compact	✔	✔		✔

A number of leading companies with their headquarters in the UK agreed to measure and report against these key indicators during 2001–2002, and to share their business experience in making them work.

WHAT TO MEASURE

The decision as to what to measure depends crucially on the overall strategy that you as a manager are adopting, and whether you are basing this on a particular code or standard such as the Global Reporting Initiative. Another influence on your decision might come when your company is:

● Part of a multinational that has already signed up for a measurement tool and is providing substantial guidance on how to fulfill this.
● Ahead of the rest of the business. They have spotted a market trend and moved ahead of the wave. Occidental in Ecuador introduced ISO 14001 as a safeguard against potential criticisms from pressure groups, although there were no

similar moves at that time in the rest of the firm.
- In a trade association or national market environment where there is peer group pressure to measure.

If you are a manager with a multinational company, you may find that your fellow managers are already using a variety of different measurement indicators.

- Swedish Match is an international group based in Sweden and one of the world's leading companies in the area of niche tobacco products. These are collectively known as Other Tobacco Products, including: smokeless tobacco, cigars, and pipe tobacco. Swedish Match's well-known brands have brought it strong market positions in selected geographic markets. In order to satisfy consumer expectations, the company developed its own best practice code, known as Gothiatek. This includes the whole process from seed to the consumer, covering issues of health, ethics, environment, quality, and transparency. It is based on ISO 9001:2000 for quality management and ISO 14000 for environment management.

HOW TO MEASURE

There are a number of questions to consider when deciding on the best measurement process to adopt for your company, business unit, or situation.

- Does my company have a code of business principles to measure against?
- Does the company belong to a business organization or to a trade association that has already produced a relevant code to measure against?
- Which of the generic codes is most relevant to my company's circumstances? Will it need adapting?
- Does the code call for external verification? What are the implications of that in terms of access to information and commercial confidentiality and in terms of external communications?

The mechanics of the measurement process can be undertaken exclusively in-house or by external consultants. Alternatively, external auditors can be brought in to verify the in-house procedures and results. The decision you make depends on your company's circumstances. Smaller firms can usually only afford to measure internally. If your business wants to be included on tender lists, you will need to show that you have achieved certain standards. This will need external verification.

A sophisticated form of measurement is a social audit. This covers the nonfinancial impacts of a company. The social audit takes the financial audit as its model, and is sometimes produced in the form of a balance sheet showing the net impact (positive or negative) on the social dimension of a company's operations. This approach is in its infancy, with differently held views as to how to quantify the considerable qualitative data associated with social impact.

Producing Reports

A small but growing number of businesses are producing environmental and social reports alongside their financial reports in order to respond to stakeholder interest.

Sometimes these relate to a particular geographical area of the company's operations, for example The Body Shop Australia and New Zealand. Other reports cover the totality of a company's environmental and social "footprint."

The consultancy Sustainability, which acts as an external verifier to a number of company reports, reviewed some 250 different environmental and social reports for its Global Reporters 2000, which surveys corporate reports and reporting. In it they identified the 50 top reports based on clarity of measuring and reporting, transparency, management, and approach. Those in the top 20 included BAA, Novo Nordisk, British Airways, Bristol-Myers Squibb, Volkswagen, ING, Eskom, and United Utilities.

WHY SHOULD YOU REPORT?
It may be a requirement to report. In Germany, for example, there are legal requirements on companies in relation to environmental impacts. French law has required social reports

for some time. There are also likely to be other drivers:

- Your company may need to respond to strong stakeholder expectations, perhaps because of previous crises.
- You might have to manage critics' misinterpretations of what your company is doing. Silence is not always golden.
- You may need help to maximize the firm's learning ability.

This is not to say that reporting is always the right choice. There may be occasions when reporting is inappropriate, for example after the first round of measurement. It may be more politic to have a trial run to familiarize the organization with the process and provide the opportunity to take remedial action without the full glare of publicity.

WHO TO REPORT TO?

The principal audiences to receive the report will be selected from key subgroups. The report may be:

- Circulated internally
- Sent to a peer learning group where participants are sharing their measurement results
- Sent to all stakeholders, perhaps as part of a leadership exercise.

WHAT TO REPORT

Some companies are now reporting against what is called the Triple Bottom Line (*see* p. 243). This is the simultaneous measurement of the financial, environmental, and social performance of the business.

FORMS OF REPORT

Some environmental and social reports are entirely paper-based and a few are entirely web-based. However, most involve a combination of formats, some with popular versions that are promoted through advertising.

   As more companies produce environmental, social, or composite triple-bottom-line reports, they will come under increasing scrutiny. The New Economics Foundation, based in the UK, which pioneered work on social auditing, issued a critical analysis of corporate reports in 2000. It alleged that less than one percent of all listed companies on either the

New York or London Stock Exchanges report on social performance, that "social reporting has been captured by the marketing departments," and that it "ignores the most important facts" (Deborah Doane, *Corporate Spin: The Troubled Teenage Years of Social Reporting*, 2000).

While this may seem as if business is damned if it does report and still damned if it does not, the pressures on companies are pushing toward higher standards of accountability and demanding hard evidence of performance. This will need to be made available to internal and external stakeholders, in forms and formats that permit more accurate benchmarking.

WHAT THE FUTURE HOLDS

The internet will enable businesses to produce real-time reports that stakeholders will be able to study by country, by issue, or by stakeholder. Stakeholders will be able to use these reports in order to compare the performance of different companies. Thus, country managers, brand managers, or plant managers will increasingly find themselves asked to contribute to an overall company social impact report. This will show how sustainable development activities are integrated into mainstream business, not least in developing countries.

EXTERNAL VERIFICATION

Many environmental and social reports are subject to external verification or to an external commentary from an acknowledged expert in the issues involved. The advantages of such external verification are that:

- It is inherently difficult to be your own judge, which is one reason why financial statements have external auditors.
- However vigorous a company is in assessing its own performance, it may not be trusted as being so by external stakeholders.
- While there may have been a genuine effort internally, some of the methodology and conclusions may be incorrect.
- External verifiers bring accumulated knowledge and experience from elsewhere.
- An external verifier may elicit fuller or more honest answers from interviewees.

However, there are potential disadvantages to this form of verification. They include:

- Losing the learning from the process of measuring and reporting.
- Compromising the company's confidentiality.
- Higher reporting costs.
- The risk of elevating the process to the point where it provokes an internal backlash before there is sufficient consensus for the underlying process.
- The lack of competent external assessors in many parts of the world, where those available may be trained with a very industrialized world view.

There are many different external verifiers and assessors. They include:

- The Institute for Social and Ethical Accounting, called Accountability.
- Some of the major accounting firms.
- Some academics in university business ethics departments have also undertaken such work. The European Business Ethics Network has members from across Europe, including academics, consultants, and unaffiliated individuals.

ENGAGING WITH YOUR STAKEHOLDERS

Measuring and reporting are essential tools for creatively engaging stakeholders. Stakeholder engagement is more than stakeholder management or one-way communication. Leading firms such as the Scandinavian healthcare company, Novo Nordisk, emphasize dialogue and the added-value that comes from seeing stakeholders as a source of ideas and insights, rather than simply a group to communicate with. How long will it be before major firms embrace this, and the traditional investor relations department in a large company becomes the section for stakeholder relations?

In the 1970s, ideas of employee empowerment and engagement began to be accepted, but faced resistance from some older managers who saw this as an abdication of leadership. Today, there is a similar rift over stakeholder engagement, but leading edge companies are already seeing the benefits from this approach.

> Economic liberalization and privatization need not lead to environmental damage if adequate space and support is provided to the civil society to act as a powerful and knowledgeable watchdog
>
> Centre for Science and Environment, India, June 2000.

Adopting the Seven Steps as a Management Approach

You may be the chairman, chief executive, director, senior manager, department head, or middle manager in a large business. Or you may be the owner or manager of a small business.

Whatever your level, the actions needed for adopting the Seven Steps as a management approach are the same, even if the scale of activity is different. The actions can be summarized as follows:

- Seek out or create triggers.
- Marshall arguments for action in a business case appropriate for your business and your market.
- Identify key stakeholders and ensure that channels of communication are open and flow both ways.
- Work with colleagues in scoping the risks and opportunities that the emerging management issues will bring.
- Commit internally and externally to every manager adopting the Seven Steps approach.
- Ensure sound governance structures are in place to oversee policy and performance across teams and business units.
- Stretch existing business processes and, where necessary, introduce new practices.
- Continue to institutionalize the approach by incorporating into aspects of people management such as remuneration.
- Forge community partnerships along with those in your supply chain, and acknowledge what the business has to learn from, as well as offer to, the community.
- Put in place effective measuring and reporting methodologies. Be honest about setbacks and celebrate successes on the road to sustainable business excellence.

Cynics might argue that, by promoting a concept of everybody's business, there is a danger it might become nobody's business. This handbook has endeavored to show that the risks are too great and the opportunities too rewarding for inaction. The task now is for you, the reader, to make it your business as well.

Peter's Story

If he had used the Seven Steps, Peter, the manager we first met at the start of this section, might have fared differently. Many of the mistakes he made may be avoided by adopting this approach.

- Peter could have incorporated the environmental improvements he made into the corporate communications plans of the business, and made sure the communications manager knew about his personal contacts with leading environmentalists. The company would have been able to alert these third party ambassadors faster and encourage them to speak up for Peter and the company.
- If he had consulted with employee stakeholders, he would have discovered anxieties about volunteering.
- If he had worked with his human resources managers, Peter might have developed a detailed action plan for recruiting, training, and promoting talented female employees and could have set targets for measuring the progress of female staff. Peter would have had the data to report back to HQ to answer activists' criticism.
- Focus group discussions with his staff about the needs of the local communities would have shown their concern about the quality of their children's education.
- A volunteer local community involvement coordinator, able to access a company-wide database of good practice, would have found examples of corporate support for schools elsewhere in the world. With this evidence, the co-ordinator might have found volunteers to help in the children's schools and have been able to brief them.
- By running training sessions with local managers, Peter would have realized their genuine misunderstanding that they were being asked to cut all existing company contributions. Together, they might have devised an exit strategy and moved to the new education focus over time.

Implementing the Seven Steps does not guarantee that there will be no risks or that all opportunities will be exploited, but it should help minimize risks and enable managers to make more of the opportunities presented to them.

SIGNPOSTS

STEP 1: RECOGNIZING THE TRIGGER

Regularly scanning international journals such as the *Financial Times, The Economist, Business Week*, and *Fortune* will provide information on events that could prove to be a trigger for action, as well as news of how competitors are acting.

STEP 2: MAKING A BUSINESS CASE

The Rocky Mountain Institute is a widely recognized NGO that seeks to provide market-led solutions to foster efficient use of resources (www.rmi.org). Business case arguments and examples with an environmental sustainability theme are available at the World Business Council for Sustainable Development (www.wbcsd.org). Information about the benefits of eco-efficiency is widely available through business organizations such as chambers of commerce and local environmental business clubs.

The business case for sound health and safety measures is well documented, but well-being is less so. Consultancy Sustainability publish *Radar*, a monthly publication that includes a regular entry on health and well-being (www.sustainability.co.uk).

Business case arguments for sensitivity to human rights issues are described in *Human Rights: Is It Any of Your Business?* by Peter Frankental and Frances House (Amnesty International UK and PWIBLF, 2000).

Business case information about women in the workforce and family-friendly work practices is available from *Opportunity Now*, a Business in the Community Campaign (www.bitc.org.uk). For general diversity issues try *The Business Case for Diversity* from Allegiant Media (www.diversityinc.com).

General business case arguments are presented in *Doing Good and Doing Well: Making the Business Case for Corporate Citizenship* by Simon Zadek (The Conference Board, 2001).

STEP 3: SCOPING THE ISSUES

For frameworks to think through the impact of the business on its stakeholders, and vice-versa, read *Building Competitiveness and Communities: How World Class Companies Are Creating Shareholder Value and Societal Value* by Jane Nelson (PWIBLF in collaboration with the World Bank and the United Nations Development Program, 1998), and *Winning with Integrity* from the Business Impact Taskforce (Business in the Community, 2000) (www.business-impact.org.uk).

How issues emerge is discussed in *When Good Companies Do Bad Things. Responsibility and Risk in an Age of Globalization* By Peter Schwartz and Blair Gibb (John Wiley & Sons, Inc., 1999).

STEP 4: COMMITTING TO ACTION

For examples of how leadership companies are committed to change, see *The Power to Change: Mobilizing Board Leadership to Deliver Sustainable Value to Markets and Society* by Jane Nelson, Peter Zollinger, and Alok Singh (PWIBLF and Sustainability, 2001).

For an explanation of the Triple Bottom Line read *Cannibals with Forks* by John Elkington (Capstone,1997). Read *Living Tomorrow's Company* by Mark Goyder (Gower, 1998) for an

explanation of the "inclusive" company. Mike Goyder is Director of the Tomorrow's Company Center (www.tomorrowcompany.com).

A number of institutions exist to help companies understand and practice corporate social responsibility and corporate citizenship. www.worldcsr.org is a portal to the international organizations. Business for Social Responsibility (www.bsr.org); CSR Europe (www.csreurope.org); and the PWIBLF (www.csrforum.org) have on-line databases of relevant information. Business organizations such as chambers of commerce are developing knowledge and expertise in the area. Visit the International Chamber of Commerce (www.iccwbo.org) and the US Chamber of Commerce Center for Corporate Citizenship (www.uschamber.org).

The UN Global Compact encourages signatory companies to report details of their support of the Compact principles. Contact the UN Global Business Compact (www.unglobalcompact.org).

For initiatives and help on eradicating corruption and bribery, contact Transparency International (www.transparency.de).

Companies can receive strategic advice and operational support through private sector consultancies such as the sponsor of *Everybody's Business*, EPPA (www.eppa.com).

Business schools and management centers are now developing competence in these areas, such as the Centre for Corporate Citizenship at Warwick Business School (www.wbs.warwick.ac.uk) and the Centre for Business and Society at Ashridge Management Centre (www.ashridge.co.uk), both in the UK, and The Center for Corporate Citizenship at Boston College (www.bc.edu).

Everybody's Business coauthor David Grayson's personal website contains speeches and articles on CSR, enterprise, and other related subjects (www.davidgrayson.net). Jonathan Cohen of the UN Staff Association produces a free, frequent, and informative roundup of CSR news. To subscribe, send a message to jcohen@unausa.org and input Subscribe to Socially Responsible Business in the subject header.

The US Environmental Protection Agency has developed a voluminous directory entitled *Resources for Promoting Global Business Principles and Best Practice: People, Organizations and Websites*.

STEP 5: INTEGRATING STRATEGY

There is a small but growing body of knowledge about the inclusion of social and ethical issues into management practices, joining more sophisticated data available on environmental management. Leading institutions include: The International Standards Organization, the European Foundation for Quality Management, and the American Productivity and Quality Center. Management Consultancy firms such as KPMG and PricewaterhouseCoopers provide a range of risk management services.

Corporate Social Responsibility: Making Good Business Sense (World Business Council for Sustainable Development, 2000) (www.wbcsd.ch) provides an excellent summary of possible action. Read also *Corporate Citizenship* by Malcolm McIntosh et al. (FT Pitman, 1998) and *The Civil Corporation* by Simon Zadek (Earthscan, 2000).

Create your own management checklists for policies and practices based on those provided by the Center for Corporate Citizenship at Boston College (www.bc.edu/bc), Business for Social Responsibility(wwwbsr.org), Business in the Community (www.bitc.org.uk), and the Social Venture Network (www.svn.org). Specialized issue-based organizations such as the UK's Employers Forum on Disability (www.employers-forum.co.uk) are also helpful.

STEP 6: ENGAGING STAKEHOLDERS

For the in and outs of building partnerships, good practical works include: *The Two-Way Street: Towards Partnerships for the Mutual Benefit of Business and Voluntary and Community Organizations* (Business in the Community and National Council of Voluntary Organisations, 1998) and *Managing Partnerships: Tools for Mobilizing the Public Sector, Business and Civil Society as Partners in Development* by Ros Tennyson (PWIBLF, 1998). *Partnership Alchemy* by Jane Nelson and Simon Zadek (The Copenhagen Centre, 2000) (www.copenhagencentre.org) showcases a number of business/community/public partnerships across Europe.

The World Bank Business Partners for Development program has been evaluating the benefits and workings of trisector partnerships (www.bpdweb.org).

STEP 7: MEASURING AND REPORTING

The measurement and reporting agenda is fast-moving. Keeping track of good practice is best achieved through the organizations noted in Step 4: Committing to Action, and specialists such as the Institute of Social and Ethical Accounting (www.accountability.org.uk), the Council on Economic Priorities (www.cepnyc.org), and The Global Reporting Initiative (www.globalreporting.org). The Ethos Institute in Brazil has developed a useful set of indicators (www.ethos.org.br). For a summary of leading practice in reporting see *Global Reporters: International Benchmark Survey of Corporate Sustainability Reporting* (Sustainability 2000).

NATIONAL ORGANIZATIONS

THE AMERICAS

Americas (general): Empresa (www.empresa.org).
Argentina: Empresa y Sociedad.
Brazil: Ethos (www.ethos.org.br).
Canada: Canadian Center for Philanthropy. Imagine Campaign (www.ccp.ca/imagine).
Chile: Acción Empressarial (www.accionempressarial.cl).
Colombia: Colombian Center for Corporate Responsibility (www.ccre.org.co).
Dominican Republic: CONEP/Alianza. Programa de Formento a la Inversión Social Empresarial.
Ecuador: Fundacion Esquel.
El Salvador: FUNDEMAS (www.fundemas.org).
Mexico: CEMEFI (www.cemefi.org).
Panama: BSR Panamá; Center for Social Investment in Panama.

Empresa Privada Para la Responsabilidad Social Empresarial.
Peru: Peru 2021 (www.peru2021.org).
US: Social Venture Network (www.svn.org); Center for Corporate Community Citizenship at Boston College (www.bc.edu/cccr).

AFRICA/MIDDLE EAST

Africa: African Institute for Corporate Citizenship (www.corporatecitizenship-africa.com).
Kenya: Centre for Promotion of Philanthropy and Social Responsibility.
Israel: MAALA – Israel Business for Social Responsibility (www.maala.org.il).
South Africa: National Business Initiative (www.nbi.org.za).
Zambia: Forum for Business Leaders and Social Partners.

FAR EAST/AUSTRALASIA

Australia: Community Business Partnership (www.partnership.zip.com.au).
India: Business and Community Foundation (www.bcfindia.org).
Japan: Keidanren: Council for Better Corporate Citizenship (www.keidanren.or.jp).
New Zealand: New Zealand Business for Social Responsibility.
Philippines: Business for Social Progress (www.pbsp.org.ph).
Thailand: Thailand Business Coalition against AIDS.

EUROPE

csr europe (www.csreurope.org).
Belgium: Business & Society Belgium (www.bensc.net).
Bulgaria: Bulgarian Business Leaders Forum (www.bblf.tlogica.com).
Czech: Czech Business Leaders Forum (www.blf.cz).
Denmark: The Copenhagen Centre (www.copenhagencentre.org).
Finland: Finnish Business & Society – STAKES Consortium – (www.stakes.fi).
France: Institut du Mécénat et de Solidarité (info@imsolidarite.com).
Greece: Diktyo – Hellenic Business Network for Social Cohesion.
Hungary: Hungarian Business Leaders Forum (www.hblf.weste1900.net).
Ireland: Business in the Community Ireland (www.bitc.ie).
Italy: Sodalitas (www.sodalitis.it).
Poland: Business Leaders Forum.
Portugal: Talentum (coordinator of the Portuguese Business Network for Social Cohesion) (www.talentum.pt).
Scotland: Business in the Community Scotland.
Spain: Fundacion Empresa y Sociedad (www.empresaysociedad.org).
Sweden: Jobs and Society (www.jobs-society.se).
Switzerland: Philias (www.philias.org).
UK: Business in the Community (www.bitc.org.uk). The Prince of Wales International Business Leaders Forum (www.csrforum.com).

All websites active at the time of writing.

REFERENCES

Books

Adkins, S., *Cause Related Marketing: Who Cares Wins*, Butterworth-Heinemann, Oxford, 1999.

Burke, E. M., *Corporate Community Relations: The Principle of the Neighbor of Choice*, Praeger Paperback, Westport, CT, 1999.

Brown, L. R., Renner, M., and Flavin, C., *Vital Signs 1998: The Environmental Trends that are Shaping Our Future*, W. W. Norton & Co., New York, NY, 1998.

Cairncross, F., *The Death of Distance*, Orion, London, 1997.

Clifton, R., and Maughan, E. (eds.), *The Future of Brands: Interbrand*, Macmillan Press, London, 2000.

Collins, J., and Porras, J., *Built to Last*, Random House, London, 2000.

Dalla Costa, J., *The Ethical Imperative: Why Moral Leadership Is Good Business*, Perseus Publishing, Cambridge, MA, 1998.

de Soto, H., *The Mystery of Capital: Why Capitalism Triumphs in the West and Fails Everywhere Else*, Basic Books, New York, NY, 2000.

Elkington, J., *Cannibals with Forks*, Capstone Press, Minnetonka, MN, 1997.

Gates, B., *Business at the Speed of Thought*, Warner Books, New York, NY, 1999.

Huntington, S. P., *The Clash of Civilizations and the Remaking of the World Order*, Simon and Schuster, New York, NY, 1996.

Klein, N., *No Logo: Taking Aim at the Brand Bullies*, Picador, New York, NY, 1999.

Matathia, I., and Salzman, M., *Next: A Vision of Our Lives in the Future*, HarperCollins, London, 1999.

McIntosh, M., Leipziger, D., Jones, K., and Coleman, G., *Corporate Citizenship: Successful Strategies of Responsible Companies*, Financial Times/Pitman Publishing, London, 1998.

Peters, G., *Waltzing with the Raptors: A Practical Roadmap to Protecting Your Company's Reputation*, John Wiley & Sons Inc., New York, NY, 1999.

Ridderstrale, J., and Nordstrom, K., *Funky Business*, Financial Times/Prentice Hall, London, 1999.

Schwartz, P., *The Art of the Long View*, Doubleday, New York, NY, 1991.

Schwartz, P., and Gibb, B., *When Good Companies Do Bad Things, Responsibility and Risk in an Age of Globalization*, John Wiley & Sons Inc., New York, NY, 1999.

Steckel, R., Simons, R., Simons, J., and Tanen, N., *Making Money While Making a Difference*, High Tide Press, Homewood, IL, 1999.

Thurow, L., *The Future of Capitalism*, Nicholas Brealey Publishing, London, 1996.

The Yearbook of International Organizations 2000, The Union of International Associations, Brussels, 2000.

Journals

Binyon, M., "Maimed by Embracing the Market," *The Times*, August 23, 1999.

Colvin, G., "Value Driven. Should Companies Care?," *Fortune*, June 11, 2001.

Crawford, R., "Adidas's Human Rights Policy Back on Track," *Financial Times*, December 20, 2000.

Crumm, D., "General Mills apologizes for feeding Souls with Cereal-box Bibles," *Miami Herald*, July 23, 2000.

Dodgson, H., *Journal of Business Research*, December 1987.

Drucker, P., "Beyond the Information Revolution," *Atlantic Monthly*, October 1999.

Epstein, J., "A Seedy Business," *Latin Trade*, October 1999.

Fisher, A., "Finding a Job that Lets You Care for an Ageing Parent," *Fortune*, February 21, 2000.

Frankel, B. "Work Life Initiatives Benefit Companies as Well as Employees," *DiversityInc.com*, October 24, 2000.

Lindahl, G., "A New Role for Global Businesses," *Time*, January 31, 2000.

Moss Kanter, R. "From Spare Change to Real Change," *Harvard Business Review*, May/June 1999.

O'Neill Packard, K., and Reinhardt, F., "What Every Executive Needs to Know About Global Warming," *Harvard Business Review*, July/August 2000.

O'Reilly, B., and Wyatt, J., "What Companies and Employees Owe One Another," *Fortune*, June 13, 1997.

Roberts, A., "NGOs: New Gods Overseas," *The World in 2001*, The Economist, 2000.

Schneider, F., "The Shadow Economy," *The Economist*, February 3, 2001.

Stroh, L., and Reilly, A., "Loyalty in the Age of Downsizing," *Sloan Management Review*, 1997.

"Best Foot Forward," *The Economist*, October 21, 1999.

"Beyond The Hague," *The Economist*, December 2, 2000.

"Corporate Hospitality," *The Economist*, November 27, 1999.

"Customs Stops Clothing Reportedly made by Children," *Miami Herald*, November 29, 2000.

"Fuel Cells Hit the Road," *The Economist*, June 24, 1999.

"Gang Sackings," *The Economist*, November 14, 1998.

"Global Most Admired Companies Report," *Fortune*, 1997.

"Levi's Open House," *Business Ethics*, January/February 1999.

"McDonald's Case Highlights Risks of Libel," *Reuters*, June 19, 1997.

"Supplement for Prince of Wales International Business Leaders Forum," *Time*, June 1999.

"Sweatshop Wars," *The Economist*, February 27, 1999.

Additional references dated in the text to:
Associated Press/Billings Gazette; Black Book; Bloomberg Financial News; BSR Global Resources Center; Business Mexico; Business Week; Christian Science Monitor; Corporate Social Responsibility Europe; Croner's Environmental Management; The Daily Yomiuri; Denver Post; Fast Company;

Financial Times; Financial Times Responsible Business Magazine; Global Exchange Newsletter; The Globe; Green Hotelier; Greenpeace Business, International Herald Tribune; Los Angeles Times; Miami Herald; Review of International Political Economy; San Francisco Examiner; US News and World Report; USA Today.

Reports

Doane, D., Corporate Spin: The Troubled Teenage Years of Social Reporting, New Economics Foundation, 2000.

Frankental, P., and House, F., Human Rights, Is It Any of Your Business?, Amnesty International UK and Prince of Wales International Business Leaders Forum, London, 2000.

Nelson, J., Building Competitiveness and Communities, Prince of Wales International Business Leaders Forum, World Bank and the United Nations Development Program, 1998.

Nelson, J., The Business of Peace: International Alert, Council on Economic Priorities, Prince of Wales International Business Leaders Forum, 2000.

Nelson, J., Singh, A., and Zollinger, P., The Power to Change, Sustainability and Prince of Wales International Business Leaders Forum, 2001.

Sparrow, O., Navigating Uncharted Waters, Chatham House Forum, 1997.

Sparrow, O., Open Horizons – The 1998 Report of the Chatham House Forum, Chatham House Forum, 1998.

Weiser, J., and Zadek, S., Conversations with Disbelievers, Brody Weiser, 2000.

A 12-Point Program for Business to Combat Depression in the Workplace – Mental Health in the Workplace, International Labor Organization, 2001.

British Government Report on Corporate Social Responsibility: Society and Business, DTI, March 2001.

Committee of Inquiry into a New Vision for Business, Committee of Inquiry into a New Vision for Business, 1999.

A Decade of Difference 1990–2000, Prince of Wales International Business Leaders Forum, 2000.

Development Beyond Economics 2000, Inter-American Development Bank, 2000.

Diageo Corporate Citizenship 2001 Guide, Diageo, 2001.

EarthTrends, World Resources Institute, 2000.

The Employment Impact of Mergers and Acquisitions in the Banking and Financial Services Sector, International Labor Organization, February 2001.

Final Report, Business Impact Taskforce, November 2000.

Futures Unit Report on Knowledge-Driven Economy, Department of Trade and Industry, 1999.

A Geography of Corporate Risk: UK Transnational Companies, Amnesty International UK, 2000.

Global Environmental Outlook, United Nations Environment Program, 1999.

Global Civil Society: Dimensions of the Nonprofit Sector, The Johns Hopkins Center for Civil Society Studies, 1999.

Human Development Indicators, United Nations Development Program, 1999.

Human Development Report, United Nations Development Program, Oxford University Press, New York, NY, 1992.

Human Development Report, United Nations Development Program, Oxford University Press, New York, NY. 1999.

Human Development Report, United Nations Development Program, Oxford University Press, New York, NY, 2000.

Latinobarometro, Corporación Latinobarómetro, 2000.

Life at Work in the Information Economy, World Employment Report, International Labor Organization, 2001.

Magnetic Attraction – The Potential of Talent and the Corporate Brand, Shared Learning Project, Stanton Marris, 2001.

The Millenium Poll on Corporate Social Responsibility, Environics International Ltd., 1999.

Reputation Management, Institute of Directors, 1999.

Second Assessment – Climate Change, Intergovernmental Panel on Climate Change, 1995.

Social Security Pensions: Development and Reform, International Labor Organization, 2000.

Sowing the Seeds of a Sustainable Future, Environment Foundation, 2000.

Standards of Corporate Social Responsibility, The Social Venture Network, 1999.

Starter Pack on Social Responsibility, Business for Social Responsibility, 1998.

The State of Food Insecurity in the World, Food Agricultural Organization, 1999.

State of the World, United Nations Population Fund, 1998.

State of the World's Children, UNICEF, 1988.

State of the World Population, United Nations Population Fund, 1999.

StrategyOne, Edelman PR Worldwide, 2000.

Survey of Energy Resources, World Energy Council, 1998.

Top 2000: The Rise of Corporate Power, Institute for Policy Studies, 2000.

The Two-Way Street, Taskforce 2002, Business in the Community and National Council of Voluntary Organizations, 1998.

Visions: Socially Responsive Investing, Neuberger Berman, 1998.

The War for Talent, McKinsey, 1998.

A Water Secure World: Vision for Water, Life and the Environment, World Commission on Water for the 21st Century, 1999.

Winning with Integrity: Guiding Principles, Business in the Community, London, 2000.

World Development Report 1999, World Bank, 1998/1999.

World Development Report 2000, World Bank, 2000.

World Bank Partners in Development, World Bank, 2000.

World Employment Report 2000, International Labor Organization, 2000.

The World Energy Assessment, United Nations Development Program, 2000.

World Population Report, US Census Bureau, 1998.

World's Most Respected Companies, Financial Times and PricewaterhouseCoopers, 1999.

Zenith Media Fact Book 1998–1999, Zenith, 1999.

INDEX

A

Aarhus Dockyard 164–65
ABB 21, 140, 152, 251
Abrinq Foundation 148
absenteeism 195, 196, 198, 215, 221, 292
accountability 33, 36, 38, 63, 69, 87, 194, 228, 266, 272, 298
acquisitions, *see* mergers and acquisitions
activism 17, 73, 85, 158, 186
  against transnationals 30, 60
  animal rights 85, 186–87
  anti-globalization 36, 37
  community 126, 215
  environmental 36, 68, 74, 104, 135
Adidas 116, 265
advertising 133, 147, 169, 179, 256, 261, 269, 291, 297
Africa 56, 58, 61, 100, 279
  aid and investment 29, 226
  health 55, 191
age 46, 48, 49, 65, 158
agriculture 51, 100, 156, 217
  alliances 236
  chemicals 133–34
  and global warming 102, 103
  intensive 97, 104, 178
  organic 106, 178
aid 30, 51
AIDS/HIV 55, 113, 137, 138, 178, 186, 191, 221, 269, 271, 279
Air France 69
air pollution 24, 55
air travel 25, 32, 100, 178, 179
alcohol industry 166–67, 227
Algeria 118
ALKA Forsikring 157
Alliance for Environmental Innovation 254, 271
alliances 154, 158, 262, 267–72, 282
Allied Dunbar 224
Amazon Watch 124
American Bar Association 88
American Express 32, 270
American General 226
Amnesty International 69, 271
Anderson, Paul 150
Angola 118

Annan, Kofi 70, 84, 100, 246
AOL Time Warner 154, 155, 279
Aracruz 277
Argentina 135
Asia 43
  politics 67
  pollution 55
  society 49, 51, 56, 61
  working conditions 116, 148–49
Association of British Insurers 78, 80
AT&T 15
auditing 116, 139, 168, 222, 246, 249, 256, 296
Australia 168, 170–71, 280
authority 64, 66, 67, 69, 72
auto industry 21, 23, 24, 46, 47, 136–37, 178, 180–84
automation 21, 185
Azerbaijan 118

B

BAA *see* British Airports Authority
Bain & Co 39
B&Q 152, 227, 270
Bamburi Cement Company 156
Bangladesh 54, 123, 204, 269
Bank of Scotland 158
banks 80, 123, 157, 158, 160, 179, 185–8, 250, 280
Barclays 186
benchmarking 210, 234, 250, 288, 298
Benetton 169
best practice 60, 136, 197, 232, 237, 250, 295
Bijur, Peter 165
biotechnology 178–79
BMW 137, 158, 278
Board, *see* directors
BOC 237
Body Shop 75, 142, 152, 288, 296
Boeing 80
Bolivia 123
The Boots Company PLC 278
BP 21, 29, 102, 181, 245, 246, 252
brainstorming 230
brand 32–3, 38, 86, 129
  differentiation 17, 152, 168, 227
  joint branding 262

life-cycle approach 151–53
loyalty 74
manager 269
rebranding 154
reputation 141–53, 168
vulnerability 17, 141, 142, 150
Brazil 29, 118, 130, 278, 291
  child labor 148
  ecology 98, 134, 135, 146, 147
  education initiatives 267, 277
  health 54, 113
  waste disposal 99, 134
bribery 119, 133, 257, 291
Bridgestone/Firestone 69, 106, 183
British Airports Authority 153, 288
British Airways 134–35, 276
Broken Hill Proprietary 150
broker, partnership 264
BT 33, 246, 250, 280
building the business 210, 225–27, 283
business case 210, 218–28, 300
Business Excellence Model 291
business impact assessment 210, 235–39
Business Impact Taskforce 292–93
Business in the Community 254
Business in the Environment 78
business needs 42–50, 224–28
business organizations 195, 245–46, 257, 266, 295
business stakeholders 88
business start-ups 255, 278

C

C&A 222
Cadbury Schweppes 277
Caja Madrid 188
Cambodia 55
Canada 82, 98, 99, 271
Cap Gemini Ernst & Young 111
care, dependant 57, 105, 108, 157
  corporate facilities 110–11
  see also childcare; elderly
Caribbean 17, 60, 61, 125, 277
Carphone Warehouse 14
cause-related marketing, *see* marketing
CERES 290, 291, 294

certification 88, 104, 143, 178, 195, 196, 250

CGNU 186

charities 203, 204, 226, 235, 269, 282

chemical industry 170–71, 237, 271

Chevron 225

chief executive officer 174, 217, 241

child labor 60, 82, 116, 120, 138, 143, 147, 148, 290

childcare 110, 115, 164, 197

China 29, 44, 80, 100, 130
  environment 82, 186
  human rights 118, 148
  information technology 16, 18

China Employee Benefits Forum 238

Chiquita Brands International 148, 251

Cisco Systems Inc. 140, 235, 279

cities, see urban areas

Citicorp 33

Citigroup Inc. 186, 265

closure 155, 156, 158, 178, 183, 188

CNN 20

The Coca-Cola Company 32, 33, 117, 152, 191, 217, 236, 246

Cold War 66

Colombia 118, 124

commitment 211, 242–47, 260, 265, 300

communication 13
  corporate 163, 174, 213, 241, 301
  manager 172–73, 175, 301
  stakeholder 172, 210, 211, 261–64, 300
  see also information technology; telecommunications

Communicopia.net 196

communism 28, 66, 90, 104, 213

community 52
  activism 126, 215
  categories of 122
  expectations 124, 184
  global 32–33
  of identity 122, 203–4, 223
  of interest 122, 184, 204, 223
  and job losses 157
  needs 211, 260, 273–75
  self-contained 111
  as stakeholder 232, 259
  see also community relations

community business 202

community relations 121–27, 137, 212–13, 249, 282, 300

addressing needs 276–80, 281, 301
  in auto industry 184
  business case for 223, 224, 226–27
  commitment to 244–45
  communications manager and 173
  in emerging economies 132, 139–40
  environmental programs 225
  fast-moving consumer goods and 191
  financial services and 188
  and industry sectors 179
  legislation 188
  measurement/reporting 250, 293–94
  partnerships 269, 271
  plant manager and 170, 171
  policy checklist 258
  and reputation 149–50
  seven Ps 276, 278
  smes and 194, 195, 201–4
  win-win scenarios 273–75
  see also corporate citizenship; volunteering

companies, see small businesses; transnational companies

company structure 23

competitors 217, 228, 230

compliance 252

computers 15, 21, 112, 140
  see also internet

Cone-Roper

conflict, see wars

connectivity 13, 32, 284–85

consistency 262, 266

construction industry 17, 119

consultation, stakeholder 210, 232–34

consumer 13, 56, 67, 228
  boycotts 74, 76, 89, 95, 116, 143, 146, 149, 158, 217, 247
  campaigns 17
  diversity 50
  eco-consumers 220
  expectations of 74–76, 98
  groups 106

consumption 97–98

control 23, 141, 142–43, 215

Control Risks Group 85

Cooperative Bank 186

core business 236–38

corporate citizenship 36, 70–73, 217, 235, 242–43

and brand reputation 143, 153
  citizenship committee 274
  corporate social innovation 254
  in emerging economies 132
  and mergers 155, 159, 160
  in process stretching 249–53
  public policy aspects 238–39
  stakeholder expectations of 74–81, 228
  see also community relations; society

corporate communications 64–72, 85–87, 141–53, 163, 172–73, 175, 260–86

corporate culture 161, 211–12

corporate finance manager 175

corporate functions 163–75

corporate giving 144, 204, 235, 265, 275, 276, 281

corporate governance 211, 232, 246, 253, 258, 267, 300

corporations, see transnationals

corruption 43, 54, 63, 66, 67, 119, 133, 257, 291

Corus 158

cost-cutting 194–95, 220, 225–26, 228

Costa Rica 18

Coverco 147–48

creative swiping 284

credibility 262, 266

credit programs 123, 179, 188, 269

crime 47, 72, 185, 195, 201, 277

crisis management 210, 214–15, 256

Credit Suisse First Boston 187

culture 179, 255
  corporate 161
  local 131, 138, 147, 168, 169, 275
  popular 32–33, 67, 73, 87

customer 13, 42, 39, 215, 233, 292
  actions 161, 217
  diversity 115
  loyalty 141, 168
  see also consumer

Czech Republic 279

D

DaimlerChrysler 24, 29, 181, 183

Danone 158

Danube Knitwear Ltd. 225

Dayton Hudson Corporation 159

De Beers 254

decommissioning 155–56, 178

deference, decline in 64–73, 108
democracy 66, 67, 126
demographics 41–61, 96, 108, 189
Denmark 164–65
desalination plants 77
de Soto, Hernando 34, 35, 60
Deutsche Bank 123
Deutsche Telekom 69
developed world, *see* industrialized
    world
developing world, *see* emerging
    economies
development 30, 41–61, 70, 96
    sustainable 73, 81, 220, 243, 258,
    291
DHL Worldwide Express 113, 277
Diageo 33 166–67, 227, 246, 269
digital divide 57, 58, 140, 179, 279,
    281
directors 217, 239, 240, 241, 246,
    247
disability issues 82, 114, 115, 179,
    200, 201, 227–28, 257, 280, 281
Discovery Channel 277
discrimination 65, 120, 179, 201,
    212, 222, 259
    legislation/regulation 82, 194, 199
    litigation 165, 226
disease 46, 54, 55, 60–61, 72, 103,
    113, 125, 178, 270, 271
    see also AIDS/HIV
disinvestment 147
Disney 33, 231
distribution 21, 130, 153, 189
diversity 114–20, 131, 164, 217, 255,
    265, 282
    see also human rights
Dominican Republic 138, 198
Dow Chemical Company 33, 170–71,
    245, 246, 265
downsizing 154, 155, 157, 159, 161,
    232
Dresdner Kleinwort-Wasserstein 23
Drucker, Peter 17, 71, 76, 284
due diligence 232, 256
Dunkin Donuts 130
DuPont 102

E

e-commerce 16, 17, 154, 180, 289
Eastern Europe 38, 66, 71–72, 104,
    212

ecotourism 101, 134, 178
ecology, *see* environment
economy 217, 243
    growth 29–30, 34, 42, 43, 44, 48,
    58, 98
Edelman PR Worldwide 69
education 43, 44, 55, 67, 72
    access to 41, 47, 50, 54, 56–57, 60
    corporate initiatives 125, 188, 198,
    212, 250, 262, 267, 275–77, 281
    campaigns 107
    and gender 56–57
    IT 140
    remedial 57, 125, 223, 226, 277
    study leave 110
    see also training
efficiency 45, 194, 196, 258
elderly 46, 48–49, 54
    care of 111, 115, 164, 197
Eli Lilly & Co 149–50, 271
emerging economies 129, 130–40
    best practice in 136, 183
    cities 44, 184
    debt 179
    demography 44, 49
    FMCG companies 191
    growth 34
    health 54, 55, 105, 113
    health and safety 106, 107
    investment 29–30, 96
    markets 136
    new business sectors 17–18
    and new technology 58
    poverty 43, 51, 52
    small businesses 34
emissions 102, 178, 182, 220, 226,
    252, 258
employability, security of 112, 225
employees, *see* workforce
employment 41
    access to 50
    changing patterns of 17–19, 108
    increasing 58–59
    nonprofit sector 37, 38
energy 24
    clean technology 22
    conservation 96, 195, 220
    consumption 97–98, 258
    industry 21–22
    renewable 22, 23, 102, 178
    see also fuel
entrepreneurialism 34, 39, 76, 272
Environics International Ltd. 74

environment 24, 64
    activism 36, 74, 104, 135, 145, 225
    NGOs 36, 69, 104
environmental management 73, 74,
    96–104, 249, 283
    business case for 220
    committing to 245
    in emerging economies 132–35
    financial services and 186
    FMCGs and 191
    industry sectors and 178–79
    investor expectations 78–80
    life-cycle approach 151, 178
    measurement/reporting 290–94
    partnerships 270, 271
    plant manager and 170–71
    policy checklist 258
    and process stretching 252–53
    and reputation 143–45
    and restructuring 155–56
    smes and 194, 195–96, 204
    suppliers and 166
    and tourism 100–1, 134–35, 153,
    156
environmental impacts 133
Environmental Index 78
environmental industries 22
environmental refugees 100
environmental regulations 22, 99, 131,
    143
environmental rehabilitation 155–56
environmental reports 296–98
environmental standards, 96, 178, 194
    ISO-14001 88, 104, 178, 196, 294
environmental task force 212
equal opportunities 65, 81, 212, 213,
    292
Eskom 221
Ethical Trading Initiative 139
ethics 13, 25
    compliance 252
    corporate 75, 120, 149, 152, 232,
    243
    ethical consumers 269
    in investment 78, 79, 178, 232
    in lending 179, 186, 187
    in trade 179, 190, 191, 259, 288,
    290
ethnic minorities, *see* minorities
European Union (EU) 22, 23, 81, 82,
    216, 266
    directives 23, 81–82, 99, 111, 182
excellence, *see* quality and excellence

expansion 153, 223
extractive sector 21–22, 71, 97–98, 102, 135, 136, 139, 140, 144–45, 156, 171, 178–79
Exxon 69, 80, 159, 290

F

family 49
family-friendly employer 157, 224
family values 90
farming, *see* agriculture
fast-moving consumer goods (FMCGs) 143–44, 152–53, 166, 168, 169, 178–79, 188–91
feedback 261, 264, 286
feminism 64
Fiat 137
financial services 48–49, 77–80, 102, 123, 152, 160, 178–79, 185–88, 230
  see also banking; insurance; pensions
fishing 238
Fleet Bank Boston 157
flexitime 157, 197
FMCG, *see* fast-moving consumer goods
food 44, 46, 50, 51, 55, 143, 277
  GM 25, 68, 69, 106–7, 178, 217
  organic 106, 178
food industry 190–91
food safety 106–7, 178, 191, 217
Ford Motor Company 21, 24, 29, 33, 69, 112, 181–184, 245, 246, 292
foreign direct investment (FDI) 29, 233
foreign exchange markets 28
foreign workers 61
forestry 156, 270, 288
  deforestation 96, 97, 98, 135
Forrester 17
France 69, 172, 296
franchise manager 175
freedom 41, 50, 90, 179
Friends of the Earth 159, 216
fuel 21–22, 88, 101, 178, 182
fuel-cell technology 24, 178, 180, 181
future 239, 285

G

Gabriel Resources Ltd. 140
Gap 116
gas industry 21, 97, 181

GDP 28, 29, 46
gender 56–57, 65, 119
  see also women
gene technology 13, 25, 178
genetic screening 179, 186–87
  GMOs 25, 68, 69, 103–4, 106–7, 146, 147, 152, 178, 217, 262
General Electric Company 16, 29, 33
General Mills, Inc. 152, 169
General Motors, 24, 29, 80, 88
Generation X 111
Germany 49, 69, 145, 157, 246, 296
Ghana 134
Gibson, Chris 21
GlaxoSmithKline 244, 257, 270
global community 32
global economy 27, 28–31
Global Exchange 167
global markets 27, 36, 70
Global Partnership for Youth Development 270
Global Reporting Initiative 291–94
global warming 24, 97, 98, 101–3, 159, 180, 252, 258
  and insurance 102, 178, 186, 220
globalization 25, 28, 41, 129
  backlash 36, 37
  global brands 31–32, 38
  global NGOs 38
  and local issues 33, 119–20
  negative impacts 71
  and working patterns 18
  see also global economy; transnationals
glocalism 33
GM 24, 29, 80, 88, 181, 225, 292
goodwill 227
government 39, 67, 216, 227
  corporate role in 238–39, 266–68, 283
  and global market economy 27
  and internet 16, 67
  lack of trust in 63, 64, 68, 69
  leadership role of 64, 65
  oppressive 66, 117, 133, 179
  scrutiny of 20
  as stakeholder 81–82, 136, 232, 266
Greece 291
Greenpeace 69, 85, 135, 144–45
Greenspan, Alan 16
Groundwork Trust 271

Grupo M 198
Guido's Pizza, Boise 204

H

Handy, Charles 243
Hanna Andersson 203
health 69, 108, 164
  mental 108, 109
health and safety 105–7, 120, 249, 258
  and auto industry 178, 181, 182–83
  in emerging economies 131, 136
  plant manager and 170
  in small business 194
  standards 146, 292
  of suppliers 138
health and well-being 105, 232
  auto industry and 182–83
  and brand/corporate reputation 146–47
  business case for 221
  and business restructuring 157–58
  in emerging economy 136–38
  fast-moving consumer goods and 190–91
  financial services and 186
  in human resources 164
  and industry sectors 178
  management issues 108–13
  partnerships 269, 270, 271
  policy checklist 258
  reporting codes of practice 294
  small businesses 195, 196–99
healthcare 50, 60, 178, 278
  access to 41, 54–55
  corporate provision 57, 105, 108, 111, 113, 124, 131, 136–47, 199, 221, 225
  and demographics 44, 46
  private sector 54
health education 54, 113
health insurance 25, 54, 178, 186, 221
Heineken 117
Hewlett Packard 117, 278, 280
Home Depot 85, 144, 270
Honda Motor Corporation 146–47
Hopkins Catering Equipment 195–96
HSBC 110, 115, 187
human resources 50, 76, 108–12, 114, 119, 157, 164–65, 173, 202,

224–25
developing 237
manager 164–65, 175, 269, 301
network programme 199
policy audit 256
human rights 50, 65, 69
auto industry and 183
and brand/corporate reputation
147–49
business case for 222
and business restructuring 158
in emerging economy 138–39
fast-moving consumer goods and
191
financial services and 187
and industry sectors 179
legislation 199
litigation costs 222, 226
management issues 114–20
measurement/reporting 293–94
partnerships 271
policy checklist 258
in process stretching 251
shareholder resolutions on 80
in small businesses 195, 199–201
suppliers and 167
see also diversity
Huntingdon Life Sciences 85, 187

I
IBM 19, 29, 32, 33, 262, 271, 280
incentives 211
India 100, 130, 134, 190
auto industry 137
consumption 98
environment 82, 127
human rights 118
investment 29
IT industry 18, 59, 131
NGOs 38
population growth 44
indigenous peoples 22, 62, 98, 119,
179, 233
Indonesia 82, 100, 118
industrialized world
consumption 97
immigration 44, 60–61
informal economy 35
new economy 18
new technology 58
population levels 44
poverty 43

industry sectors 18, 39, 177–91, 215,
284
inequality 29–30, 57, 70
gender 72
of opportunity 43
wealth 43, 50–58
infant mortality 46
informal economy 34–35, 60, 193
information 63, 69
access to 67, 101, 106, 179
corporate programs 134
flows 174
freedom of 66–67
market intelligence 230
media 20, 69
NGO sources 69
stakeholder 228
information technology 14–20, 23,
193
industry 17–18, 59, 131, 178–79
NGOs and 85–86
Telematics 183
infrastructure 44, 159, 171, 233, 238,
283
ING 186
innovation 228, 254–55
insurance 157, 178, 179, 185, 198
corporate 107, 139, 195
discrimination in 226
and genetic screening 25, 186–87
and global warming 102, 178, 186,
220
mapping management issues 230
and pensions 49, 152
integrity 262
Intel 18
Interbrand 32, 142
interconnected management 163,
174–75, 240
Interfaith Center on Corporate Social
Responsibility 80
intergovernmental institutions 83–84,
231, 266
International Center for Alcohol
Policies 227
International Labour Organization 58,
114, 120, 160, 185, 271, 294
International Paper 159
internet 16, 32, 143, 204, 240, 279
access 58
business advice 195
chat rooms 30
financial services 185

freedom of information 67, 108
hate sites 179
interactive communication 261
learning via 225
reporting via 298
and working practices 19, 115
see also e-commerce
interpersonal skills 282
investment 58
in education 56
in emerging economies 29–30, 96,
233
and environmental risk 186
ethical 78, 79, 178, 232
generation of 236
public sector 30
social, see corporate citizenship
in suppliers 166–67
urban 45
Investor in People logo 198
investors 173, 216
staging boycotts 77
response to interests of 232
as stakeholders 77–80, 138
see also shareholders
Ireland 166–67
Israel 203
Italy 44

J
Japan 44, 99, 291
job creation 58–59, 216, 236, 292
job losses 154, 155, 157–58, 160,
178, 183, 185
job security 109, 112, 160, 183,
258
job-sharing 110
jobs market, informal 34–35, 60
joint venture 119, 154, 158, 179, 236,
289

K
Kakum National Park, Ghana 134
Kellogg's 32, 168–69, 270
Kenya 156
Kids Line 168
Klein, Naomi 30
Korea 99, 149, 291
KPMG 15, 111, 116

L

labeling 143, 168, 178, 190
labor 18
  cheap 130–31
  forced/indentured 80, 120, 167
  regulations 131
  rights 69, 138
  shortages 44, 60
  standards 116, 119–20, 138, 147
  surplus 60
  see also child labor
Laing, John 227
land claims 119, 139
land damage 156, 157, 178
Lapeyre 135
Latin America 57, 60, 61, 64, 148
layoffs 157, 158, 160, 161, 235, 258
leadership 64, 65, 68–69, 211, 247
learning 112, 225, 284
  life-long 81, 105, 198, 232, 283
leave 110, 111, 158, 164, 198
leisure industry 178–79
leveraging 285
Levi Strauss & Co. 138, 148
liberalization 27, 28, 35, 71
license to operate 227, 233, 283
life expectancy 46, 49, 55, 72
literacy 56, 57, 127, 198
litigation 167, 172–73, 178, 222, 226
  employee 76, 116–17, 165, 221, 226, 288
Littlewoods 251
Lloyds TSB Bank 14, 250
loans 80, 123, 140, 188
  ethical lending 179, 186, 187
lobbying 266
local business systems 236
local government 69, 202, 227, 232, 269
Lockheed Martin 117
logos 31, 148, 198, 288, 289
Los Angeles 88
Lowe's 144
Lucent Technologies 80

M

McDonald's 31, 33, 85, 172–73, 254,
McKay Nursery 200
McKinsey & Company 36, 39
Malaysia 118

managers 163–75, 185, 215, 282, 285, 289
  commitment of 244, 260, 265
  initiating change 209
  local 215
  making business case to 228
  and oversight group 246
  of privatized businesses 36
  reporting 298
  skills and training 283–85
  of small businesses 193–204
Mandela, Nelson 70
manufacturing 13, 21–24, 131, 143, 152, 179
  Global Manufacturing Principles 139
  measurement codes 290
mapping 230, 249
marketing 152, 163, 179, 189
  alliances 154
  cause-related 141–42, 145, 168–69, 204, 235, 259, 269, 276, 283
  cultural sensitivity 147
  responsible 255
  and sales 74–76, 141–53, 158, 168–69, 175
markets 27–39, 96, 104
  diversity in 50, 200–1, 222
  expanding 42
  global 27, 36, 80
  local 33
  stability 42
  transition in 34, 51
Marriott Hotels 223, 280
Mars 191
Mason, Tim 145
Mattel, Inc. 139, 143
measuring 211, 250, 264, 287–99, 300
media 16, 67, 173
  business 213
  community involvement 203–4
  criticism 20, 38, 214–15, 288
  freedom of 66–67
  global 20, 67, 98, 106
  new technology 31
  popular 87, 90
  protests 95
  public attitude toward 68, 69
  trade 230
medicine
  and demographics 46, 49
  drugs and medication 178–79

  freedom of information 67
  new technology 25, 36
  preventative 54
mental health 108, 109, 271
mentors 110, 112, 171, 251, 258, 265, 278, 279
mergers and acquisitions 29, 119, 154–61, 178, 217, 232, 255
  in auto industry 181, 183
  failures 160–61
  in financial services 185
Merrill Lynch 186
Mexico
  environmental issues 82, 134, 153
  healthcare 113, 136–37
  human rights 118
  informal economy 34
  migrant workers 200
  social programs 123
Michelin 158
Microsoft 17, 33, 69, 117, 279, 280
migration 44, 50, 60–61, 200, 203
Minera Yanacocha 171
mining 137, 140, 150, 171
minorities
  business ownership 117, 203, 251, 269
  discrimination 165
  markets 50, 222
  rights 65, 199
  in workforce 50, 265, 282
Mitsubishi 29, 77, 153
Mitsui 29
Mobil 159
monitoring 231, 246
  see also measuring
Monsanto Corporation 69, 147, 263
Montreal Protocol 216
Morgan Chase, J.P. 256, 265
Morgan Stanley 186
motivation 18, 76, 110, 164, 211
motor vehicles 24, 178, 179, 180–84
  hybrid 178, 180, 181, 182
  Super Ultra Low Emission Vehicle (SULEV) 182
  traffic congestion 179, 180–81, 184
Motorola 18
MORI 70–71, 76
multiculturalism 50, 61
multinational companies, *see* transnationals

Muslims 50, 138
Myanmar 117, 118

N

Nabisco 144, 145
Nambarrie 204
National Westminster Bank Plc. 188
Natura 142
natural resources 21–22, 97–98, 130, 178, 258
Nedbank 188
Nelson, Jane 235, 246
networks 195, 199, 203, 233, 234, 283, 285
New Zealand Post Office 130
Newbold, Yves 139
Newmont Mining Corporation 171
news media 20, 31, 85
Nextel 117
Nigeria 118, 140
Nike 69, 116, 141, 148–49
Nissan Motor Co. 29, 183
noise 178, 184
nongovernmental organizations (NGOs) 27, 31
    activism 36, 85, 186, 223
    business links with 126, 138, 140, 213, 223, 247, 254, 269–70, 272
    business skills of 39
    communication technology 85–87
    and communities 124
    environmental 36, 69, 104
    expectations of 85–87
    influence of 69
    and the internet 86
    legitimacy questioned 126
    market power of 37–38
    pressure, as trigger 216
    public sector role of 39
    public trust in 68–69, 85
    scrutiny of 38, 87
    and technology 38
    tracking development of emerging issues 231
    and transnationals 38
    verification role of 116, 167
Norsk Hydro 237, 271
Northern Ireland 271
nonprofit sector 37, 38, 39
Novartis 133

O

OECD 35, 83, 294
oil industry 21, 97–98, 144–45, 181
Olson, James 180
outsourcing 23, 149, 154
oversight, see monitoring

P Q

packaging 81–82, 143, 166, 172, 178, 190, 195, 220, 254, 258
Pakistan 118, 271
Papua New Guinea 55, 137, 150
parental leave 110, 111, 158
partners, domestic 88, 158
partnerships 84, 173, 282
    added credibility via 262
    building 211
    business 228, 289
    business-community 121, 125–26, 223, 235, 273–74
    business-NGO 126, 168, 223, 254, 262, 269–70, 272, 273
    in development 70
    and privatization 36
    public-private 81, 185, 202
    stakeholder 260, 267–72
Pepsi 30
pensions 46, 48–49, 60, 78, 152, 185
people management 210, 224–25, 237, 276–80, 282, 300
personal development 225, 283, 292
Peru 34–35, 99, 171
Petzetakis, A. G. 158
pharmaceuticals 68, 103–4, 138, 147, 153, 178–79, 187, 270, 271
philanthropy 235, 281
Philippines 73, 82, 118, 217, 236
Phillips-Van Heusen Corporation 120
Pioneer 158
Pitney Bowes 256
Placer Dome 137
planning applications 223
plant 179, 184, 215, 220, 238
    or unit managers 137, 140, 150, 156, 159, 163, 170–71, 269
policy
    auditing and extending 249, 255–59
    change, mastering 286
    implementing 285–86
pollution 96, 101, 103, 178, 212

air 24, 55
    cleanups 156, 157, 171
    motor vehicles 180, 181–82
    prevention 220
    standards 106
    water 82
population 41, 43–50, 97, 180
poverty 42–43, 47, 51, 52, 121, 277
    healthcare/education access 54–57
    and informal economy 60
    and job creation 58–59
    and privatization 71–72
power, corporate 276–80
premises 276–80
Premier Oil 117
presentations 208
PricewaterhouseCoopers 116, 139, 253
privatization 27, 28, 35
    in emerging economies 130
    managers in 36
    and poverty 71–72
    public expectations 67
processes, review/stretching 248–54, 300
Procter & Gamble 115, 143, 159, 226, 291
product 238, 276–80
    crises 210, 214, 217
    development 222
    differentiation 141, 152, 217
    launches 189
    safety 106–7, 146, 178, 221, 233
product life-cycle analysis 99, 151, 178, 190, 233, 258
production 21–24, 97, 189
    see also manufacturing
productivity 46, 55, 57, 59, 194–95, 221, 265, 292
profit 225, 226–27, 276–80
promotion 152, 276–80
Prudential 78
public policy 211, 238–39, 241, 260, 266–67
public-private partnership 81, 185, 202, 233
public relations 172–73
public sector 30, 39, 49, 67, 233, 267–68
    corporate contribution to 125
    privatizations 35–36
publicity 213
purchasing and supply 116, 119, 137,

138–39, 147, 163, 171, 180, 202, 251, 276–80, 290–91
manager 166–67, 175, 269
see also suppliers
Putnam, Robert 67
quality and excellence 88, 211, 228, 250, 253, 272, 291
quarrying 156

R

racism 65, 147, 212, 217, 226
Rasmussen, Poul 81
rebranding 154, 164
recruitment 123, 171, 222, 224, 228, 282
  costs 194, 195
  difficulties 215
recycling 96, 143, 152, 153, 172, 178, 195, 202, 258
  legislation 23, 81–82, 99
Reebok 119
refugees 60–61, 100, 103
regulation 99, 131, 194, 210, 214, 220, 252, 288
regulatory agencies 36, 81–82, 216
religion 73, 152, 158, 169
  demographic change 50
  environmental groups 80
relocation 232, 233
repetitive strain injury 137, 178
reporting 80, 211, 250, 294, 296–300
reputation 124, 131, 135, 138, 170, 222, 232, 289
  building 210, 227–28
  life-cycle approach 151–53
  profile survey 241
  protecting 129, 141–53
  risk 253
research and development 181, 237, 283
restructuring 129, 154–61, 183
retail sector 116, 119, 143, 145, 147
retailing 143, 178–79, 189
retirement 48
Rio Tinto 246, 254
risk management 107, 138, 211, 232, 253–54
roads 24, 179, 180
Robertson, Pat 158
Roddick, Anita 75
Romania 66, 140
Royal Bank of Scotland 187

Royal Dutch/Shell 29, 33, 181, 236, 246, 278
  Brent Spar 72–73, 85, 144–45
  communication campaign 261
  compliance 252
  emissions costing 102
rural areas 51, 179, 190, 201
Russia 35, 71–72, 98, 118, 159
Rwanda 271

S

Saint Gobain 135
Sainsbury's 110, 143
Saipan 167
sales 152, 163, 168–69, 175, 194–95, 225
San Francisco 88
San Miguel Food Group 236
Sara Lee Corporation 89
satellites, communications 14, 85, 178
Saudi Arabia 118
scandals 63
scenarios 210, 239
Schering AG 153
scholarships 188, 198
scoping 210, 229–41, 256, 300
scrutiny 20, 31, 38, 63, 64, 87, 104, 141, 150, 266, 297
Seattle 36, 37, 68, 88
Seaview Hotel and Restaurant, Isle of Wight, (UK) 202
security 47, 139, 170, 171, 179, 195, 223
Sedgwick 238
self-regulation 56
service sector 13, 131
Seven-Step Process 209–12
sexism 65, 147, 212
sexual harassment 119, 139
sexuality 64, 65, 82
Shanghai 44
shareholders 193
  activism 77–78, 144, 212, 216
  added value 211, 243
  making business case to 228, 247
  resolutions 80, 116, 216
  see also investors
Shell, *see* Royal Dutch/Shell
shelter 50
Shoney's Inc. 226
sickness 57, 164, 165, 195, 196, 215, 221

Siemens 33, 108, 134, 219
Sierra Club 69
Skandia 112
skills 52, 56–57, 105, 237, 283–85
  reskilling 112, 292
  transfer 29, 60, 132, 171, 191
small businesses (smes) 15, 34, 193–204, 251, 289, 292
social audit 296, 297
social exclusion 43, 70, 81, 277
social investment, *see* corporate citizenship
social reports 250, 296–98
Solvay S.A. 135
sourcing 152, 179, 190, 191, 223
  measurement codes 290
South Africa 137, 158, 217, 221, 277
  bank loans 188
  government initiatives 216, 267
South African Breweries 140, 227, 251
South America 116
Spain 184, 188, 191
Sparrow, Dr. Oliver 16, 28, 98
sponsorship 198
State Street 33
stakeholders 39, 41, 72, 95, 161
  board representation 246
  communication 172, 210, 261–64, 284, 300
  consultation 210, 232–34
  engagement of 211, 228, 260–86, 299
  expectations 74–90, 208, 209, 215, 232, 297
  human rights of 114
standards 78, 96, 178, 182, 198, 217, 222
  international 237
  Investors in People 198
  ISO 14001 88, 104, 196, 260, 294
  SA8000 291, 294
Starbucks Coffee 147–48, 262
Statoil ASA 84
stock exchange 219, 253
strategy 129–61, 218
  integrating 211, 248–59
stress 18, 105, 108–9, 112, 160, 221
subcontractors 23, 116, 131, 149, 250
Sumitomo Bank 80
suppliers 177, 178, 179, 217, 247
  in auto industry 180, 183, 184
  communications with 173
  diversity 191, 222

human resources manager and 164
measurement in 289
networks 233, 283
plant manager and 171
purchasing manager and 166–67
reputation risks 119, 142, 143, 152
stakeholder interests of 232
standards 119–20, 194, 251, 259, 289
working conditions 116, 138, 152, 222
supply, *see* purchasing and supply
supply chain management 251
Sutherland, Peter 85
swarming 88
sweatshops 116, 147, 167
Swedish Match 295

T

Taco Bell 152
Taiwan 99
take-back legislation 23, 220
Tanzania 153
Tata Group 19
technology 13–25, 36, 96, 131
auto industry 180, 181, 182–83
cleaner 96, 181, 220
development/transfer 237
energy 22
manufacturing/production 21–24
medical/genetic 25
NGOs and 38
see also information technology
telecommunications 13, 14–15, 58, 124, 279, 281
telecommuting 108, 110, 115, 281
Telefónica de Espana 120, 250
Telenor 269
telephone 14, 58, 168, 280
call centers 19, 185
mobile phones 14, 140, 178, 269
text messaging 14–15, 73
television 16, 20, 21, 277, 278
telecommuting 108, 110, 281
Tesco 145, 279
Tetrapak 172
Texaco Inc. 33, 117, 140, 165, 217, 265
Texas Instruments 18
Thailand 271
Thames Water 133, 280, 285
Thatcher, Margaret 104

3M 220, 246
TIAA-CREF 78
tobacco industry 136
Tokyo 45, 158
tourism 125, 178–79, 223, 270, 291
ecotourism 101, 134, 178
and environment 100–1, 134–35, 153, 156
and leisure sector 25, 45, 87, 100, 125, 134, 153, 223
toy manufacturers 113, 139
Toyota Motor Corporation 24, 181, 183, 277
trade 28
fair/ethical 179, 190, 191, 259, 290
traffic congestion 24, 179, 180–81, 184, 201
traffic safety 146–47, 178
training 60, 133, 164, 167, 194, 211, 213, 223, 249, 251, 258, 283–85, 292
retraining 112, 159
transnationals 29, 30–31, 41, 60
health and safety issues 107
human rights issues 117, 120
measurement indicators 292–93
NGOs and 38
OECD guidelines 83
reputation of 131, 289
as standard bearers 132–33
welfare provision 57, 123
transparency 87, 133, 138, 191, 194, 211, 228, 266, 282, 288
transportation 21, 24, 25, 45, 123, 130, 178–79
Travelsphere Ltd. 201
triggers 210, 214–17, 239, 240, 300
Trotman, Sir Alex 21
trust 64, 65, 67, 68–9, 287
between partners 272
building 138, 211, 227, 228, 234, 289
consumer 74–75, 228
in NGOs 68–69, 85
TRW Inc. 136–7
Turkey 118
TXU 245, 292

U

Uganda 204
Ukraine 35
unemployment 58, 155, 217
Unilever 153, 189, 190, 238, 277
Union Camp 159
Unipart Group Limited 112
Unisys 226
unit manager, *see* plant manager
United Kingdom 19
financial services 186, 187, 188
partnerships 271
public attitudes 67, 70–71
waste disposal 99
United Nations
Declaration of Human Rights 114
Development Programme 71
Environment Programme 291
Global Compact 84, 245–46, 294
Industrial Development Association 137
UNICEF 172, 276
United States
Clean Corporate Citizenship 143
Community Reinvestment Act 188
corporate carer facilities 111
Customs Service 82
Federal government 266
migrant workers 200
partnerships 271
public attitudes 65, 67, 70
universities, corporate 112, 225, 283
tendering process 140
Unocal 117
urban areas 179
brown field sites 156
industrial pollution 156, 157
multiculturalism 61
population growth 44–45
poverty 51
smes in 201
traffic congestion 180–81, 184
youth 47
utilities 45, 178–79, 217, 221, 245

V

value 219
added 114, 131–32, 211, 234, 243
values 63–90, 96, 106, 204
changing 64–73
corporate 18, 76, 155, 161, 224, 243

local 119
  and motivation 76
  universal 70, 73
vandalism 195, 201, 274
Van den Bergh Foods 277
The Vanguard Group, Inc. 78
verification 116, 131, 147–48, 167,
  222, 291, 295–96, 298–99
Vietnam 55, 149
visibility 30–31, 38, 150, 237
Voice of the Red Sea radio station
  203–4
Volkswagen 33, 153
volunteering 149–50, 198, 213, 223,
  259, 276, 280, 282
  employee response to 225, 265
  manager's support for 164, 171,
  269
Voss Fabrik S.A. 256

W

wages 116, 120, 200, 224, 259, 292
  bonuses 265
Wal-Mart 29, 31, 116, 152
war 43, 60, 95, 117, 126, 133, 139,
  254
  over water 100, 103
waste disposal 23, 99, 106, 150, 153,
  178, 220, 254
  cost-saving 226
  small businesses 194, 195
  waste water 55

water 46, 52, 55, 133, 179, 258, 271
  pollution 82, 83
  shortages 95, 100, 101, 103
wealth inequality 43, 50–58
Welch, Jack 16, 76
welfare systems 18
  corporate 57, 123, 131
  271, 280
WH Smith 277
win-win culture 209, 211, 228, 243,
  269, 273–75, 285
women 49, 52, 65, 115, 138, 212,
  265, 269, 301
Women Against Gun Control 89
work/life balance 18, 76, 105, 108,
  110–11, 157, 164, 197, 221, 292
workforce 42, 111
  action, as trigger 217
  aging 49
  commitment 260, 265
  communication with 213
  conduct 164, 165
  and demographic change 50
  developing 225
  diversity 115, 131
  environmental contributions 196
  expectations of 76
  involvement in scoping 240–41
  loyalty 76, 164, 225
  migrant workers 60–61, 200
  motivation 18, 76, 164, 198, 221
  and restructuring 157, 160–61
  retention 18, 164, 195, 197, 198,

  215, 221, 222, 224–25, 292
  satisfaction, measuring 288
  skilled 56
  as stakeholders 232, 301
working conditions 179
  consumer interest in 147, 148–49
  in emerging economies 183
  of suppliers 116–17, 138, 152, 292
working practices 153, 232, 258
  24-hour day 18, 19, 108
  long-hours culture 18–19
  at NGOs 38
  and staff motivation 221, 224
  in smes 197
  see also work/life balance
World Alliance for Community Health
  137
World Bank 133, 270
World Economic Forum 84, 102, 217
World Health Organization 270,
  271
World Trade Organization 36, 99
World Wildlife Fund 69, 144, 145,
  238

X Y Z

youth 32–33, 47, 49, 67, 270, 271,
  278
Zambia 60
Zimbabwe 134, 139

ACKNOWLEDGMENTS

Picture credits

The authors and publishers would like to thank the following for kind permission to reproduce photographs and artwork:

PHOTOGRAPHS: *a* = above; *c* = center; *b* = below; l = left; r = right; t = top

Jacket: **Getty Images**: Ken Fisher front, back, and spine.

Section Openers: 10/11 Courtesy of **The Discovery Channel Global Education Fund**: Gilbert Awekofua (Kampala, Uganda); 92/93 **Panos Pictures**: Chris Stowers; 206/207 **Getty Images**: Jeff Corwin

2 **Panos Pictures**: Liba Taylor; 4 **Popperfoto**: Reuters / Chris Helgren; 5 **Magnum**: Hiroji Kubota *b*; **Frank Spooner Pictures**: Liaison / Andy Hernandez tr; 6/7 **Getty Images**: Stuart McClymont; 12/13 **PA Photos**: European Press Agency; 14 **Stockbyte**; 15 **Hulton Archive**: Fox Photos *bl*; **Popperfoto**: Reuters / Savita Kirloskar br; 18 **Associated Press AP**: Kent Gilbert Stringer; 19 **Financial Times**: David Ahmed; 20 **Corbis**: Francoise de Mulder; 22/23 **Corbis**: Morton Beebe, SF; 24 **Telegraph Colour Library**: Nono; 26/27 **Frank Spooner Pictures**: Bouvert / Merillon; 28 **Corbis**: Marc Garanger; 30 **Panos Pictures**: Trygve Bølstad; 31 **Panos Pictures**: N Peachey; 32 **Panos Pictures**: Chris Stowers; 34 **Frank Spooner Pictures**: Liaison / Swersey; 36 **Corbis**: Reuters NewMedia Inc; 37 **Corbis**: Reuters NewMedia Inc; 38 **PA Photos**: Stefan Rousseau br; **Popperfoto**: Reuters / Livio Anticoli *bl*; 39 **Panos Pictures**: Crispin Hughes *bl*; **Frank Spooner Pictures**: Job Roger br; 40/41 **Corbis**: Stephanie Maze; 42 **Telegraph Colour Library**: Michael Dunning; 43 **Popperfoto**: Reuters / Damir Sagolj; 45 **Corbis**: Roger Ressmeyer; 47 **Getty Images**: Michael Busselle; 48 **Corbis**: Robert Maass; 49 **Panos Pictures**: J Hartley; 50 **Corbis**: Michael Freeman; 51 **Agence France Presse**: Joel Nito; 53 **Panos Pictures**: J Hartley; 54 **Associated Press AP**: Greg Baker; 56 **Corbis**: Stephanie Maze; 57 **Panos Pictures**: Javed A Jafferji; 59 **Associated Press AP**: Namas Bhojani; 60 **Popperfoto**: Reuters / Apichart Weerawong; 61 **Corbis**: Morton Beebe SF; 62/63 **Associated Press AP**: Denis Doyle; 66 **Popperfoto**: Reuters / Charles Platiau; 68 **Corbis**: Adrian Arbib; 70 **PA Photos**: Fiona Hanson tl; **Popperfoto**: Reuters / Andreas Meier *bl*; 72 **Financial Times**: Ashley Ashwood; 73 **Popperfoto**: Reuters / Erik de Castro; 75 © **The Body Shop International plc**; 77 **Associated Press AP**: Denis Poroy; 79 **Corbis**: Howard Davies; 81 **Corbis**: Michael S Yamashita *b*; **Popperfoto**: Reuters / Christine Grunnet tr; 83 **Corbis**: Premium Stock; 84 Courtesy of **The United Nations Global Compact** *cl*; Courtesy of **The United**

Nations tl; 85 **Frank Spooner Pictures**: Alain Morvan; 86/87 **Corbis**: David & Peter Turnley; 87 **Panos Pictures**: Crispin Hughes; 89 **Corbis**: David H Wells; 94/95 **Greenpeace Images International**: Sims; 96 **Popperfoto**: Reuters / Gregg Newton; 97 **Corbis**: Mark Jenkinson; 98 **Panos Pictures**; 99 **Magnum**: P. Jones-Griffiths; 100 **Panos Pictures**: Bruce Paton; 101 **Popperfoto**: Reuters / fsp / HO-Jet Propulsion Lab / NASA; 104 **PA Photos**; 105 **Getty Images**: Nick Dolding; 106 **Popperfoto**: Reuters / Savita Kirloskar; 107 **Popperfoto**: Reuters / Jeff J Mitchell; 110 Courtesy of **HSBC Bank plc**; 112 Courtesy of **Unipart Group Communications**; 113 **Science Photo Library**: NIBSC; 114 **Getty Images**: Billy Hustace; 117 **Panos Pictures**: Jan Banning *bl*; **Popperfoto**: Reuters / Apichart Weerawong br; 121 **Corbis**: Ed Kashi; 122 **Telegraph Colour Library**: Josef Beck; 123 **Panos Pictures**: David Dahmen; 124 Courtesy of **Amazon Watch**: The U'wa; 125 **Corbis**: Jonathan Blair; 127 **Panos Pictures**: Howard J Davies; 128/129 **Popperfoto**: Reuters / Guang Niu; 130 **Associated Press AP**: Lois Raimondo; 133 Courtesy of **Thames Water Utilities Ltd**; 134 **Corbis**: Kevin Schafer; 135 **Greenpeace Images International**: Emmanuel; 136 **Panos Pictures**: Chris Stowers; 137 Courtesy of **BMW South Africa**; 138 **Corbis**: Roger Ressmeyer; 140 **Corbis**: Michael S Yamashita; 141 **Colors**: James Mollison; 144 **Greenpeace Images International**: Cox br; Sauch *bl*; 145 **Popperfoto**: Reuters / Greenpeace *bl*, br; 146 **Corbis**: Stephanie Maze; 148 **Associated Press AP**: Moises Castillo tl, tr; **Corbis**: Owen Franken tc; 149 **Corbis**: Anna Clopet tr; Courtesy of **Eli Lilly and Company** br; 150/151 **Panos Pictures**: Chris Sattleberger; 153 **BAA Picture Library / In-Press Photography**: Steve Bates *bl*; 153 **Corbis**: The Purcell Team br; **Still Pictures**: Hartmut Schwarzbach bc; 154/155 **Popperfoto**: Reuters / Mel Nudelman; 156 Courtesy of **Baobab Farm Ltd**; 157 **Panos Pictures**: Michael J O'Brien; 158 **Corbis**: Tim Wright; 159 **Getty Images**: Andy Sacks; 162/163 **Associated Press AP**: Chien-Min Chung; 165 **Popperfoto**: Reuters / Sam Mircovich; 166 **Telegraph Colour Library**: Tom Tracey; 169 **Corbis**: Bob Kirst; 170 **Getty Images**: Keith Wood; 172 **Telegraph Colour Library**: V.C.L. / Chris Ryan; 175 **Getty Images**: Tim Flach; 176/177 **Corbis**: Bill Ross; 181 **PA Photos**: Owen Humphreys; 182 **Corbis**: Tim Wright; 186 **Financial Times**: Jim Winslet; 187 **Science Photo Library**: Ed Young; 188 **Still Pictures**: Mark Edwards *bl*, br; 189 **Corbis**: James Marshall; 190 **Corbis**: Tim Page; 191 **Corbis**: Michelle Chaplow; 192/193 **Getty Images**: Andy Sacks; 194 **PA Photos**: Michael Walter; 196/197 **Getty Images**: Lori Adamski Peek; 200 Courtesy of **McKay Nursery Company**: Robin Almanza; 202 Courtesy of **The Seaview Hotel and Restaurant, Isle of Wight** tl, tr; 208 **Agence France Presse**: Mauricio Lima; 210 **Corbis**: Jonathan Blair *bl*; Left Lane Productions *clb*; Peter Barrett *cla*; 211 **Corbis**: Jeff Albertson *cra*; Lawrence Manning *crb*; Reuters NewMedia Inc tr; **Getty**

Images: Jon Bradley *br*; 212 **Getty Images**: Laurence Monneret; 214 **Corbis**: Peter Barrett; 216 **Corbis**: Philip Gould; 218 **Corbis**: Left Lane Productions; 219 **PA Photos**: European Press Agency; 220 Courtesy of **3M**; 221 Courtesy of **Eskom, South Africa**; 222 Courtesy of **C&A**: SOCAM / Fishburn Hedges; 223 Courtesy of **The Kaua'i Marriott Resort & Beach Club, Hawaii**; 226 Courtesy of **Procter & Gamble**; 229 **Corbis**: Jonathan Blair; 236 **Corbis**: Owen Franken *c*; Paul A Souders *bl*; 237 Courtesy of **Norsk Hydro plc**; 240/241 **Telegraph Colour Library**: Eric Pearle; 242 **Getty Images**: Jon Bradley; 247 **Corbis**: Phil Schermeister; 248 **Corbis**: Lawrence Manning; 258 **Corbis**: Randy Faris *l*; **Financial Times**: Tony Andrews *r*; 259 **PA Photos**: European Press Agency *l*; **Getty Images**: George Hunter *r*; 260 **Corbis**: Jeff Albertson; 263 **PA Photos**: European Press Agency; 269 Courtesy of **Diageo plc**; 270 **Science Photo Library**: David Nunuk; 276 Courtesy of **British Airways**; 277 Courtesy of **The Discovery Channel Global Education Fund**: Gilbert Awekofua (Kampala, Uganda); 278 Courtesy of **The Prince of Wales International Business Leaders Forum**: BOC; 279 Courtesy of **Microsoft**; 287 **Corbis**: Reuters NewMedia Inc; 288 **Panos Pictures**: Crispin Hughes; 290 **Still Pictures**: Al Grillo; 301 **Getty Images**: Laurence Monneret.

ARTWORKS

15,65 **KPMG Peat Marwick**; 16 **Dr. Oliver Sparrow, Chatham House Forum**; 16 **Department of Trade and Industry**; 17 **Forrester Research Inc.**; 21 **Zenith Media**; 25 **International Air Traffic Association**; 33 **Interbrand**; 35, 44, 48, *The Economist*; 46 **World Bank**; 46, 51 *Financial Times*; 49, 52 **United Nations Development Programme**; 55 **US Census Bureau**; 57 **Inter-America Development Bank**; 58 **International Labour Organization**; 64 **Latinobarometro**; 65, 74 **Environics International Ltd.**; 71, 76, 261, **MORI**; 118 **Amnesty International**; 243 **John Elkington**; 284 **Harvey Dodgson**.

Text credits

The authors and publishers would like to thank the following for kind permission to reproduce text:

Accenture; Adbusters; Asian Development Bank; The Associated Press Ltd.; Bradley Googins, Center for Corporate Citizenship at Boston College; Business for Social Responsibility; *Business Week*; Civilization Magazine; Council on Economic Priorities; Capstone Press; Cone/Roper; CSR Europe; Custom Publishing; Diversity Inc. Allegiant Media; Dr. Oliver Sparrow, Chatham House Forum; The Conference Board; Control Risks Group; *The Economist*; Edelman PR Worldwide; Environics International Ltd; *Financial Times*; Fortune Magazine; Fleischman Hillard; Food and Agricultural Organization of the United Nations; Global Exchange newsletter; Greenpeace; HarperCollins; Institute of Policy Studies; Inter-American Development Bank; Interbrand; John Wiley & Sons UK; Johns Hopkins University; Latin Trade Magazine; Linda Michaels Ltd.; Manufacturers Alliance/MAPI and National Alliance of

Manufacturers; Miami Herald; MORI; Nicholas Brealey Publishing; W. W. Norton & Co. Inc.; Oxford University Press; Phillips Van Heusen; PWIBLF; Random House; Richard Steckel; Royal Dutch/Shell; Texere Publishing; UNHCR: UNFPA; UNICEF; United Nations; World Bank; World Energy Organization; World Resources Institute; Worldwatch Institute (www.worldwatch.org); World Water Council; The Yomiuri Shimbun.

19 "Companies Cast Worldwide Net", *USA Today*, 24 April 1997. Copyright © 1997, USA Today, reprinted with permission; 35 "The Shadow Economy", *The Economist*, 3 February 2001, reprinted with permission of Dr. Friedrich Schneider, University of Linz; 40, 42 UNDP, *Human Development Report 2000*, Oxford University Press, New York © 1999 by United Nations Development Programme; 44 *The State of Food Insecurity in the World 2000*, reprinted by permission of the Food and Agriculture Organization of the United Nations; 51, 148, 200 Malcolm McIntosh et al., *Corporate Citizenship: Successful Strategies of Responsible Companies*, 1998, by permission of Pearson Education; 58 *Life at Work in the Information Economy*, World Employment Report, International Labour Organization, 2001. Copyright © International Labour Organization, 2001; 72 Michael Binyon "Maimed by Embracing the Market", *The Times*, © Times Newspapers Limited (23rd August 2001); 78 *Bloomberg Financial News*, 21 December 1999, © 2000 Bloomberg L.P. All rights reserved. Reprinted with permission. Visit www.Bloomberg.com; 111 *International Workforce Management Study: Extracts from International Workforce Management Study, Capitalizing on the Workforce Revolution*, a Cap Gemini Ernst & Young Study prepared by Yankelovitch Partners Inc.; 138 "Levi's Open House", *Business Ethics*, January/February 1999, www.business-ethics.com; 173 "McDonald's Case Highlights Risks of Libel" Copyright © Reuters Limited, 19 June 1997; 199 *Los Angeles Times*, 24 February 1999, by permission of Los Angeles Times; 254 Reprinted by permission of Harvard Business Review, from *From Spare Change to Real Change* by Rosabeth Moss Kanter, May/June, 1999. Copyright © 1999 by Harvard Business School Publishing Corporation. All rights reserved; 66 Hernando de Soto, "Mystery of Capital". Copyright © 2000 by Hernando de Soto. Reprinted by permission of Perseus Books Group; 70 P. Schwartz and B. Gibb, *When Good Companies Do Bad Things*, 1999. Translations by permission of John Wiley & Sons. All rights reserved; 76 James Collins and Jerry Porras, *Built to Last*, published by Random House Business Books. Reprinted by permission of The Random House Group Ltd. Reprinted in the US and Canada by permission of HarperCollins Publishers Inc. Copyright © 1994 by James C. Collins and Jerry I. Porras; 76 J. Ridderstrale and K. Nordstrom, *Funky Business*, 1999 by permission of Pearson Education; 204 Tod Wilkinson "Eat a Slice of Pizza: Help Save the Environment". Reprinted by permission of Tod Wilkinson. This article first appeared in The Christian Science Monitor, online at www.csmonitor.com; 123 *World Bank Development Report 1998–1999*. Reprinted by permission of World Bank; 243 Charles Handy, *Sowing the Seeds of a Sustainable Future* by permission of Charles Handy and the Environment Foundation.

Publisher's acknowledgments

Dorling Kindersley would like to thank the following for their help and participation in this book:
Editorial: Corinne Asghar and Mary Lambert. **Design**: Nigel Duffield and Steve Woosnam-Savage. **Index**: Chris Bernstein. **Picture Research**: Louise Thomas. **Proofreading**: Ann Kay. **Illustrators**: Martin Darlison and Tom Coulson, Encompass Graphics Ltd.

Authors' acknowledgments

A book like *Everybody's Business* only happens because of the help and stimulating ideas of many people. We are grateful for the patience of family and friends whom we have neglected while the book was being finalized; and to those who have responded quickly to frequent requests at short notice to comment on examples, pictures, and graphics.

One of the reasons for producing *Everybody's Business* is a belief that a lot of good material has been produced that deserves to be more widely shared. That is why we approached chairman of the *Financial Times* David Bell for advice, and it was he who recommended a partnership between Dorling Kindersley and the FT, both Pearson Group companies. We were delighted when Christopher Davis, as head of Dorling Kindersley, confirmed his desire to publish the book, and expressed his personal support for its theme.

Many of the concepts in *Everybody's Business* have emerged from discussions with colleagues and from conversations with business and community leaders around the world too numerous to mention. It draws considerably on the work of others either directly – in which case we have tried to give credit accordingly – or indirectly, in the form of inspiration. For both contributions, we are most grateful.

We want particularly to thank Julia Cleverdon (BITC), Robert Davies (PWIBLF), and Liz Spencer (EPPA), who have encouraged us and lent organizational support.

In addition, special thanks to the following for reviewing text, and sharing ideas and material:

Sue Adkins, Jan Ahlskog, Mallen Baker, Amanda Bowman, Linda Borst, Barbara Brodell, Stephen Brooks, Geoffrey Bush, Jonathan Cohen, Geoffrey Colvin, Chris Cowls, Kieran Daly, Peter Davies, Aiden Davey, Tom Delfgaauw, Richard Edelman, Vernon Ellis, John Elkington, Peter Frankental, Kevin Gavaghan, Clare Gleeson, Brad Googins, Charles Handy, John Heaslip, Frances House, Belinda Howells, David Irwin, Sandra Kowalchek, Neil Jeffery, Marta Lagos, Dorothy Mackenzie, Michael Magan, Patrick Mallon, Marcela Manubens, Melody McClaren, Jacqui McDonald, Nancy McGaw, Malcom McIntosh, Doug Miller, Jane Nelson, Alok Singh, Shanker Singham, Susan Simpson, Oliver Sparrow, Michael Stewart, Richard Steckel, Ros Tennyson, Per Utterback, David Vidal, Gerry Wade, Anne Watts, Paul Wilden, Bob Worcester, Chris Yapp, Simon Zadek and Peter Zollinger.

Research was aided by Julia Egerer, Karen Gomersall, Rocco Renaldi and Nathan Macwhinnie.

Thanks too go to Gail Greengross (BITC), Sally Mindelsohn, Joe Phelan, Leon Taylor (PWIBLF), Amanda Harvey (EPPA), Ibis Alvarez, and Monique Arenas (Steel Hector & Davis LLP) for their logistical support. We have had valuable in-kind help from DEEP, Steel Hector & Davis LLP, EPPA, Diageo, DHL Worldwide Express, and TMP Worldwide.

At Dorling Kindersley, Stephanie Jackson and Adèle Hayward have coordinated a hardworking team of editors and designers for each of the three sections of *Everybody's Business*, working in parallel to meet ambitious deadlines. The responsibility for any omissions and errors rests with us.

We are relieved to say that we are both still friends after all the challenges of transatlantic writing and editing and texts getting lost – despite The Revolution of Technology – in cyberspace!

David Grayson, London and Adrian Hodges, Miami, August 2001

The views expressed in Everybody's Business are those of the authors, and do not necessarily reflect those of the partner institutions or sponsor. Information on corporate practices is sourced directly from companies or from material in the public domain and is reproduced in good faith. Inclusion does not constitute a direct endorsement from the authors, partners, or sponsor.

Everybody's Business website

At www.everybodybusiness.net, you can find a template presentation of the issues that a busy manager might want to share with colleagues. There is also a sample chapter, thanks to the generosity of EPPA and Dorling Kindersley.

From the site, you can hot-link to a number of the leading web resources about corporate social responsibility via www.worldcsr.com and to the sites of our partner organizations, Business in the Community and the Prince of Wales International Business Leaders Forum.

You will also find some more examples and checklists for action.

Most importantly, we will be posting updates – and for that we need your help. We want our site to get smarter with use, so please send us your experiences of applying the *Everybody's Business* approach, of using the Seven-Step Process, and of interesting practices that you spot.

Email us at **everybodybusiness@eppa.com**

AUTHORS

David Grayson and Adrian Hodges have experience working in business, non-governmental organizations, and the public sector, and have participated in partnerships scanning all three sectors. They were colleagues at Business in the Community (BITC) in the early 1990s and share a common belief in the power of business to contribute to social change. They speak regularly on the subject, and recent assignments have taken them to Australasia, the Americas, Europe, and the Middle East.

DAVID GRAYSON started his working life in management with Procter & Gamble, before going on to co-found Project North East – an innovative British NGO that has operated in 40 countries. He was the first joint Managing Director of The Prince's Youth Business Trust, ran The Prince's Innovation Trust, and chaired the UK's National Disability Council. He remains a director of BITC and is an associate of the pan-European consultancy EPPA. He is happiest on, in, or preferably under, water in hot climates.

ADRIAN HODGES is a marketing and communications professional who specializes in issues of corporate responsibility as they relate to international business strategy and practice. He lives in Miami, Florida, from where he directs the Americas operation of The Prince of Wales International Business Leaders Forum (PWIBLF). He was previously head of communications for global cosmetics retailer The Body Shop International. Inspired by a brief season with the National Youth Theatre in the UK, he started his working life in arts management, from where he made the link to the world of business through corporate sponsorship.

SPONSOR

EPPA (www.eppa.com) is delighted to sponsor *Everybody's Business*, recognizing the need for a practical guide to enable managers to make corporate social responsibility a reality.

E   P   P   A

Founded in 1987, EPPA has offices throughout the EU and CEE, and is the leading pan-European consultancy on public policy, corporate social responsibility, and change management.

EPPA is committed to helping clients achieve sustainable business excellence by mastering continuous, externally driven change. An important source of change is social values and political behavior. EPPA works closely with clients to ensure that internal strategic development and planning accurately foresees, and takes sufficient account of, changes in customer expectations, and regulatory and legislative requirements.

For organizations whose competitive advantage depends on anticipating societal and political developments as a key component of their strategy, EPPA is uniquely well-placed to assist.

PARTNERS

Everybody's Business is published in association with The Prince of Wales International Business Leaders Forum and Business in the Community.

THE PRINCE OF WALES
INTERNATIONAL BUSINESS
LEADERS FORUM

THE PRINCE OF WALES INTERNATIONAL BUSINESS LEADERS FORUM is a nonprofit organization that promotes international leadership in responsible business practices to benefit business and society. The Forum works strategically with leaders in business, civil society, and the public sector in transitional and emerging economies in order to achieve social, economic, and environmentally sustained development. Over 60 major international companies from a broad range of business sectors and regions of the world constitute the Forum's core membership. Senior executives from these companies constitute a board and member's council. The Forum encourages continuous improvement in responsible business practices, develops geographic or issue-based partnerships to take effective action on a range of social, economic, and environmental issues, and contributes to an enabling environment, providing the conditions for these practices and partnerships to flourish.

President: HRH The Prince of Wales
Vice Chairman of the Board: Vernon Ellis
CEO: Robert Davies
A company registered in England,
no. 2552695
Registered charity no. 102411915–16

15 Cornwall Terrace
Regent's Park, London NW1 4QP
Tel: +44 0(20)7467 3600
Fax: +44 0(20)7467 3610
Email: info@iblf.org
Website: www.iblf.org

BUSINESS *in the* COMMUNITY

BUSINESS IN THE COMMUNITY (BITC) is a unique movement of companies across the UK committed to continually improving their positive impact on society. A core membership of 700 companies includes 70 percent of the FTSE 100 largest companies. Members of BITC are committed to developing business excellence by continually improving, measuring, and reporting the impact their business has on the environment, workplace, marketplace, and community. They also develop community excellence by actively engaging in partnerships to tackle disadvantage and create enterprising communities. Since its creation in 1982, BITC has championed socially responsible business practices. BITC initiated the International Business Leaders Forum in 1990, and now works closely with partner organizations in CSR Europe and internationally. The prestigious annual BITC Awards for Excellence have become the premier awards of their kind.

President: HRH The Prince of Wales
Chairman: Sir Peter Davis
CEO: Julia Cleverdon CBE
Registered charity no. 297716137

137 Shepherdess Walk, London N1 7RQ
Tel: +44 0(20)8600 2482
Email: information@bitc.org.uk
Website: www.bitc.org.uk